100 THINGS NEBRASKA FANS SHOULD KNOW & DO BEFORE THEY DIE

Sean Callahan

TRIUMPH
BOOKS

Library of Congress Cataloging-in-Publication Data

Callahan, Sean.
    100 things Nebraska fans should know & do before they die / Sean Callahan ; [foreword by] Dave Rimington.
        p. cm. — (100 things...fans should know)
    ISBN 978-1-60078-835-2 (pbk.)
    1. University of Nebraska-Lincoln—Football—History. 2. University of Nebraska-Lincoln—Football—Anecdotes. 3. Nebraska Cornhuskers (Football team)—History. 4. Nebraska Cornhuskers (Football team)—Anecdotes. I. Title. II. Title: One hundred things Nebraska fans should know and do before they die.
    GV958.U53C35 2013
    796.332'6309782293—dc23

                                        2013021532

This book is available in quantity at special discounts for your group or organization. For further information, contact:
    Triumph Books LLC
    814 North Franklin Street
    Chicago, Illinois 60610
    (312) 337-0747
    www.triumphbooks.com

Printed in U.S.A.
ISBN: 978-1-60078-835-2
Design by Patricia Frey
Photos courtesy of AP Images unless otherwise indicated

This book is dedicated to the great teachers and coaches at Saints Peter & Paul grade school and Daniel J. Gross High School in South Omaha.

Contents

Foreword *by Dave Rimington* ix

Introduction xv

1 The Sellout Streak 1

2 Tom Osborne 3

3 Bob Devaney 7

4 Nebraska's Dominance from 1993 to 1997 10

5 The Game of the Century 12

6 The Walk-On Program 16

7 The Best Ever? 1971 vs. 1995 Huskers 19

8 Leading the Nation in Academic All-Americans 21

9 The Blackshirts 23

10 Nebraska's First National Championship 26

11 The 1994 National Championship 29

12 Osborne's Perfect Ending 32

13 The Tunnel Walk 35

14 Johnny Rodgers 38

15 Tom Novak 41

16 Mike Rozier 43

17 Tommie Frazier 45

18 Eric Crouch 48

19 Going for Two in the Orange Bowl 50

20 Boyd Epley and the Nebraska Strength Program 52

21 The Outland Trophy Winners 55

22 Bowl Game History 58

23 Barry Switzer vs. Nebraska 60

24 George Flippin 62

25 Dave Rimington 64

26 Grant Wistrom 67

27 Rich Glover 70

28 Bob Brown 71

29 Brook Berringer 73

30 Matt Davison's Miracle Catch 76

31 Suuuuuh! 78

32 Hang Out With College Football's Classiest Fans 81

33 NU's Greatest Upset Victory 83

34 Frank Solich 85

35 Devaney's First Big Win 88

36 Will Shields 91

37 The Fumblerooski and the Bouncerooski 93

38 10 Great Huskers Quarterbacks 96

39 1994 Colorado at Nebraska 98

40 Herbie Husker, Lil' Red, and the Bugeaters 102

41 Turner Gill 105

42 Texas: The Big 12's Villain 107

43 The 1983 Scoring Explosion Offense 110

44 Defensive Coordinator Charlie McBride 112

45 I-Back High 115

46 Offensive Line Coach Milt Tenopir 120

47 Unsung Heroes: Nebraska Fullbacks 125

48 The Four Food Groups: Runza, Valentino's, Fairbury,
and Colby Ridge 128

49 2001 Nebraska at Colorado 130

50 Kenny Walker 132

51 The First Family: The Swanson-Ruuds 134

52 Bo Pelini 137

53 Lawrence Phillips 140

54 The Oklahoma-Nebraska Rematch 143

55 Nebraska Switches to a 4-3 Defense 145

56 The 1994 Orange Bowl 147

57 Trev Alberts 149

58 Listen to Mr. Football's Classic Call 151

59 The Peter Brothers 154

60 Bill Callahan 157

61 Watch HuskerVision 160

62 JUCO Recruiting Success 163

63 Black 41 Flash Reverse Pass 167

64 Neil Smith and Broderick Thomas 170

65 Coach Jumbo Stiehm 172

66 Don "Fox" Bryant 174

67 Alvarez, Kiffin, and Other Coaching Legends With

Husker Roots 176

68 Mr. Nebraska Football 180

69 The 1941 Rose Bowl 182

70 Mr. Touchdown 184

71 Road Trippin' Through the Big Ten 186

72 Freshman Football 189

73 1982 Nebraska at Penn State 192

74 The Legionnaire Club 195

75 Remembering the Orange Bowl 198

76 Kicker/Punter U 201

77 "The Brown Brothers" 204

78 Athletic Director Steve Pederson 207

79 The Worst Loss in Program History 209

80 Nebraska's Partnership With Adidas 212

81 The 2003 Alamo Bowl 214

82 Clarence Thomas: The Highest Husker Fan in the Land . . . 217

83 *Sports Illustrated* Cover Boys 222

84 Huskers Football, Tokyo Style 226

85 Skyboxes, Skyboxes, and More Skyboxes 228

86 Rex Burkhead 232

87 Enjoy the Big Red Breakfast 235

88 The Kick 238

89 Visit Misty's on Friday Nights, the Sidetrack Band,
and Barry's 240

90 Star Gazing for Recruits 242

91 The Big Red Invades Notre Dame 245

92 Harvey Perlman and the Move to the Big Ten 247

93 One Last Time: Nebraska vs. Oklahoma 250

94 The Crazy Comebacks of 2012 252

95 The Fish Bowl: 24–7 Media Coverage 254

96 The Gotham Bowl 257

97 20 Straight Years in the Super Bowl 259

98 Roy Helu Breaks Single-Game Rushing Mark 261

99 Black Friday Football 263

100 Your Guide of Where to Stay and Eat for Husker
Games 265

Acknowledgments 268

Sources 270

Foreword

I still remember the day Tom Osborne called me for the very first time. My mother said, "Coach Osborne is on the phone," and my heart just stopped, and I was like, *What?* I had no idea Nebraska was even looking at me. It was my junior year, and I had broken my femur my first game. I had a pretty good sophomore year at Omaha South High School and then I hurt my leg. I wasn't sure if anybody was even going to look at me. It was pretty special to get that call. Coach Osborne said they'd like to have me if I'm able to heal. *Wow*, I thought. It was a very special time for me.

I grew up listening to Nebraska games with Lyell Bremser on the radio. I usually would listen out in the yard. My first recollection of following Nebraska was in the 1969 Sun Bowl, and the Huskers beat Georgia pretty handily. I became a fan at that point, but I didn't go to a Nebraska game until I got recruited by them. I just used to listen to the radio, and it fascinated me the way Lyell Bremser painted the picture of Nebraska football. At that time there wasn't a lot of hype around Nebraska. It was important to the people in the state, but it wasn't the national phenomenon that it became after the national championships. Back then even Kansas games were tough. It was a lot of fun.

Johnny Rodgers was a natural hero for everybody growing up in Nebraska. He did some things that you don't see today. It was just phenomenal to watch him on his punt returns. Rich Glover was another guy I was just in awe of because of how quick he was off the ball and the way he was able to make plays. Those two guys combined—to me, that was Nebraska football. Nebraska also had a pretty good offense with Jeff Kinney at running back and Jerry Tagge at quarterback. At that time I wasn't really a follower of offensive line play. I was pretty much just following whoever had the football and who was making the tackle. It wasn't until later that I started looking at the history of the offensive line and the center position in particular.

I really didn't know much about that until I started getting recruited. I looked at guys like Tom Davis, Rik Bonness, and Kelly Saalfeld when I got to Nebraska and knew I wanted to play center. These were the guys I wanted to follow and look up to and do the best that I could. I didn't want to embarrass myself at that time because these guys were great players and a lot of them were All-Americans and I just wanted to follow in their footsteps.

Then I met coach Cletus Fischer, who coached at Omaha South way back in the day. He was just a guy who you could trust. He was no-nonsense and just told you how it was going to be. I bought into the program as soon as I talked to those guys. I was ready to roll.

When I first got to Nebraska, I was pretty lucky to be put on the varsity side about two weeks into camp. I knew I had a lot to learn at that time. I knew I was just getting by on being a physical player, but I didn't really know what I was doing. It took a while, and then I hurt my knee. It was frustrating, but I really wasn't ready to play right away anyway. On the first five plays I ever played, I probably went the wrong way three times before I blew out my knee. It wasn't like I went out there and dominated. I just kind of grew into the position. I had the physical tools, but it took me a while to learn the blocking schemes. The coaches didn't tolerate mistakes. You couldn't jump offside. If you jumped offside in that era, they would pull you out of the game regardless of who you were. They didn't want mental mistakes. Most guys wouldn't even see the field on the offensive line until their third year.

My first start came during my sophomore year. It took some time for me to get on the field. I was really nervous. My parents were there, and my brothers and sisters were all watching. I just wanted to do a good job and hold up my end of the bargain.

I never felt pressure being a local guy from South Omaha. The only pressure I felt was that I never wanted to let down my teammates. We worked so hard together that I wanted to make sure I was doing what I was supposed to do, and that's what I concentrated on. I didn't really worry about the people I knew in South Omaha or my parents. The only people I worried about were my coaches and my teammates because they were counting on me, and the center position is where it all starts. You have to get the ball to the quarterback every play and call the offensive line plays. I just wanted to do my job and I was so nervous doing it that I really never got nervous about what was going on in the stadium.

We didn't have the Tunnel Walk or anything like that back then. We just ran out onto the field, but even then without all the bells and whistles that they have now, just running out in front of 76,000 people—when you are used to 2,000 or 3,000 back in high school—was quite a deal. You could feel the hairs on your neck stand up and you would go into another mode. You realized this was the real deal. That lasted a couple plays, and then it felt like being back at practice.

For me as a player, the Oklahoma series really stood out over my career. It was always a tough game for us. I remember it took Coach Osborne until 1978 to beat Oklahoma. It was always the game of the year and the last game of the season. During my first year in 1978, we beat the Sooners during the regular season and then we had to play them in the Orange Bowl. Just to be on the sideline for that game was really special. John Ruud's hit on the kickoff and the things that happened that day were wild. That was where I wanted to be, and I wasn't even playing yet. That opened my eyes that this is a special game.

Our luck against Oklahoma turned when we brought in Turner Gill, Mike Rozier, and Irving Fryar. We just had a great offense and we were able to finally turn the tables on Oklahoma and start beating them handily at the end.

When I watch Nebraska today, I don't think there is a rival like Oklahoma anymore. I think the Wisconsin game could be a big one because of the Nebraska connections there, but I don't think there's going to be a game like Oklahoma. We played the Sooners every year, and it was the end of the year and it was always a big game. Nebraska vs. Oklahoma is a lot like Michigan vs. Ohio State. That was the game in the Big Ten, and Nebraska vs. Oklahoma was the game in the Big 8.

What was neat about those Nebraska vs. Oklahoma games was the winner got to go to the Orange Bowl. Holding those oranges in your hand represented being a champion. For a Nebraska kid, going to Miami was exciting because a lot of us had never seen the ocean before. Just being in 90-degree weather in December was exciting. South Beach was a different lifestyle than what we were used to. It wasn't ideal for us, though, because we'd leave the freezing weather and go into the heat down there and it was like doing camp all over again because you couldn't replicate that heat and humidity.

When I go back and reflect on my career at Nebraska, maybe the thing I'm most proud of is being an Academic All-American. That was something I worked at, but I didn't camp out in the library to do it. I did what I had to do, showed up to class, and was able to earn that.

Another thing I was proud of during my era was that we were able to defeat the Sooners and put them on the defensive. Before that it was a monkey on Coach Osborne's back, and he couldn't beat those guys. The Sooners would go out to the field with a Frisbee and toss it around like the game wasn't even a big deal for them. Finally we were able to match up with their talent, and they couldn't mess around before the game like they used to. We got to the point where *we* could be tossing the Frisbee around, but we never did it. Oklahoma had to come out and play us straight up.

I remember winning my first Outland Trophy in 1981. When I won it, I didn't even realize I was up for it. It was just a huge honor to win that. I had the goal when I came to Nebraska to become a starter, and after I accomplished that, I wanted to be All-Big 8, then All-American. I was fortunate enough to be able to do all of that.

Today I am honored to have my own award given to college football's top center. It's a real special thing. I hope people enjoy the award. Before the trophy was put together the only centers who won anything were myself, Jim Ritcher, and Chuck Bednarik. Before the Rimington Trophy, there were only three other centers in the history of college football who won any national awards.

The Rimington Trophy has been able to shed some light on the center position, and another reason I think it is important is because it raises a lot of money for cystic fibrosis. We've been able to raise close to $3 million, so I'm real proud of it. We've been holding the event since 2000, and the first guy to win the award was a Nebraska guy—Dominic Raiola. That was really exciting for me.

As I look at Nebraska today and what makes Nebraska special, to me it's still the walk-on program. They were able to bring that back, and you see a lot of guys who have made contributions to the program through the walk-on program. I think it's important. As we try to be the elite football program in the country, we should never forget that the walk-on program has done more for this football team than any other thing. I really believe that it's the heart and soul of what we do, and it probably doesn't get as much attention as it should. It's about self-made guys who want it so bad that they put the time in and do it themselves. Those are the players who will always push the scholarship guys, and they are the backbone of the team. They are the ones who raise everybody else to a higher level. They may not start, but the guys who are there and put the time in and start pushing the scholarship guys make Nebraska different than just about any other program out there.

A lot of these players who were walk-ons at Nebraska took that same work ethic into life and have done some fantastic things in the business world because they know how to work, and they'll continue to strive. They aren't concerned with being the name guy and they are okay with just being a guy on a team and pushing everybody forward. That's always been important. That's what makes us different than any other program, and for a while, I think we forgot about it. With coaching restrictions it's tough to organize it, but you have to find a way to still get those guys to Nebraska.

To me Nebraska is about persevering. You may not be the greatest athlete, but you find a way to keep it up and keep working and go to classes and do the right things. If you work hard and keep a positive attitude, great things can happen. What I learned at Nebraska was: Don't worry about where you are right now. Just worry about getting better and try to get better every day. You are going to have ups and downs, but you have to keep persevering. You'll eventually get to where you want to be. It just takes time and a lot of effort, and you appreciate it more when you put in the work.

—Dave Rimington

Introduction

Growing up in Nebraska, I can remember going to my first Husker game with my dad like it was yesterday. It was during the 1988 season against Utah State. I was eight years old, and I remember being overwhelmed by the amount of people and the red in Memorial Stadium. I remember watching Husker All-American quarterback Steve Taylor effortlessly move the ball down the field.

Growing up in Omaha, I always heard my dad talk about how he was a walk-on at Nebraska from 1975 to 1977 for coach Tom Osborne. I didn't really know what that meant at the time. Though he never got into a game, being part of the Husker football program for three years is a great part of my dad's life.

In 1991 my dad and I attended the Washington game together, and by 1993 we got season tickets—section 16A, Row 88, seats 5 and 6. From 1993 to now, I have only missed a handful of home games and I've attended every road game since 2000.

As I watched Osborne's 1993 team go undefeated during the regular season, I immediately fell in love with what was going on. I was spoiled to be able to watch some of the greatest teams in college football play each Saturday afternoon. I didn't know what losing was. From 1991 to 1998, Nebraska only lost two home games—against Washington and Texas—and I happened to be at both of them.

Like a lot of people, I wanted to work in sports media when I got to college and I was lucky enough to get several early opportunities at the University of Nebraska to shape my career to where it's at today. I tell people I have the best job in Nebraska because I get paid to talk about Husker football on TV and the radio, along with being the publisher of HuskerOnline.com.

When I was first approached by Triumph Books in September of 2012 to take on this project, I didn't know what to think. I really wanted to write this book, but being a first-time author, naturally had some fears about trying to complete this daunting task. As I thought about it more, however, it became a pretty easy decision for me to say yes. Maybe the biggest challenge was condensing the great history of Nebraska football into 100 things.

There are several great moments and players that have been left out of this book because in all reality there's that much history when it comes to Nebraska football. Covering the team from 1999 to now, I've seen and been around one of the more unique eras of Husker football. There's a lot of history from the recent era that has never been captured in a book before. I think Husker fans will really enjoy what's inside as I've certainly learned more while putting this book together. I hope you enjoy.

1 The Sellout Streak

Nothing defines what is great about Nebraska football more than the sellout streak. Heading into the 2013 season, the Huskers have sold out an NCAA-record 325 consecutive games at Memorial Stadium. The streak dates all the way back to November 3, 1962 when the Huskers took on Missouri in front of a crowd of 36,501 during Bob Devaney's first season.

On September 29, 1979, NU reached the 100-consecutive sellout mark when it played Penn State. The Huskers hit the 200 mark on October 29, 1994 against Colorado and 300 straight on September 26, 2009 when they played Louisiana-Lafayette. They are on target to hit 400 consecutive sellouts some time in 2024.

Each milestone was a celebration—a celebration of the greatest fans in college football. The sellout streak is a true testament to Nebraska fans. The sellout streak is what bridges the past and the present together.

The amazing thing about the streak is Memorial Stadium will have a seating capacity in 2013 of just more than 91,000. On Husker football Saturdays, Memorial Stadium is the third largest city in the state. Nebraska's population is just 1.86 million, which means one out of every 20.4 people is in Memorial Stadium on gameday. "The greatest fans in football history," former rival and Oklahoma head coach Barry Switzer said in Memorial Stadium during NU's 300th consecutive sellout. Added legendary ABC broadcaster Keith Jackson: "The whole nation of college football stands in admiration."

Former head coach and fullback Frank Solich even commended Huskers fans during the 300th consecutive sellout. It was the first

Putting the Streak into Perspective

Here are some fun facts to chew on about Nebraska's sellout streak, which began on November 3, 1962.

- There have been 10 U.S. Presidents since 1962. John F. Kennedy was in office when the Nebraska sellout streak began.
- In 1962 actress Marilyn Monroe died of a drug overdose at the age of 36.
- The price of gas in 1962 was 28 cents per gallon. A postage stamp cost four cents.
- The sellout streak began just one day after the Cuban Missile Crisis was resolved, which took the U.S. and the Soviet Union to the brink of nuclear war.
- The average price of a house in the U.S. was $12,500.

Heading into 2013 Nebraska's home record over its 325 straight sellouts is 282–43 (.868 winning percentage).

time Solich had done anything like that since being fired from NU in 2003. "Keep filling up Memorial Stadium, keep winning football games and championships, and go Huskers," Solich said. Through the streak NU has seen their stadium capacity increase by big numbers. Memorial Stadium went from a seating capacity of 31,000 in 1962 to nearly 74,000 by 1972. The original stadium only had seating on the east and west sides. A four-series project that began in 1964 enhanced the stadium by adding seats above the north and south end zones, which brought the capacity to 74,000.

In 1999 NU added skyboxes and club seating on the west side to bring the capacity to 78,000. In 2006 Nebraska expanded its seating in the north end zone and added more skyboxes to bring the capacity to more than 85,000. In 2013 NU added skyboxes, club seating, and another balcony to bring the stadium capacity to 91,000.

Very few teams can continue to expand their stadium at a rapid pace like the Big Red. When schools like Florida State or Florida play lower profile games, you will see thousands of empty seats. The fans just don't care. "It's easy to be a fan when you are winning national championships. Anybody can be a fan," Husker fan and Supreme Court Justice Clarence Thomas said. "I've been to some Southeast Conference games, and the thing that really jumps out to me is just how empty the stadiums are when people aren't interested. The thing I love about the Huskers is we could be playing a high school, and we show up."

The challenge for NU in keeping their sellout streak alive is to continue to evolve the gameday atmosphere. "The social aspect of Nebraska football is vital to our success in keeping the sellout streak," associate athletic director Paul Meyers said. "You have to make sure your ticket is in high demand. Otherwise people start cherry-picking games."

As for growing the stadium to more than 100,000, Meyers doesn't see that day coming any time soon especially if it would put the sellout streak at risk. "You'd have to really convince me to go higher," Meyers said. "We've done a lot of homework on that number and we're pushing it to the limits to go where we are at. I suspect you'll see that number for a long time."

2 Tom Osborne

To say retired Nebraska head coach and athletic director Tom Osborne had an illustrious career is to put it mildly.

Osborne was part of all five of Nebraska's national championship teams and captured three as a head coach in 1994, 1995, and 1997. He won 255 games in 25 years and finished with a .836 winning percentage. He reached both 200 and 250 wins faster than any other coach in college football history. His teams captured 13 conference championships and appeared in 25 straight bowl games, including 17 major bowls. Over his 25 years, Osborne never had a season with less than nine wins. Under Osborne's watch the Huskers won 11 national rushing titles, six Outland Trophies, three Lombardis, one Heisman, one Butkus, and one Johnny Unitas Award.

As an administrator Osborne helped restore stability to the athletic department when he took over in 2007. He hired head coach Bo Pelini and played an instrumental role in getting the Huskers an invite to join the Big Ten in 2010.

When you talk to Osborne about his career at Nebraska, however, it's not the individual achievements or team accomplishments he remembers the most. It's the relationships he's made with so many of his former players and the process of developing young men for life. Osborne said he cherishes those friendships and relationships more than any championship ring. "I would say not a week goes by where I don't hear from three to 10 players, and so those relationships continue," Osborne said at his retirement party in March of 2013. "People forget about the championships and the wins and the losses. If you were to name the Heisman Trophy winner 10 years ago or the national champion 15 years ago, it would probably be pretty hard to name them, but the relationships persist. I guess that's one of the great things about coaching I'll always appreciate."

Osborne even shared a story at both his retirement party and the 2013 Nebraska Coaches Clinic about being with former head coach Bob Devaney during his death in 1997.

As Devaney and Osborne shared their final words together, they didn't talk about football. Instead they talked about family, and Devaney asked Osborne to say a prayer for him as a tear rolled down Osborne's cheek. "We didn't talk about games or championships or awards. We talked about relationships," Osborne said. "At the end of things, that's really what it all comes down to and whatever impact it might have had on players. So often times players

Legendary coach Tom Osborne stands between the back-to-back national championship trophies he earned after the 1994 and 1995 seasons.

will bring up stuff that seemed to be really important to them that they still remember from 20 to 30 years ago, and I have no recollection of that conversation or that comment, but it tends to stick with them, and I guess that's important."

What former defensive coordinator Charlie McBride remembers most about Osborne was his unique gift to remember names and faces, which made each player over the years feel important. "If you asked Tom during the season to write down every person on the team's name, their parents, and where he was from, he could probably do that," McBride said during Osborne's retirement party. "Tom used to go into the freshman locker room all the time when they were new. We would all go on occasion. He'd go every day to see how the kids were doing. He was always checking on them. He knew everybody's name. That manner I think brought a lot of his players closer to him by the fact every time he'd see them he would use their name and things like that. It doesn't sound like a big thing, but when players are young and they don't know if they're even being noticed in a program like this, they appreciated it. I think that was kind of the start of things."

McBride also said what made Osborne successful was his extreme attention to detail in every aspect of life. "I don't know if I know a more disciplined person than Coach Osborne in every facet," McBride said. "It goes from if he tells you something, that's what it is. There's no messing around with it. If he tells another person he's going to do something, he does it. He's one of those people that I appreciated immensely because he let you coach."

Even Osborne's biggest rivals had an extreme amount of respect for him and how he ran his program. "What I want to say about Tom and what he accomplished in his career at Nebraska in 25 years is it's the greatest 25 years any football coach has ever had in college football," former Oklahoma head coach Barry Switzer said at Osborne's retirement party. "He cast a shadow longer than anybody that's ever coached the game. You don't win like what he won and not be the best."

"Tom set the standard for everybody," legendary Kansas State head coach Bill Snyder said. "I can't think of anybody who spent 25 years coaching the game and never won less than nine ball games in any of those 25 years. That's an unbelievable statistic, and he always did it the very, very right way. That's what everybody appreciates—to be successful the right way."

Some feel that as great as Osborne's accomplishments were as a head coach that what he did during his time as an athletic director from 2007 to 2012 was equally as impressive. Under Osborne's watch, Nebraska built an $18.7 million basketball practice facility, a $4.75 million indoor baseball/softball practice center, a $8.7 million renovation to the Nebraska Student Life Complex, a $63.5 million renovation to the east side of Memorial Stadium, and a $20.5 million Devaney Center renovation to configure it for volleyball. He also helped lead the charge to get voters to approve the $160 million dollar Haymarket Arena in downtown Lincoln.

"As good as he was and as great of a football coach as he was, he might have been a better administrator," Nebraska alum and Wisconsin athletic director and former head coach Barry Alvarez said. "The program was in shambles, and I think people around the state were very alarmed with what was going on. With Tom coming back, he put everybody at rest and everybody at ease and righted the ship. I think you could look at him as a great football coach, but you could also look at him as somebody that stabilized and got the athletic program back in order."

3 Bob Devaney

When head coach Bob Devaney arrived in Nebraska in 1962, the Huskers had only experienced three winning seasons over the previous 21 years. From 1941 to 1961, the Huskers' highest number of wins in a season was six. Previous head coach Bill Jennings left the program in shambles with a 15–34–1 record over five seasons. Before Devaney got to Nebraska in 1962, the Big Red had only played in two bowl games—the 1941 Rose Bowl and the 1955 Orange Bowl.

The task for Devaney was no doubt tall, but the fiery Irishman from Saginaw, Michigan, was up for the challenge. In 14 seasons as a high school coach in Michigan and five years as a coach at Wyoming, Devaney had never experienced a losing season. Devaney was a winner and he immediately brought that mentality with him to Nebraska. Little did anyone know at the time Devaney would be the man to take Husker football and the Nebraska athletic department to places they've never been before. "[Devaney] put Nebraska on the college football map," said Walter Bingham, former college football editor for *Sports Illustrated.*

Immediately within his first season, Devaney led the Huskers to a 9–2 record—the most wins Nebraska had won since going 10–0 in 1903. Devaney caught the eyes of everyone when he took the Big Red into Ann Arbor and beat Michigan 25–13 in only his second game at NU. The Huskers would go on to lose to both Missouri and Oklahoma in 1962, but they did manage to qualify for the Gotham Bowl and beat Miami 36–34 for the first bowl victory in school history.

Devaney followed that up with a 10–1 record and a Big 8 title in 1963 capped off by a 13–7 win against Auburn in the Orange Bowl. The next three seasons the Huskers would go 9–2, 10–1, and 9–2. They played in the Cotton, Orange, and Sugar Bowls. Within Devaney's first five seasons, NU was 47–8 and they played in five bowl games.

Adversity, however, hit in 1967 and 1968 as the Huskers had back-to-back 6–4 seasons and failed to qualify for a bowl game. After NU lost to rival Oklahoma 47–0 during the final game of the 1968 season, a group of boosters actually circulated a petition, trying to get Devaney fired. In 1968 fans didn't have message boards or talk radio shows on which to vent their frustrations. Instead they circulated silly petitions.

Two things, though, would happen by 1969. No. 1, assistant coach Tom Osborne would convince Devaney to switch to the I-formation on offense. No. 2, Osborne also convinced Devaney to implement college football's first known strength and conditioning program by hiring Boyd Epley to head the operation. These two moves by Devaney changed college football as we know it.

By 1969 Devaney had the Huskers back on track again. That same OU team that beat Nebraska 47–0 the previous season got embarrassed in Norman, Oklahoma, by the Big Red 44–14. The Huskers qualified for the Sun Bowl in El Paso, Texas, and beat Georgia 45–6. This started an NCAA record streak of 35 consecutive years of playing in a bowl game.

Devaney had a unique ability to motivate players and a gift to work the room with boosters. Everybody was now on board. He was a perfect fit for Nebraska, and little did anyone know that the best was yet to come. "Bob had the ability to get along with any group of people from the working class to the higher end and he had a presence about him…He was just a real special man," former Nebraska linebacker Tom Ruud said. "He knew how to deal with people and get the most out of them."

In 1970 the Huskers would go on to win their first of two straight national championships, going 11–0–1 after beating LSU 17–12 in the Sugar Bowl. Devaney's 1971 team followed that up with a dominating 13–0 record, winning a second consecutive national title. During that magical run, NU beat No. 2 ranked Oklahoma 35–31 in the "Game of the Century" and No. 2 ranked Alabama 38–6 in the Orange Bowl. Many consider the 1971 Huskers as one of the greatest teams of all time.

During Devaney's final season in 1972, he brought Nebraska its first Heisman Trophy winner in wide receiver Johnny Rodgers. Defensive lineman Rich Glover also captured the Outland and Lombardi Trophies that year, and defensive lineman Larry Jacobson won the Huskers' first Outland Trophy the previous year.

In 11 seasons Devaney's teams won or shared eight Big 8 championships and were invited to nine bowl games. Devaney finished with a 101–20–2 record over that period. In 30 years of coaching, he never had a losing record.

During his time at Nebraska, the University of Miami tried to woo Devaney in 1965 as did the NFL's Los Angeles Rams, New England Patriots, Denver Broncos, and Pittsburgh Steelers. Never once did Devaney consider leaving, and he eventually moved into a dual role of head coach and athletic director in 1967. He held the athletic director title until 1993.

In 1973 Devaney would name Osborne his successor, which was another legendary move that changed the history of Nebraska. Osborne was the complete opposite of Devaney in terms of personality, but the two had an extremely close relationship until Devaney's death in 1997. "[We] always had a healthy respect for each other," Osborne told the *Omaha World-Herald* after Devaney died. "I've always supported Bob; I've always been loyal to him. In return he's done the same for me. Our relationship was very unique in that respect."

When Devaney passed away on May 9, 1997, his funeral was aired on statewide public television. It was a day that touched all Nebraskans because Devaney changed the culture of the state.

"Bob Devaney was an inspiration to Nebraskans," former Governor and U.S. Senator Ben Nelson told the *World-Herald* after his death in 1997. "He made pride in Nebraska and pride in football the same. He helped Nebraskans believe that we could be No. 1 in football and whatever we did. He'll be missed personally and by all Nebraskans."

Nebraska's Dominance from 1993 to 1997

When you talk about the history of college football, no team has had a run of dominance like Nebraska did from 1993 to 1997. Over that five-year period, the Huskers went 60–3, won three national championships, and had one runner-up finish. In 1996 NU lost to Texas in the Big 12 championship game; otherwise the Big Red would've played for the national title five consecutive years. The only other two losses over those five years came to Florida State in the 1994 Orange Bowl and in 1996 at Arizona State, who won the Pac-10 title that season.

During that 60–3 period, the Huskers outscored their opponents by an average of 42.8 to 14.6 and scored 50 or points 18 times. In comparison NU only scored 50 points or more five times during Bo Pelini's first five seasons as head coach. Defensively the Blackshirts were equally as dominant, holding opponents to seven points or less in 19 games from 1993 to 1997. There was a span during the 1997 season against Texas Tech, Kansas, and Oklahoma where Nebraska outscored those teams by a margin of 133–7.

Another amazing statistic shows the excellence of Nebraska's line, which only allowed a total of 36 quarterback sacks (.57 per game) in five seasons while the NU defense sacked the quarterback 231 times for an average of 3.7 per game (counting bowl games). The 1995 Huskers did not allow a quarterback sack the entire season. Nebraska rushed for 21,453 yards on the ground during those five seasons (counting bowl games) for an average of 340.5 yards per game and 5.9 yards-per-carry.

Some people have tried to compare the recent Alabama teams to Nebraska's dynasty of the '90s. Under Nick Saban the Crimson Tide won three national championships (2009, 2011, and 2012) in four years just like Nebraska, but their five-year record is 61–7. USC's dynasty under Peter Carroll went 82–9 from 2002 to 2008 and won back-to-back national championships in 2003 and 2004 and finished second in 2005. The Trojans' best five-year run in that period was 59–6 from 2003 to 2007, but the Trojans only had one undefeated season (2004).

Nebraska was a true dynasty that had everything you could ever imagine. There was a legendary head coach in Tom Osborne; star quarterbacks in Tommie Frazier and Scott Frost; dominant running backs in Lawrence Phillips and Ahman Green; Outland Trophy-winning offensive linemen in Aaron Taylor and Zach

Wiegert; and All-American defensive linemen in Jason Peter, Jared Tomich, and Grant Wistrom. Even NU's kicker Kris Brown went on to be a successful NFL player. There were really no flaws with the Huskers during that period.

The further Nebraska gets away from 60–3, the more Husker fans have come to realize it may never be duplicated again. Twelve-game regular seasons along with the addition of conference championship games have made it much more difficult to go undefeated. "What we were able to do, losing three games in five years, I certainly don't want anyone to break that record and I don't know if anybody will break that record," said offensive lineman Matt Hoskinson, who was part of all five seasons of the 60–3 run. "We played in four national championship games and won three of them and, probably minus a flu bug hitting our team [against Texas, we] would've played in five national championships in five years.

"[My teammates and I] do talk about it, and we do think about it. I tell my 10-year-old's team that I was a part of something special in college football that will never be done again. We understand our place in history and the teams that we had. A lot of it had to do with mentality, and a lot of it had to do with coaching and just the way kind of everything came together. We were just there at the perfect time."

5 The Game of the Century

There have been several big games in college football over the years that have attempted to call themselves "The Game of the Century," but there's really only one that deserves to carry that title. The 1971 Nebraska vs. Oklahoma game in Norman, Oklahoma, was a No. 1

Celebrating 50 Years

It was announced in November of 2012 by Oklahoma and Nebraska officials that the two historic football programs will play a home-and-home series in September of 2021 and 2022 to celebrate the 50th anniversary of The Game of the Century. The Huskers will visit Norman on September 18, 2021 while the Sooners will come to Lincoln on September 17, 2022.

"Our rivalry with Oklahoma has been one of the great traditional matchups in the history of college football," former Nebraska coach and athletic director Tom Osborne said. "The games between the two schools were generally to decide a conference championship, and many times helped determine the national champion. Those matchups were always played with great intensity on the field but with a great deal of respect from both sides and among the fan bases."

With the Huskers no longer in the Big 12, it will be the first scheduled matchup between the two schools since the 2010 Big 12 title game in Arlington, Texas. "Classic rivalries like Oklahoma-Nebraska are part of college football's historic fabric," OU athletic director Joe Castiglione said in a statement. "The ability to rekindle a fabled series between two tradition-rich programs and two extremely loyal and passionate fan bases was very important to both universities."

vs. No. 2 matchup that ranks as one of the greatest college football games of all time. Very rarely does a game with this much hype live up to the billing, but the 1971 Game of the Century did that and more.

A national television audience of 55 million viewers tuned in to watch the Thanksgiving classic on ABC. In comparison 26.4 million viewers watched Alabama vs. Notre Dame in the 2012 BCS National Championship Game, and 35 million viewers watched USC play Texas for the title in 2005.

Seventeen of the 22 players on the field that day were first team All-Big 8 selections. It was a game that defending national champion Nebraska won 35–31—highlighted by future Heisman Trophy winner Johnny Rodgers' legendary first-quarter punt

Joe Blahak (27) delivers a block to help spring Johnny Rodgers (20) for a first-quarter punt return for a touchdown in The Game of the Century, which took place on Thanksgiving of 1971.

return. Rodgers broke free for a 72-yard return to put the Huskers up 7–0 and set the tone of this classic. The Game of the Century featured five lead changes in all as Husker running back Jeff Kinney scored the game's winning touchdown with 1:38 left in the fourth quarter.

There was only one penalty the entire day—a 5-yarder committed by Nebraska. There were no holds, personal fouls, or face-mask penalties. The 55 million viewers that day witnessed two heavyweights play football in its purest form. "Was it the Game of the Century? Yes, I think so. It certainly was to me," Oklahoma running back Joe Wylie told *The Oklahoman* years later. "You had to be blind, deaf, and dumb not to recognize what this game meant. It was for the national championship. It was for everything."

Coming into the game, OU was No. 1 nationally in scoring offense while Nebraska was No. 4. The Sooners led the nation in total offense at 563 yards per game while the Huskers led the country in total defense, allowing just 171 yards per game. It was strength vs. strength. NU's talented defense featured two Outland Trophy winners on the defensive line—Larry Jacobson and Rich Glover. In all the 1971 Blackshirt defense had seven All-Big 8 players and four All-Americans. OU's explosive offense was led by All-American running back Greg Pruitt and All-American quarterback Jack Mildren. Glover and Jacobson squared off up front against All-American Oklahoma center Tom Brahaney.

Amazingly, though, it wasn't the top-ranked defense that won the game for the Big Red. NU's ground control offense kept the ball away from Mildren and the Sooners explosive wishbone attack. "Supposedly, that was the greatest Nebraska defense ever, but it wasn't their defense that held us to fewer points than our average. Their offense did that," Wylie told *The Oklahoman*. "Nebraska held the ball so long, especially in the second half, that we didn't get as many possessions as we normally did. I've said on several occasions that when you played Nebraska, it was a very clean game—very hard-hitting but very clean. Their players did not talk to you. They just played hard."

In today's college football world, the top games—like the 9–6 final score we saw in 2011 when Alabama and LSU squared off in a No. 1 vs. No. 2 matchup—are typically low scoring because that's the style most teams in the Southeastern Conference play. The 1971 Game of the Century was much more engrossing. "To me that game was football the way football was meant to be played," Glover told the *Omaha World-Herald*. "It had everything you could ask for in a game. We'd go up, and they'd come back. They'd go up, and we'd come back. It was like the team that had the ball last was going to be the one that won."

What also stands out about that legendary game was the immense amount of respect both programs had for one another. There have been multiple reunions and events where Oklahoma and Nebraska players have gathered together years after The Game of the Century to celebrate this special day in college football's history. "We were both great teams," Glover said. "No one was out there talking. Oklahoma was coming off the football. We were coming off the ball. Both teams took the other's best shot, and they still kept coming back for more."

Each year around Thanksgiving, The Game of the Century is honored and remembered by college football fans around the country. The late Beano Cook of ESPN said the best description of the 1971 Game of the Century came from Dave Kindred, who wrote for *The* (Louisville) *Courier-Journal*: "They can quit playing now, they have played the perfect game."

Glover said the older he gets, the more he realizes how special that game was in college football's history. "Still, I don't think any of us at the time knew just how important that game would turn out to be," Glover told the *Omaha World-Herald*. "There was a lot of hype before the game, but all that mattered to us was that we came out with the win. Now, whenever Thanksgiving comes around and replays of that game flash back on the TV, it's nice to think back on it. It's like, *Wow! I took part in that.* But at the time, I don't know if we thought it would ever be such a big deal."

6 The Walk-On Program

When Tom Osborne became Nebraska's head coach in 1973, he knew Nebraska was different than most major college football programs. With a population of around 1.9 million people, only the state of West Virginia currently has a smaller population base than Nebraska among BCS football schools. And although Nebraska does not have beaches or mountains, it does have great facilities and support that will rival any school in the country. Osborne's idea was to create a culture within the program of high-profile out-of-state recruits and surround them with in-state, walk-on players.

Osborne thought that if you could instill Nebraska values and attitude into your football program, it would carry over to players from out of state. "It's something that he believed in and it goes back to kids that grew up watching Nebraska football," former walk-on offensive lineman Matt Hoskinson said. "You played football at a small-town Nebraska high school and to have the opportunity to wear the Scarlett and Cream and just be a part of something that's been a part of your life for a long time is a really, really big deal."

Most teams in college football only carry a handful of walk-on players because of the cost to house additional players. That's never been the case with Nebraska. In 1986 NU had 206 players on their roster, 191 in 1990, and 168 in 1995, according to *Omaha World-Herald* records. Even with 143 players on the roster in 2013, NU still carries nearly 60 walk-ons to go with their 85 scholarship recruits. No team in college football even comes close to this number. Those 60 walk-on players in the program must pay for their own room, board, books, and tuition, which is $17,106 per year for in-state and $29,856 for out-of-state students, according to the University of Nebraska's website.

"Loyalty. Motivation. Willingness to sacrifice," were the words Osborne used to describe the walk-on program over his coaching tenure. That meant many of those walk-on players had to find summer jobs along with taking classes and attending workouts. It, though, was all part of the master plan. In Osborne's eyes the work ethic of the Nebraska walk-on players would rub off on the rest of the team and create a culture unlike anywhere else.

Osborne's other major ideology with the walk-on program was that all players were treated the same. It didn't matter if you were a five-star running back from California or a walk-on long snapper from Bassett, Nebraska. That wasn't always the case at other schools as NU's coaches can remember at the 1982 Orange Bowl against Clemson when the Tigers coaching staff didn't even let their walk-on players ride the bus to practice each day with the scholarship players. "Tom told us that everybody was going to be treated equally," said the late Dan Young, who coached offensive line and kickers for Osborne, "and that we needed to take extra time to let the walk-ons know they weren't going to be whipping boys. Once they got the pads on, you didn't know who was on scholarship and who wasn't."

Over the years there have been many great walk-on success stories like defensive end Jared Tomich (1995–1996) or kicker Alex Henery (2010). They are two of six Huskers walk-ons who went on to become first team All-Americans. There have also been 12 walk-on players, who have gone on to become Academic All-Americans, including fullback Joel Makovicka (1997–1998) and defensive end Jeff Jamrog (1987).

When Bo Pelini took over in 2008, he did his best to make sure the walk-on program stayed alive and well at Nebraska. One of Pelini's first hires in 2008 was Jamrog, who is currently NU's director of football operations and oversees NU's walk-on recruiting each year. From 2008 to 2011, Jamrog and Osborne actually found a loophole that allowed all incoming walk-on players to get free summer school and housing, which was a huge boost. However, in 2012 the NCAA ended that summer bridge program because many Southeastern Conference schools were taking advantage of it and using it the wrong way.

The Best Ever? 1971 vs. 1995 Huskers

A great debate among Nebraska fans is which national championship team was more dominant—the 1971 or the 1995 Huskers. Both teams won back-to-back national championships as the '71 Huskers had a 13–0 record, and the '95 team had a 12–0 mark.

The 1971 team had victories over No. 2 Oklahoma, No. 3 Colorado, and No. 4 Alabama. NU handed the Sooners and Crimson Tide their only losses of the season in 1971 while CU lost to OU and Nebraska. The 1995 team had wins over No. 2 Florida, No. 5 Colorado, No. 7 Kansas State, and No. 9 Kansas. The 1971 team had two first-team AP All-Americans and eight overall. The 1995 team had three first team AP All-Americans and five overall. The 1971 team also had eight first team All-Big 8 selections, and three players made the second team. The '95 team had seven on the first and four on the second.

The biggest difference between the two teams was how they played. The 1971 team had the No. 1 defense in the country, giving up just 209.5 yards per game and outscoring their opponents by an average of 39–8. The 1995 team was more driven by their offense, averaging 556.3 yards per game and outscoring opponents by an average of 52.4 to 13.6.

In 2006 ESPN did its own breakdown of the greatest college football teams of all time. Out of 32 teams, the '71 and '95 Nebraska teams made it to the championship round, and the '95 team won by a fan vote of 82.5 to 17.5 percent. ESPN *College GameDay*'s Kirk Herbstreit expressed his anger during the broadcast that two Nebraska teams were picked as the greatest of all time, clearly accusing Huskers fans of ballot stuffing. The '71 Huskers beat out

Vince Young's 2005 Texas Longhorns team in the semifinals, and the '95 Nebraska team beat out the 2001 Miami Hurricanes. "This is ridiculous," Herbstreit said. "The '04 USC team losing to the '71 Nebraska team and then the '05 Texas team losing to them also? You have '01 Miami, '05 Texas, and the '04 USC team and you aren't going to throw one of them a bone?"

An uninformed Herbstreit and Lou Holtz also talked about how the '71 Huskers ran the option, but NU was actually more of a balanced attack during that era. Jerry Tagge, the 1971 Nebraska quarterback, said he had no problem with some of Herbstreit's opinions, but to call the Huskers an option offense during that time was simply wrong. NU threw the ball 41 percent of the time in 1971. "[Herbstreit] has all of 15 years of history. Young people are not going to remember us," Tagge told the *Omaha World-Herald* in 2006. "But obviously there were a lot of older folks who voted who remembered.

"I had a problem with two things he said. One, we did throw the ball. We were 50-50. Tom Osborne was a passing guru back then. We were very efficient in throwing the ball. The other thing was our defense. We had a great defense. The one thing I remember is every time the offense ran onto the field, we were at the 35 or 40-yard line. Our field position was phenomenal. That was because of our defense."

What stands out about the 1995 Huskers is they only trailed in one game all year, and it was against Washington State very early in the season. NU dismantled Kansas State 49–25, Colorado 44–21, and Kansas 41–3. The latter two teams were in the top 10 at the time. In the national championship game against No. 2 Florida, the Huskers played a nearly flawless game, winning 62–24. "I have no memory of anybody dominating like Nebraska did this year," late Texas coach Darrell Royal told the *World-Herald* when talking about the 1995 team. "We had three national championships and we got out by the hair of our chinny-chin-chin three times a season.

Nebraska? They were standing over there looking for the water bucket by the fourth quarter in all of their games."

"They brought college football to a different level," retired Notre Dame sports information director Roger Valdiserri told the *World-Herald*. "I don't know if anybody will ever catch up to them."

The truth of the matter is nobody will ever know which team was better, but it will continue to serve as great debate fodder for years to come. Most of the younger generation gravitates toward the 1995 team, but people who have seen both argue the '71 Huskers definitely belong right up there.

Sporting News ranked the 1971 Nebraska team the greatest of all time in 2011 while the 1995 team was fourth in their rankings. ESPN's Page 2 also ranked the 1971 team as the greatest ever in 2002. ESPN's fan vote in 2006 ranked the 1995 team No. 1 as did *Parade* magazine.

8 Leading the Nation in Academic All-Americans

When you visit the University of Nebraska, a lot of different awards and accolades will jump out at you. NU has won five national championships in football, three Heisman Trophies, and nine Outland Trophies, but maybe its most impressive honor wasn't achieved on the football field. Heading into the 2013 season, the Huskers currently lead the nation with 302 CoSIDA Academic All-Americans with 104 of those coming in football.

The next closest school to Nebraska is Notre Dame with 227 overall Academic All-Americans while Penn State has the second-most football Academic All-Americans in the Big Ten at 51. In order to be eligible for Academic All-American honors, a student-athlete must maintain a 3.30 grade-point average along with being a varsity starter or key reserve.

If you visit Lincoln, one of the first things you will see in the West Stadium hallway is a giant wall that honors NU's Academics All-Americans. Each Academic All-American is featured with an oil-painted portrait along a wall that sits outside NU's dining facility and student life complex. Within Memorial Stadium itself, Nebraska's overall number of football Academic All-Americans is prominently scrolled across the north end zone.

When you talk about recruiting tools, Nebraska's Academic All-American history in football is a huge selling point to prospective athletes and parents. Playing sports at the NCAA level is about being a student-athlete, and NU's rich tradition of Academic All-Americans defines that more than anything.

Several of Nebraska's Academic All-Americans also were extremely successful on the field. Some notable Academic All-Americans were: offensive lineman Dave Rimington (1981–1982), defensive end Trev Alberts (1993), safety Mike Brown (1999), offensive lineman Aaron Graham (1995), defensive end Grant Wistrom (1996–1997), running back Rex Burkhead (2011–2012) and defensive end Kyle Vanden Bosch (1999–2000). All of these players were either All-Americans on the field, major award winners, or All-Conference over their careers at Nebraska.

Three of NU's current team doctors and orthopedic surgeons were Academic All-Americans at one time—Pat Clare (1960), Tom Heiser (1975), and Scott Strasburger (1983–1984). Both Pat Tyrance (1990) and Rob Zatechka (1993–1994) are also former Husker Academic All-Americans who went on to become successful doctors. Current director of football operations Jeff Jamrog was an Academic All-American in 1987. The list goes on and on, and the exclusive fraternity that defines being a student-athlete continues to grow at Nebraska.

Current head coach Bo Pelini has done his part to maintain the academic tradition at NU. When Pelini first arrived to Nebraska in 2008, he kept attendance records of every class and even showed up to a few buildings to make sure certain players were attending. Pelini's focus on academics has paid off. Heading into the 2013 season, the entire football team has a cumulative 3.2 grade-point average. "Everything counts in this program. From the time you wake up in the morning until the time you go to bed at night, we're going to hold you accountable in every aspect of what you do," Pelini told the *Lincoln Journal Star* in 2008.

9 The Blackshirts

When former Nebraska head coach Bob Devaney sent Mike Corgan to a local downtown sporting goods store, he had no idea of the monster it would eventually create.

The NCAA implemented rule changes following the 1963 season that would allow teams to go back to two-platoon football, so that players wouldn't have to play both offense and defense. After a 56–0 win against South Dakota in the 1964 season opener, Devaney made the decision he would no longer play his starters both ways but instead split up the practice field with offensive and defensive sides. "We just decided that we would be more efficient if we started platooning," Devaney told the *Lincoln Star*. Devaney's fear was Nebraska's program would fall behind if it didn't stop using players both ways.

Corgan, who was known for his frugality, worked out a deal with the sporting goods store to purchase black pullovers for the starting defense. The joke was Corgan got a bargain on the jerseys because nobody wanted them.

Defensive assistant coach George Kelly said when players first began practicing with the defense they wore gray pullovers. It wasn't until the first-team unit was divided up that the black pullovers were used to identify the starting defense. It served as a way to motivate the players on the lower units. From that moment on, a Nebraska legend was created that still stays with the program today. Each season since 1964, NU's starting defense has been identified as the "Blackshirts," a nationally recognized term to anyone associated with college football.

When defensive coordinator Charlie McBride came to Nebraska in 1977, the Blackshirts slogan took on more marketing and pizzazz. The Blackshirt logo would eventually be identified by a skull and crossbones. "I can't remember exactly, but it kind of started to get publicized after a guy from Omaha came to me about making an official Blackshirt insignia," McBride said. "We had something initially, and it was really bad. What happened was everyone started coming out with Blackshirt T-shirts and everything like that. Then one year we played Oklahoma, and I remember they made Blackshirt handkerchiefs that were like towels, and everyone had one. It kind of boomed from there, and when they started writing about them in the paper, they didn't refer to them as the Nebraska defense. They used the 'Blackshirts.' The press started picking that up, and the TV started picking that up. I'm not the guy that started it, but I was there when it was being promoted more and I probably instigated some of the promotion."

McBride, though, did start the tradition of putting the 11 Blackshirts in the defense's lockers on the Monday before the first game to let them know they were the starters. "The top 11 guys got Blackshirts, and that's the way it went," McBride said. "We handed them out the Monday of the first game. Everybody would come down and see what was in their locker. Most of the guys would come down, and they pretty much knew who it was going to be. It was kind of an unwritten rule that there were only 11 of them given out, but as time went on, we might have three guys play equal at a position like defensive end, so we ended up maybe giving one to Mike Rucker, even though he wasn't actually a starter."

Another tradition McBride added was rewarding senior defensive players with Blackshirts at the bowl game each year. "Then as time went on, we started having a Blackshirt picture taken at the bowl game. What we did was: Every senior player on defense got a Blackshirt at the bowl game for practice," McBride said. "Maybe some of them didn't get Blackshirts before. I remember one defensive back that I gave one to at the bowl had never had one before, and he started to get tears in his eyes and cry. I think at that point I started to realize what that thing really meant to a lot of these kids. As time went on they had a little decal that went on the back of the helmet. Everybody on the defense got that. It was round, about the size of a quarter on the back of your helmet."

It's a tradition that Bo Pelini still carries on to this day, but it's been altered somewhat from the Devaney and Tom Osborne days. Instead of giving the starting 11 their Blackshirts the Monday before the first game, Pelini hands out the jerseys after he feels they've earned them by playing "Blackshirt quality football." During some years under Pelini, the Blackshirts haven't been given out until November.

As many as 18 players have earned Blackshirts under Pelini in 2011, and as few as 11 did in 2012. Pelini's justification for handing out more than 11 Blackshirts is that his defense features several players who play starting-type roles depending on the opponent each week.

The Blackshirt slogan has carried a lot of weight for Nebraska during the last 40 years. It's something that high school players take notice of when they are on their official visits. "It was a big deal. On my recruiting visit, everybody was talking about being a Blackshirt, what it takes to be a Blackshirt," former All-American linebacker Lavonte David said during his NFL Combine draft interview in 2012. "The tradition of the Blackshirts goes way back, way back. You gotta earn it; you've gotta prove to the coaches that you're capable of getting the Blackshirt and to your teammates as well."

10 Nebraska's First National Championship

Heading into the 1970 season, it appeared Nebraska's program had turned the corner. NU finished 1969 by winning seven straight, including a 44–14 drubbing of rival Oklahoma and a 45–6 beating of Georgia in the Sun Bowl. Before the 1970 season began, future All-American Husker linebacker Jerry Murtaugh predicted the Big Red would capture the national championship. It was a bold prediction, considering NU started the season ranked No. 9.

The Huskers opened the year with a 36–12 victory against Wake Forest and then they traveled to the Coliseum to take on USC, who had defeated Nebraska 31–21 in 1969, and was ranked No. 3 going into their matchup in 1970.

With a 21–14 lead in the fourth quarter, Nebraska lined up for a chip shot field goal attempt to put the game away, but a bad snap kept USC alive. The Trojans would march down the field to score and tie the game at 21–21, and that's where things ended up. "We should have won the game," future Heisman Trophy winner Johnny Rodgers said years later.

It was a devastating early blow to Nebraska's national title hopes, but NU still moved up one place in the polls to No. 8 after the tie. And in a way, the tie to USC helped ignite the Huskers, who went on a nine-game winning streak. During that run in 1970, the Huskers avenged a 1969 loss to Missouri by beating the 16th ranked Tigers 21–7.

In the Big Red's homecoming game with No. 20 Kansas State, the Huskers took down the Wildcats 51–13. Ranked No. 3 going into the final week of the regular season, the Huskers beat a young Oklahoma team 28–21. (A year later the same two teams would play in The Game of the Century.)

Prior to the Orange Bowl, the Huskers were still ranked No. 3 behind Texas and Ohio State. Back in those days, the UPI released their final poll before the bowls, so Texas already had their top spot wrapped up while OSU was No. 2 and NU No. 3. The Associated Press poll waited until after the bowl games to release their rankings. There also wasn't a BCS ranking system in 1970, matching up the No. 1 and No. 2 ranked teams in a bowl game. The Big 8 (Orange Bowl), Southwest (Cotton), SEC (Sugar), Pac-10 (Rose), and Big Ten (Rose) Conferences all had locked-in bowl game agreements for their league champions.

That meant Texas and Ohio State could not match up in a bowl game. The Longhorns played No. 6 Notre Dame in the Cotton Bowl, the Buckeyes took on No. 12 Stanford in the Rose bowl, and the Huskers played No. 5 LSU in the Orange Bowl.

The Orange Bowl always kicks off at night in Miami, which meant the results of the Cotton and Rose Bowls would be known before NU and LSU squared off. As the Huskers left the hotel in Miami for the Orange Bowl, they already knew Notre Dame had upset Texas 24–11 in the Cotton Bowl. As they boarded the bus, they were aware that Stanford was giving Ohio State all they could handle. According to media relations director Don Bryant, tension was extremely high on that bus ride as a huge traffic jam slowed Nebraska's arrival to the stadium. "Minutes dragged on, and the buses couldn't move," Bryant wrote in *Tales from the Nebraska Sidelines*. "The silence was suddenly shattered as Husker middle guard Ed Periard jumped out into the aisle and yelled, 'Get this damn bus rolling!'"

Finally during pregame warm-ups, word got around that Stanford had beaten Ohio State 27–17, meaning all the No. 3 Huskers had to do was beat No. 5 LSU to win the national championship. That was the beauty of the old bowl system. It was almost like a mini-playoff on New Year's Day to decide the national champion. The chips fell the right way in 1970 for Nebraska, and everything set up perfectly for Bob Devaney and his squad. Bryant wrote that Devaney and his staff had to do their best to calm down the team in the locker room after news of the Rose Bowl became known.

With NU trailing 12–10 in the fourth quarter to LSU, Husker quarterback Jerry Tagge engineered a 67-yard drive and scored the winning touchdown from a yard out with 8:50 remaining. "I can still see Tagge reaching that ball over the goal line," Ross said years later. Junior linebacker Bob Terrio preserved the Huskers' 17–12 victory by intercepting a Bert Jones pass with 45 seconds left as NU finished the year 11–0–1.

Even after the game, there was some uncertainty about what the AP voters would do as Notre Dame head coach Ara Parseghian made a strong push to pollsters to select the Irish as the No. 1 team. "I was afraid Ara's comments might influence the voters, but I guess the writers are too smart to take some coach's word," Devaney said. "The writers knew who was best."

Nebraska also received an endorsement from president Richard Nixon, who proclaimed the Huskers No. 1. About 8,000 fans celebrated at the NU Coliseum on January 14, 1971. The following day Devaney addressed a crowd of about 2,000 fans who attended the football banquet at the Pershing Auditorium in Lincoln. "This is one of the few times in my life I can't think of anything funny to say. This 1970 team of ours is the finest football team I've ever had the opportunity to be a part of," Devaney said.

According to the *Lincoln Journal Star*, Devaney ended his speech with a reminder to underclassmen that "back-to-Earth day starts tomorrow," meaning preparations for the 1971 season began immediately.

11 The 1994 National Championship

For years Nebraska head coach Tom Osborne and his players had to constantly hear how they couldn't win the big one. Whether it was critical games with Oklahoma or bowl matchups against Miami and Florida State, the Big Red couldn't get over the hump. Heading into the 1994 Orange Bowl against Miami, NU had lost seven consecutive bowl games, and the Huskers were 0–7 in bowl games against FSU and Miami since 1983.

The running joke around college football was the Huskers were "bowl impaired." Naysayers thought of NU as a program that built up their win total against weaker Big 8 programs, and when it came time to play elite teams in the Orange Bowl, they couldn't compete with those athletic squads.

In 1993 the light bulb started to come on for Osborne and his team. After switching to the 4–3 defense and behind the emergence of quarterback Tommie Frazier, Nebraska took Florida State to the wire for the national championship in the Orange Bowl. The Huskers too a 16–15 lead with 1:16 left in the fourth quarter but failed to close the deal, losing to the Seminoles 18–16 on a field goal in the game's final minute.

Even though Nebraska lost that game to Florida State for the national championship, it came away hungrier than ever to finish the deal in 1994. NU's theme for the season was "Unfinished

Business." It became a T-shirt slogan, which grew familiar to everyone in the state.

After each drill Nebraska would put an extra 1:16 back on the clock to remind them of their painful defeat against Florida State. 1:16 drove the Huskers the entire offseason to get better. "I remember those workouts in the first week of January being as intense as ever because we wanted to get back to the Orange Bowl," offensive lineman Aaron Graham told the *Omaha World-Herald*. "We knew we were going to do whatever it took to get back."

The 1994 season was filled with all sorts of obstacles, including losing starting quarterback Frazier for eight games with blood clots. Backup quarterback Brook Berringer stepped in for Frazier, and the offense didn't miss a beat. The 1994 Huskers were determined to get back to Miami, and it showed that entire season as they continued to win big games when the odds were stacked against them.

NU opened that season with a 31–0 statement victory against No. 24 ranked West Virginia in the Kickoff Classic in East Rutherford, New Jersey. A couple of weeks later, the Huskers took down No. 13 UCLA 49–21. Even when Berringer went down, NU found ways to win. On the road at No. 16 Kansas State, the Huskers beat the Wildcats 17–6 with walk-on Matt Turman starting at quarterback. A couple of weeks later, Nebraska beat No. 2 ranked Colorado 24–7 in Lincoln. To this day it's considered one of the best regular season victories in school history. Before getting to the Orange Bowl, NU had to take care of business at Oklahoma and gritted out a 13–3 victory in Norman against their Big 8 rival.

When the stage was set in the Orange Bowl, Frazier had finally recovered from his blood clot problems. Osborne would name Frazier the starting quarterback over Berringer, but both players had an equal role in the Huskers victory, nearly splitting the snaps 50-50.

The Hurricanes had a defense that featured future NFL stars like linebacker Ray Lewis and defensive tackle Warren Sapp. Early on the Big Red fell behind 10–0 and 17–7. The Huskers stuck with the plan, and the game came down to the fourth quarter—exactly how Osborne predicted it would. Nebraska wore down Miami's talented defense, and fullback Cory Schlesinger had two fourth quarter touchdowns to give Osborne and the Huskers a 24–17 victory and their first national championship since 1971. "I don't think I've ever been around a team that knew where it was going and what it wanted to do from January 1 on," Osborne told the *Omaha World-Herald*. "These guys were focused from the beginning on getting back down here and winning the game."

The monkey was finally off Osborne's back. The past bowl experiences against teams like FSU and Miami prepared Nebraska for 1994, and the hard work paid off. "No matter what happened," Osborne said, "our guys showed pretty good character, a good work ethic, and a lot of determination. I'm proud to be associated with them. We felt if we could be close going to the fourth quarter that we had an excellent chance."

For Osborne it was an emotional moment. He had come so close to winning the national championship in 1981, 1983, and 1993. Finally his day had come. "I'm a person who puts a lot of emphasis on my faith," Osborne said. "I don't talk about it much, but I would like to express my thanks to God and to the players and the character they had."

It was only fitting Osborne's first national title would come against the Hurricanes, a team that stole the 1983 national championship right out of his hands. "It's a great way to close it out—to play Miami in Miami and finally beat them," Osborne said. "We've had a terrible time with those folks."

12 Osborne's Perfect Ending

In December of 1997, Nebraska head coach Tom Osborne shocked the college football world by announcing his retirement. Heading into the Orange Bowl against Tennessee, Osborne had put together a remarkable 59–3 record over five seasons, and it didn't look like the well was going to run dry any time soon.

Ranked No. 2 behind 11–0 Michigan, the 12–0 Huskers were set to square off against No. 3 Tennessee team led by All-American quarterback Peyton Manning. The Nebraska players not only wanted to send Osborne out as a winner, but they also wanted to give him an unprecedented third national championship in four years. In order for that to happen, they would have to beat the Volunteers and beat them convincingly to steal some votes from the Wolverines.

In most scenarios with the score 28–10 in the third quarter, teams adopt a conservative game plan. But the 1998 Orange Bowl was different because NU couldn't afford to let up if it wanted a chance at the title. Even with a comfortable lead late in the third quarter, Nebraska's players saw Osborne show emotion unlike ever before. "I've never really seen him the way he was tonight," senior defensive tackle Jason Peter told *Sports Illustrated*. "He came and got in everybody's face. That's very rare. Coach Osborne usually just says, 'Come on, let's go.' But he just grabbed me and said, 'Enough is enough! You guys have got to go out there and get the damn ball back. We've got to score some more points!' When we heard that, we didn't want to do anything but win this game for him."

After Tennessee scored to make it 28–10, NU responded with two more touchdowns to jump up 42–10. All the way up until the

Homegrown Offensive Talent

On the 1997 national championship team, nine of the 11 offensive starters came from the state of Nebraska. The 1997 offense defined what Nebraska football was about. It was a mixture of high profile in-state players—like quarterback Scott Frost and running back Ahman Green—along with overachieving walk-ons. All five of NU's starting skill players hailed from the state of Nebraska.

QB—Scott Frost (Wood River, Nebraska)
RB—Ahman Green (Omaha, Nebraska)
FB—Joel Makovicka (Brainard, Nebraska)
WR—Jeff Lake (Columbus, Nebraska)
WR—Lance Brown (Papillion, Nebraska)
TE—Tim Carpenter (Columbus, Nebraska)
TE—Vershan Jackson (Omaha, Nebraska)
OL—Eric Anderson (Lincoln, Nebraska)
OL—Josh Heskew (Yukon, Oklahoma)
OL—Aaron Taylor (Wichita Falls, Texas)
OL—Jon Zatechka (Lincoln, Nebraska)
OL—Fred Pollack (Omaha, Nebraska)
OL—Matt Hoskinson (Battle Creek, Nebraska) Note that Hoskinson rotated in as sixth man on the offensive line.

game's final seconds, Osborne was on his guys, who eventually won it for him 42–17.

Michigan beat Washington State 21–16 the day before in the Rose Bowl, and the Huskers did their part by not just beating Tennessee but making a statement, giving Tennessee the worst loss it had suffered over the last two seasons. Only one other time in his four years at Tennessee had Manning suffered a 25-point loss (1995 vs. Florida).

Following the win Osborne said he wasn't going to do any lobbying for his team to be voted No. 1, but that didn't stop his players. "If anybody can honestly find it in their heart not to vote us No. 1, that's their problem," senior defensive end Grant Wistrom said. "If you're just going to give it to Michigan because they haven't won in 45 years, then we don't want it anyway."

Quarterback Scott Frost sounded like a political candidate doing whatever he could to steal some late votes. "I don't think there's anybody out there with a clear conscience who can say that Nebraska and that great man Tom Osborne doesn't deserve a national championship for this—at least a share," Frost said.

The voters must have listened or taken notice of NU's 42–17 victory against Tennessee. Nebraska edged Michigan by receiving two more first-place votes to take over the No. 1 spot by a margin of 1,520 to 1,516 in the CNN/*USA TODAY* Coach's Poll. The Wolverines would finish No. 1 in the AP poll by a margin of 51½ to Nebraska's 18½ total first place votes. It was a split national championship, which has only happened one other time since 1997.

"It certainly is very gratifying," Osborne said. "Most all of us were in doubt. From our standpoint it couldn't have worked out any better. I'm really pleased for the University of Michigan, strangely enough. They very much deserve to be national champions…I have respect for both polls. It's just sad we're still dealing with polls. You wish there was just one [poll] or a playoff."

For the senior leaders like Wistrom, Frost, and Peter, sending Osborne out not only with a win, but also a national championship was the perfect ending to the best 25-year run in college football history. The Tennessee win was Osborne's 255th in 25 seasons. No coach has ever won that many games in 25 years. "These guys were playing for Tom and for all of his former players. They knew that there wasn't one guy in the last 25 years who would love to trade places with them," defensive coordinator Charlie McBride told the *Lincoln Journal Star*. "They had the honor of playing in Tom's last game and they showed it."

"This is the first game we played strictly on emotion," Wistrom said. "We wanted Tom to go out on top. We played all 60 minutes on emotion."

13 The Tunnel Walk

When HuskerVision's Jeff Schmahl, football recruiting coordinator Steve Pederson, and media relations director Chris Anderson got together for their first meeting about creating what is now known as the Tunnel Walk, nobody really knew what to expect. The HuskerVision big-screen boards were brand new, and no other team in college football had a specialized entrance like the Tunnel Walk, the team's march from the locker room under the North Stadium tunnel onto the field.

Schmahl knew the Tunnel Walk had the potential to be something special, but nobody could've predicted the type of impact it would have in building up the overall stadium atmosphere. "The first time we did the Tunnel Walk for that first game, I think people were just in shock," Schmahl said. "I can even remember that it didn't quite have the reaction that I was hoping for. I was in the control room, but I can hear what's happening because we have mics out on the field. I had at least one camera focused on the crowd, so I could kind of watch and see what the crowd's reaction was. There was almost just this shock of just what's going on?"

One of the early challenges of creating the Tunnel Walk was finding the perfect song for the team to take the field to. After listening to several different songs, it was Anderson who suggested the song "Sirius" by the Alan Parsons Project. It's was the same song the Chicago Bulls used to introduce their starting lineup, and they still use it today. "It was Chris Anderson who gets the credit for coming up with the Sirius music," Schmahl said. "She was the one who said, 'I think I've found it.' I don't remember who else was in there, but I remember Steve and I and Chris and as soon as we played it we were like, 'That's it. That's the one.' Our search ended there in terms of finding the music. That was one of the things we wanted. We wanted some music that would build and we wanted some music that had some really good bass and something that people could participate in and clap along with as well. As soon as we heard that song the first time, we were done."

The other thing both Schmahl and Pederson wanted to capture was the behind-the-scenes moment of the entrance when the team took the field. Schmahl's big thing was making sure to capture the team coming through the tunnel and slapping the lucky horseshoe that's been in the stadium nearly since its inception. Pederson wanted to make sure the fans lined up along the ropes greeting the team out of the tunnel were also part of the moment. "The idea of creating an entrance was mine in terms of sticking a camera into the tunnel," Schmahl said. "The thing that really triggered my mind was just the cool thing of the players hitting the horseshoe… It wasn't even as much as the team coming out of the tunnel and touching that horseshoe, but it was taking the fans to a place they can't go when they're in their seats. That's what I wanted to do with the visual of the Tunnel Walk."

Nebraska's first ever Tunnel Walk was the UCLA game in 1994. The next week they played Pacific, and by that point, Schmahl, Pederson, and Anderson realized they had struck gold. "As soon as the music came on this time the crowd exploded," Schmahl said. "It's kind of funny when I look back at what we did. Now the Tunnel Walk and the animation gets more complicated every year, but that first year, all we used were just three flashes on the screen followed by this star effect, and then there was the team. It was just a simple, simple little effect."

Schmahl said it was Dave Snitily from the advertising agency Snitily Carr in Lincoln, who came up with the simple flash effect that now has become the signal to tell Memorial Stadium the team is ready to take the field. "It was only about 20 minutes before the

The Impact of the Tunnel Walk on Recruiting

Over the years countless different top prospects mention their experience of the Tunnel Walk as one of the highlights of their official visit.

One notable recruit who mentioned Tunnel Walk on his official visit was Detroit Lions defensive tackle Ndamukong Suh, who starred at Nebraska from 2006 to 2009. Suh took his official visit to NU for the Kansas game in 2004. "The Tunnel Walk was intense...very intense," Suh said following his official visit. "The fans at Nebraska were one of the loudest crowds that I've ever heard. I couldn't even hear the person sitting next to me."

It's these types of small moments during a recruiting visit weekend that give Nebraska an edge in landing high-profile recruits like Suh.

first Tunnel Walk and Dave [Snitily] was playing with it and said, 'Hey, Jeff, how about if we put this flash effect on the screen first, so that we kind of bring attention to the team first?' I said, 'Okay, let me see it.' He hits it, and I said 'Yeah, that looks good. Let's see what happens when you hit it three times.' He hit it three times, and then the star effect, and that's what we used. For a couple of years, we always used that little flash effect to always signify the beginning of the Tunnel Walk. In year two it had the national championship trophy bursting through the ground on the 50-yard line. Then again it was very simplistic. It took about 15 seconds, but the crowd got to celebrate the national championship in that moment."

And ultimately that's what the Tunnel Walk is about—creating a moment at each and every home game. "What you want to do in the entertainment industry is give people goose bump moments," Schmahl said. "If I tell you right now to get goose bumps, well, you can't. You can't give yourself goose bumps. Yet when you get them, it feels really good. It's your body giving you a sensation that

'I really like this.' That's one of the really cool things the Tunnel Walk did and still does is you get goose bumps. It makes you feel good and makes you want to stand up and yell even louder. I think even the opposing teams got goose bumps and I think that's when opposing teams started to do [their own Tunnel Walks]."

Winning three national championships in four years also didn't hurt in trying to create those "goose bump moments" Schmahl was talking about. "We created a monster," Schmahl said. "Then when you win national championships and you have national championships to play with and you've got literally the most exciting years of Nebraska football, I kind of got to build the Tunnel Walk around those things. There was this aspect when [HuskerVision directors] Kirk Hartman and Shot Kleen and I would say, 'Yep, we did it again this year, but dang it, I don't know how we are going to outdo ourselves next year.' That was always one of the big things for people to see the new Tunnel Walk. There was always pressure to put together an even better Tunnel Walk. It started out very, very simple and got more complex and involved."

14 Johnny Rodgers

Not very many players could manage to steal the spotlight from legendary coach Bob Devaney in his final game at Nebraska, but that's exactly what Johnny "the Jet" Rodgers did in the 1973 Orange Bowl against Notre Dame. Rodgers, who became the Huskers' first Heisman Trophy winner a month earlier, put on perhaps one of the greatest individual performances in Orange Bowl history that night against the Irish.

Rodgers ran for three scores as an I-back, caught a touchdown pass from Dave Humm as a wide receiver, and threw a 52-yard touchdown pass to Frosty Anderson as the No. 9 Huskers routed No. 12 Notre Dame 40–6. It was the perfect way for the Big Red to send out Devaney and the perfect way for Rodgers to cap off the greatest career in program history. "Here we were, little ol' Nebraska playing the Irish. It was a big game for us," Rodgers told the *Omaha World-Herald* years later. "We wanted to make sure they had respect for us, so we gave it all we had. We pounced on them early, and I don't remember playing all that much in the second half. It was definitely satisfying to end things that way."

At the turn of the millennium in 2000, the *World-Herald* would label Rodgers the "greatest Husker player of the century." It's hard to argue that as Rodgers won the school's first Heisman Trophy and helped lead Nebraska to back-to-back national championships in 1970 and 1971 and three consecutive Orange Bowl victories. "He is still the best player I have ever seen at any level," Jerry Tagge, the starting quarterback in 1970 and 1971, told the *World-Herald* in 2001. "Without him that year, we don't win the national championship. We were pretty cocky and confident. We knew we were good. But if Johnny had gotten hurt during the season and not been able to play anymore, the feeling would have changed in a hurry."

Tom Osborne, who was Devaney's offensive coordinator, had similar words to describe Rodgers' value to NU's two national championship teams of the 1970s. Osborne said Rodgers gave the Huskers an X-factor in big games. He produced key plays in the biggest moments. His punt return for a touchdown in The Game of the Century against No. 2 ranked Oklahoma in 1971 set the tone for No.1 ranked Nebraska's 35–31 victory in Norman, Oklahoma. It's considered one of the all-time great plays in college football history.

Later that same season in the Orange Bowl against No. 2 ranked Alabama, Rodgers had another big kickoff return for a touchdown that sparked the Huskers' 38–6 win to capture their second consecutive national championship. "Johnny was always worth about 10 to 14 points a game," Osborne told the *World-Herald* in 2000. "Without him there was no assurance you would score. But with him even if we didn't score on offense, we were going to score on a punt or kickoff return."

As crazy as it sounds now, Osborne remembers that it wasn't a sure thing that Devaney was going to offer a scholarship to Rodgers when he came out of Omaha Technical High School in 1969. "I can remember a debate we had in a recruiting meeting that year," Osborne told the *World-Herald*. "It was between Johnny and another guy up in Omaha, [who] I think was named McWhorter or something like that. They were both similar players. They weren't very big—160 pounders. At one point there was some question as to which way we ought to go."

It's safe to say Devaney and Osborne made the right call on Rodgers. The Omaha native would go on to finish his career with 143 catches for 2,479 yards receiving and 25 touchdowns. Rodgers still holds the career and single-season (942 yards) receiving yards records along with the career and single-season (11) touchdown reception records. Rodgers returned seven punts and one kickoff for a touchdown and finished his career with a school-record 5,586 all-purpose yards. He averaged 13.8 yards per attempt on 406 career all-purpose touches. "Johnny probably could impact a football game more ways than anybody I've ever coached or been affiliated with," Osborne said. "It might be on a kick return, on a punt return, on a pass reception, on a reverse. He was just a great competitor."

15 Tom Novak

The description by legendary Husker play-by-play announcer Lyell Bremser perfectly encapsulates the late Tom Novak. "My eyes have never seen Tom Novak's equal at any position," the late Bremser once said. "As football players go, the Good Lord made Tom Novak, then threw away the mold."

The South Omaha native played fullback, center, and linebacker and is considered the toughest, most rugged Nebraska football player in program history. He is the Huskers' only four-time All-Conference selection (1946–1949) and was also named an All-American in 1949. Novak's No. 60 was retired in 1949, and no player has worn that number since. The only other permanently retired number at NU is Bob Brown's No. 64, but that didn't happen until 2004.

Novak appropriately earned the nickname "Trainwreck." "He simply loved to hit," former Husker teammate and trainer George Sullivan told the *Lincoln Journal Star* after Novak died in 1998. "He was one tough mogul on the football field. I remember hearing that Tom Harmon, All-American at Michigan, said he was looking forward to playing in the pros after the college All-Star Game, so he wouldn't have to practice against Novak any more. Tom just didn't have many pain fibers in football, baseball, or any sport."

Considered the best Nebraska player before the days of hard helmets and face masks, Novak played in the days of single-platoon football, meaning he never left the field. In 1947 Novak played in all but 30 minutes the entire season. He was also a three-time All-Conference selection in baseball as well, leading the Huskers to conference championships in 1948 and 1950. "The Novaks in

South Omaha were legendary," former Husker and South Omaha native Dave Rimington said. "[Novak] was one tough guy—a lot tougher than me. I was a big guy, but this guy was the real deal as far as a mean, nasty football players that you wouldn't want to mess with. He's the original star local athlete at Nebraska. The other one would be Johnny Rodgers."

Maybe the story that describes Novak in a nutshell came during the 1947 Notre Dame game. Nebraska lost that day 31–0 in South Bend, Indiana, as the Fighting Irish would go on to win the national championship that season. According to reports from that game, Novak had 17 tackles during a string of 21 plays. Eventual Notre Dame Heisman Trophy-winning quarterback Johnny Lujack definitely knew who Novak was after that game. "He didn't tackle people. He just ran over you," former Novak teammate Moon Mullen told the *Journal Star*. "The 1947 Notre Dame team, that won the national championship and beat us 31–0, called him their all-time opponent. Those South Bend fans gave him a standing ovation that day. I run into some of those guys—[All-American Notre Dame tackle] George Connor, for instance—and they always ask about Novak. Tom had this national reputation that he built every time he played. Tom was the kind of guy—he'd come to the sideline, his face all messed up, and ask the doctor to put his nose back in joint, so he could get back on the field."

Even up until his death in 1998, Novak showed toughness. In 1976 Novak was in an accident that paralyzed him and he battled numerous illnesses during that period. It was a 22-year battle for "Trainwreck", one that he eventually lost—but not without a fight.

The late Bobby Reynolds, also a former NU All-American, once described Novak as "the Dick Butkus before there was a Dick Butkus." Former Nebraska sports information director Don Bryant also had high words of praise for Novak. "Tom was without question the toughest guy I ever knew. He was the toughest football player I've ever seen," Bryant told the *Journal Star*. "He was the same way as a catcher. You didn't want to slide into the plate, and he often intimidated batters."

Novak turned down three different offers from the NFL, according to the *Journal Star* and went into the trucking business immediately after college. Each year the spirit of Novak is honored when the Tom Novak Award is given to the Husker senior who "best exemplifies courage and determination despite all odds." The award is presented annually at the Outland Trophy dinner in Omaha each January.

16 Mike Rozier

When running back Mike Rozier was coming out of high school in Camden, New Jersey, the entire football world was recruiting him. Once word got out, however, that Rozier was not going to meet the minimum NCAA GPA requirements to be eligible as a freshman, everybody dropped off of him except one person. "Everyone forgot all about me but Nebraska," Rozier said in a 1983 Independent Press Service article. "Tom Osborne suggested that I go to junior college to get my marks up. And he kept in touch with me to see how I was doing."

Little did Osborne know he was laying down the foundation with the player who would eventually become the best running back in school history.

Rozier attended Coffeyville Community College in Kansas for the 1980 season. It was a huge change from Camden. He rode a Greyhound bus cross country and was dropped off in Coffeyville, which seemed like the middle of nowhere. "Everything was in one building," Rozier remembers when he arrived in Coffeyville.

"There wasn't anything out there. It was hot. The bushes had all dried up. The grass had all dried up. There was no green grass."

Rozier was so miserable in Coffeyville that he nearly quit football altogether, but he decided to stick it out. He would go on to lead Coffeyville to a perfect 9–0 record, rushing for 1,157 yards and 10 touchdowns on 157 carries. All of a sudden, Rozier was back on the map, and all of those people that forgot about him a year ago reappeared into his life after his All-American freshman season at Coffeyville.

Rozier, however, never forgot that Osborne was the only coach to stick with him after word got out that he wouldn't be eligible. Osborne's loyalty toward Rozier made it an easy decision for him to attend Nebraska. "Nebraska stuck with me," Rozier said, "so I stuck with Nebraska."

Not only did Rozier stick with the Big Red, he would go on to shatter every single running back record in school history. He finished his career with a school-record 4,780 rushing yards and 49 touchdowns. During his senior season in 1983, he set the Nebraska record by rushing for 2,148 yards and 29 touchdowns en route to being named the Huskers second Heisman Trophy winner—joining wide receiver Johnny Rodgers who won the 1972 Heisman. To this day no other player has ever rushed for more than 4,000 yards in his career or 2,000 yards in a single season at Nebraska.

What was remarkable about many of Rozier's numbers was that he was pulled out early in the second half of a lot of games because the Huskers had such big leads. Rozier finished his career with a 7.16 yards-per-carry average on 668 attempts. That was an NCAA record all the way up until 2005 when USC running back Reggie Bush finished his career with a 7.3 yards-per-carry average.

Rozier was officially inducted into the College Football Hall of Fame in 2006. He played seven years in the NFL, earning Pro Bowl honors in 1987 and 1988 for the Houston Oilers. "Mike was one of the greatest running backs I've seen," Osborne told the *Omaha*

World-Herald at the time of Rozier's Hall of Fame induction. "He had great ability to make people miss while continuing up field without much deviation in his path. He had great balance and always had a great deal of fun playing the game and was enjoyable to be around."

17 Tommie Frazier

One word best describes Nebraska quarterback Tommie Frazier over his illustrious career from 1992 to 1995—winner. Frazier finished his career at NU with a remarkable 33–3 record as a starter, including an 11–2 mark against ranked teams. He's considered the best quarterback in NU school history and one of the best college football players of his generation.

During Frazier's four-year career, Nebraska played in three straight national championship games and won four Big 8 conference titles. Frazier was a unanimous All-American and captured the Johnny Unitas Golden Arm Award in 1995 as the Huskers won back-to-back national championships. The only thing missing from Frazier's trophy case was the Heisman.

Frazier lost out on the award to Ohio State running back Eddie George by a margin of 1,460 to 1,196. The Heisman voting happens in December, a month before the bowl games are played. After Nebraska's 62–24 victory against Florida in the Fiesta Bowl, people realized the wrong player may have won the Heisman. "I wasn't going into the game to prove anything," Frazier said after rushing for 199 yards and passing for 105 yards against the Gators. "At the time people thought Eddie George was the best player. Maybe he was, but that's not for me to say. Some voters might

The best quarterback in program history, Tommie Frazier finished his Husker career with a very impressive 33–3 record as a starter. (Getty Images)

change their minds now; some might not. It's over now. I'm ready to go on with the rest of my life."

Frazier certainly left his mark on the college football world in the third quarter of the Fiesta Bowl with a play that Husker fans simply refer to as "the Run." With the score 42–18 in favor the Big Red, Frazier dashed for a 75-yard touchdown run while breaking seven Florida tackles. After Johnny Rodgers' punt return against Oklahoma in The Game of the Century, Frazier's run that night in Tempe, Arizona, is considered one of the greatest individual plays in school history. "That's the way I want to be remembered," Frazier told the *Omaha World-Herald* following the Fiesta Bowl, "as a player who gave everything he had, no matter what the situation was."

From the moment head coach Tom Osborne recruited Frazier following NU's 1991 loss to Miami in the Orange Bowl, No. 15 was bound for greatness. No other true freshman has ever started at quarterback for Nebraska, and Osborne officially handed him the keys to the car on October 24 against Missouri during the 1992 season. That ended up being one of the biggest program-changing decisions in Osborne's coaching career as NU went 27–1 in Big 8 play from 1992 to 1995. Frazier brought a certain swagger to the football field. "The thing that Tommie brings to the game more than anybody else," Osborne said, "is a presence and a confidence and a competitiveness and an intelligence that very few players have."

When Frazier's career was over, the *Sporting News* called him one of the 10 best college football players of the century. He earned induction into the College Football Hall of Fame in 2013. "I had a great career at Nebraska, and there's no better way to end it," Frazier said as he hoisted his second consecutive national championship trophy in 1995.

18 Eric Crouch

The day was August 30, 1999. Nebraska head coach Frank Solich made what he called "the toughest decision in his 30 years of coaching." NU was preparing to open the 1999 season on the road at Iowa, and that Monday, Solich named junior Bobby Newcombe the starting quarterback over sophomore Eric Crouch. In 1998 Newcombe was the starting quarterback, but he went down with an injury, and Crouch started five of NU's final seven games and did an excellent job in Newcombe's place.

The 1999 team was a national championship contender, and the only thing that had to be decided was the quarterback race. When Solich picked Newcombe, rumors immediately swirled about Crouch's future.

Crouch drove back to Omaha that day and spent time with his former high school coach Fred Petito at Omaha Millard North. It was an extremely difficult time for Crouch, and he turned toward one of the closest people in his life for advice. Immediately Solich got word that Crouch was in Omaha talking to Petito about his future. Without hesitation Solich and wide receivers coach Ron Brown jumped in their car to meet with Petito and Crouch at Millard North. Solich blew off his scheduled time slot on the Big 12 coaches' conference call along with his speaking appearance at the Extra Point Booster Luncheon in order to meet with Crouch and Petito that Monday. In so many ways, Solich and Brown talked Crouch off the ledge and convinced him the quarterback race was still ongoing. "They just wanted to know how he was doing," Petito told the *Omaha World-Herald* in 1999. "I've seen him down before. And I've always seen him bounce back. That is athletics. This is a disappointment for Eric. But I don't think it's a setback."

Petito's instincts were correct. In the first two games of the season against Iowa and California, Crouch outplayed Newcombe, even though he saw limited snaps at quarterback. The icing on the cake came during the Cal game when in a span of less than eight minutes Crouch ran for a touchdown, threw a touchdown pass, and caught a touchdown pass from Newcombe.

The following week a very dangerous Southern Miss team came to Lincoln, and Solich made the decision to move Newcombe to wide receiver and named Crouch his new starting quarterback. "They both feel very comfortable about moving into the roles that we've asked them to move into," Solich, the Huskers' second-year coach, said at his weekly press conference. "It will give us a chance to have two great football players on the field at the same time getting multiple snaps."

Solich's decision to make a midseason switch from Newcombe to Crouch at quarterback paved the way for the Omaha native to become Nebraska's third Heisman Trophy winner. He earned the award in 2001 despite the fact the Huskers lost 62–36 in the regular season finale to Colorado. Crouch also won the Walter Camp Player of the Year award and the Davey O'Brien Quarterback of the Year award in 2001. He finished his career with 3,434 rushing yards and 59 touchdowns to go along with 4,481 yards and 29 touchdowns through the air. Crouch led the Big Red to the 1999 Big 12 championship and in 2001 he led the Huskers to the Rose Bowl where they lost to Miami for the national championship.

A disgruntled Newcombe continued to play wide receiver but never let his frustration affect the overall chemistry of the football team. In a 2009 interview, Newcombe said he hasn't attended a Husker football game since his career ended in 2000.

As Crouch hoisted his Heisman at the Downtown Athletic Club, Solich reflected on that difficult month in 1999 when he ultimately made the right decision. "Everyone associated with our program thought that Eric was very deserving of the award, and now the rest of the nation honored him as well," Solich said. "We are proud of what he accomplished not only on the field but how he lives his life. He's a great athlete and a great young man."

19 Going for Two in the Orange Bowl

Perhaps no play defined Tom Osborne in his coaching career more than his decision to go for two in the final seconds of the 1984 Orange Bowl against Miami. The 1983 Huskers are considered one of the all-time great teams not to win a national championship as they fell that night 31–30 in the Orange Bowl.

After falling behind 17–0 and then 31–17, the No. 1 Huskers scored a touchdown with 48 seconds left to pull within one point of the No. 5 Miami Hurricanes. Overtime did not exist in college football in 1984, so Osborne's options were to either kick the extra point and accept a tie or go for two and attempt to win the game. If NU would've kicked the extra point and tied Miami, it more than likely would've received enough votes to finish No. 1 in the polls.

However, going for the tie wasn't even a thought. Backup quarterback Craig Sundberg stood right behind Osborne after Jeff Smith's touchdown made it 31–30. "The thing I remember is there was no issue or no conversation about if we were going to go for two or not," Sundberg said. "I am not sure how well this has been documented, but we would always practice a two-point play for every game, so that was the play we would run…The play you saw there, where Jeff Smith and Scott Kimball go out for a pass, is the play that we designated for that game as the two-point play. There wasn't any conversation or doubt. It frankly never even crossed my mind to kick the extra point."

Even 25 years later, Osborne didn't question his decision to go for the win. But as Osborne thinks about it today, he often wonders what would've happened if the overtime rules had existed. "You would want to see what would happen in overtime," Osborne told the *Omaha World-Herald* in 2008. "We had kind of gained the momentum in the game at that point. In spite of losing Mike Rozier earlier in the second quarter, we were gaining control of the game."

Even Miami fully expected Osborne to go for two considering the circumstances of how the rules worked. "There was no doubt in Tom Osborne's mind, and there was no doubt in my mind. It was a championship game, and he went after it like a champion," Hurricanes coach Howard Schnellenberger said afterward.

It was a career-defining decision for Osborne in a lot of ways. His decision to go for two sent a message to the entire state of Nebraska as to what he was all about. Osborne was about the process, and to win a national championship you had to earn it. Backing into the national championship by kicking an extra point just wouldn't have felt right. "If I had gone for the tie, there was no guarantee that Nebraska would get the votes," Osborne said 25 years later. "If you go for the tie and you finish second or third, you look like an idiot. If you are going to play for a championship, you play to win. I don't think I could have voted for a team that knew it had backed into it. In football you don't play for a tie."

20 Boyd Epley and the Nebraska Strength Program

It was 1968. Nebraska had just lost their final regular season game of the season at Oklahoma 47–0. Head coach Bob Devaney was searching for answers. For the second year in a row, NU finished 6–4 overall and 3–4 in conference play. For the second year in a row, Devaney's Huskers were not going to a bowl game after playing in five straight from 1962 to 1966.

Devaney knew he had to find a way to give Nebraska an edge, and he turned to a young assistant coach named Tom Osborne for advice. Osborne suggested Devaney implement some sort of strength and conditioning program, and the perfect man for the job was a former Husker track athlete named Boyd Epley. Osborne noticed that Epley and a few other Husker student-athletes were having great success rehabbing injuries by lifting weights, and it was something that might help the entire football team in their overall development. "In 1968 Nebraska lost their final game of the season 47–0 at Oklahoma on national television," Epley said. "They realized they needed to do something, and that's when Tom [Osborne] gave me a call, and that's why Coach Devaney was receptive to his suggestion. If they would've won that game, they might not have felt the need to make a change."

Devaney told Osborne he'd give Epley the 1969 season to show him what he could do. Epley was paid a salary of $2 an hour and he was only paid to work two hours a day in the afternoon. Little did anyone know that the decision to hire Epley would be a program changer—and really a landscape-changing decision for all of sports as we know it. "One year later in Norman, Oklahoma, after lifting weights Nebraska beat Oklahoma 44–14," Epley said. "It was on their field and it was the worst loss they had had in history up to that point. That's when everybody started to notice something was going on at Nebraska."

All of a sudden, Osborne and Devaney looked like geniuses. Teams around the country began to take notice of Nebraska's rapid rise in strength and conditioning. Nebraska would then take it to another level by implementing the first ever offseason strength and conditioning program in college football. "There wasn't an offseason program before 1969," Epley said. "They didn't lift weights during the season and they did not lift weights in the summer and they did not stick around in the summer. Guys went home. They came into the fall and they would have fall camp to try and get people into shape at the last minute. Nebraska was the first school to lift weights during the regular season with a program, and we were the first to have summer conditioning. Coach Osborne caught onto this and went to the physical education department and made me an instructor, and the athletes actually got credit for taking summer conditioning as a class. I encouraged them to stick around, and they were able to continue their scholarships if they were on scholarship, and this made it financially feasible for them to stick around town and work out four days a week."

Epley's phone started to blow up. Coaches like Woody Hayes, Barry Switzer, and Jackie Sherrill began calling Epley to figure out what they were doing at Nebraska to gain such a physical advantage over their opponents. Husker offensive linemen were knocking opponents seven or eight yards off the ball, and people wanted to know how.

Schools were trying to lure away anyone associated with Epley and his strength program. In the 1970s Arkansas hired Jim Williams away from Epley, UCLA hired Donn Swanbom, and Miami hired Steve Bliss. In 1976 Epley hired Mike Arthur and was able to pay him full-time as a second strength coach, so other schools couldn't steal him away from NU. Arthur still remains with the strength program today.

Nebraska's first weight room was just 900 square feet in North Stadium and featured a Universal Gym machine, five dumbbells, and one set of weights. In 1981 Nebraska's weight room moved to West Stadium and would be remodeled again in 1988. In 2006 NU moved the weight room back to North Stadium, and at more than 17,500 square feet, it is still one of the most impressive facilities in the country.

Epley would retire from Nebraska in 2006. In 35 years working under Devaney, Osborne, and Frank Solich, the Huskers won 356 games and five national championships. Under Epley's watch NU produced 46 All-American offensive and defensive linemen, a true testament to Nebraska's weight room development and "Husker Power."

Epley also founded and started the National Strength Coaches Association in Lincoln, which now has more than 33,000 members. When Epley retired from NU in 2006, he went to work fulltime for the NSCA in Colorado Springs, Colorado, and still works for them today. While at Nebraska Epley was credited with inventing four different weight room machines used today across the country. Epley invented the leg sled; the Jammer, which is a part of Hammer Strength equipment; the multi-purpose Half Rack; and the Transformer, which allows athletes to squat without a spotter because of an electric mechanism that catches the bar if you lose control of the weight.

When Epley goes back to that 1968 phone call from Osborne, asking him to start Nebraska's strength program, it's pretty amazing how far things have evolved over the last 45 years. "There's no way anyone could've imagined how this would impact Nebraska or the rest of the world," Epley said. "Nowadays every athlete in every sport and every coach is impacted by what Bob Devaney and Tom Osborne did."

21 The Outland Trophy Winners

Perhaps no award signifies Nebraska's strength as a football program more than the Outland Trophy. Since 1971 NU has produced a nation-leading nine Outland Trophies highlighted by a run from 1981 to 1983 when they won the award three consecutive years. The Outland Trophy defined what Nebraska football was all about during their great championship seasons. It is awarded annually to college football's top down lineman, and consequently NU has been one of the most dominant programs up front in college football history.

Former offensive line coach Milt Tenopir worked with five of Nebraska's eight Outland winners and considers the award more than just an individual honor. "The Outland Trophy is a nice award, but I think it's more of a team award," Tenopir said. "I think it has to do more with the success you have in your program. The fact that we were doing what we were doing offensively really highlighted linemen, and it was pretty hard to pass up guys if you watched guys on film knocking the crap out of people every time they took off from the ball."

The Huskers' first Outland winner—defensive tackle Larry Jacobson—coincided with the 1971 national championship season. In 1972 defensive lineman Rich Glover won NU's second Outland Trophy and also took home the Lombardi Award. That same season Johnny Rodgers captured the Heisman Trophy, and the Huskers completed a 33–2–2 run from 1970 to 1972, winning three consecutive Orange Bowls and two national championships.

When your program wins at the highest level, players are going to receive the highest honors. Nebraska's next run of Outland winners came from 1981 to 1983. Offensive lineman

Nebraska's Connection to Three Major Awards

Each year the state of Nebraska features three major college football awards dinners—two in Omaha and one in Lincoln.

Since 1997 Omaha has hosted the Outland Trophy dinner at the Downtown Doubletree Hotel. Each January the Downtown Omaha Rotary Club helps put together the event where they honor not only the current Outland winner, but they also present a trophy to a past Outland winner. The Outland winner from 1946 to 1989 did not receive an authentic Outland Trophy, so the Downtown Omaha Rotary Club brings in a past winner to honor each year.

When Ndamukong Suh accepted his Outland in January of 2010, more than 1,000 people attended the dinner. Past Outland winners like Larry Jacobson, Zach Wiegert, and Dave Rimington are regulars at the dinner at each year.

Rimington also has his own trophy called the Rimington Trophy—given to college football's top center. Each January Rimington hosts his event in Lincoln at the Rococo Theater. Husker offensive lineman Dominic Raiola won the first Rimington Trophy in 2000.

The most recent award added with Nebraska ties was the Jet Award started in 2011 by former Heisman Trophy winner Johnny Rodgers. Each April the award honors college football's top return specialist. The dinner is held at the downtown Hilton in Omaha.

Dave Rimington—the only college football player to ever win two straight—won back-to-back Outlands in 1981 and 1982. Offensive lineman Dean Steinkuhler followed that up by winning the Outland in 1983. The Huskers didn't win a national championship in any of those seasons, but they were in contention all three years, compiling a 33–5 record and some gaudy rushing numbers to go with it.

Former strength coach Boyd Epley worked with 48 different All-American Nebraska linemen and seven Outland Trophy winners. "Those offensive linemen at one time went 15,000 workouts without a miss, without any of them missing a workout,"

Epley said proudly. "That work ethic is why Nebraska is unique. There were coaches that came from all around that watched that work ethic and tried to copy it and take it back to their facility, and they weren't able to do it. It was the willpower and the work ethic of Nebraska athletes that made Nebraska special."

After Steinkuhler, NU would go another nine years before offensive lineman Will Shields captured the Huskers' sixth Outland Trophy in 1992. Offensive lineman Zach Wiegert followed that up by winning the award in 1994, and offensive lineman Aaron Taylor won the Huskers' eighth Outland in 1997. Both Wiegert and Taylor were on national championship teams while Shields, who made 12 consecutive Pro Bowls with the Kansas City Chiefs, is arguably the most decorated NFL player the Huskers have ever produced in the modern era. Nebraska's ninth and most recent Outland came from defensive tackle Ndamukong Suh in 2009. Considered one of the most dominant defensive players of his generation, Suh is the only player not associated with Bob Devaney or Tom Osborne to win an Outland Trophy at Nebraska.

Without NU's line play up front, Epley still believes that Nebraska never would've had the type of success they did under Osborne and Devaney. "The linemen are an important part of any football team," Epley said. "Because of their run philosophy and Coach Osborne was trying to recruit linemen that would help with their running game, it tied in very well to the philosophy and need to have a great strength program. I have videos still where some of our linemen are blowing the opponent off the line seven or eight yards at a time. It was just amazing."

22 Bowl Game History

From 1969 to 2003, Nebraska appeared in a bowl game for 35 consecutive seasons. That extends to 42 of the last 44 seasons overall, heading into 2013. To put it into perspective, Alabama's longest streak is 25 years, Texas' is 12 years, Ohio State's is 15 years, and Oklahoma's is 14 years. The 35-year bowl streak defines the stability Tom Osborne and Bob Devaney built into the Nebraska program during their tenures. Almost every national power has a rebuilding year at some point, but from 1969 to 2003, that never happened at Nebraska.

Only Michigan and Florida State have played in bowl games in 30 consecutive years or more. The Wolverines had a streak of 33 straight years playing in a bowl game, but Huskers fans can thank Rich Rodriguez and a few down seasons in the 2000s for ending their run at 35. Following the 2012 season, Florida State currently has a streak of 31 consecutive bowl game appearances, but during their lean years in the mid 2000s, the Seminoles were able to get into two bowl games with 6–6 records. During Nebraska's 35-year bowl streak, only one team had less than nine wins, and that came in 2002 when the Huskers went 7–6 in the regular season.

During Nebraska's 35-year bowl streak from 1969 to 2003, the Huskers played in 14 Oranges Bowls, six Fiesta Bowls, three Sugar Bowls, and one Rose Bowl—or in today's terms 24 BCS bowl games. Nebraska played in an NCAA record 17-straight New Year's Day bowl games from 1981 to 1997, which is a record that likely will never be touched again since bowl games are now staggered throughout December and January.

Only Alabama (60) and Texas (51) have played in more bowl games than Nebraska as the Huskers are currently tied with

Warm Weather Bowl Prep

Before the days of massive indoor practice facilities, preparing for a bowl game in December could be pretty challenging for Nebraska because of the frigid temperatures in the home state.

Former head coach Bob Devaney had an interesting way around that. In 1964 (Cotton Bowl) and 1966 (Sugar Bowl), Devaney took his team to Brownsville, Texas, for bowl practice, and in 1965 (Orange Bowl), NU practiced in Scottsdale, Arizona, and stayed at the legendary Camelback Inn.

Shortly after that the NCAA passed legislation that only allowed schools to practice within 100 miles of the game site.

Tennessee at 49 all-time bowl game appearances following the 2012 season. With 25 losses, however, Nebraska has dropped more bowl games than any team in college football history. From 1988 to 1993, NU lost seven straight bowl games under Osborne before winning four in a row to close out his coaching career.

Twenty of Nebraska's 49 bowl games have been played in the state of Florida. Miami has been the Huskers most common bowl game opponent; the two teams have played six times from 1962 to 2002. NU has also played Florida State four times and LSU and Alabama three times in bowl games.

The Orange Bowl is the bowl Nebraska has played in the most, which makes sense as the Big 8 champion used to receive an automatic invite there. The Huskers have played in 17 Orange Bowls, and only Oklahoma has played in more with 18. From the 1991 to 1997 seasons, the Huskers played in six Orange Bowls over a seven-year period. Nebraska also has had six appearances in the Fiesta and four in the Sugar and Cotton Bowls.

23 Barry Switzer vs. Nebraska

From 1973 to 1988, no two coaches or programs gave college football better theater than Oklahoma's Barry Switzer and Nebraska's Tom Osborne. Over that 16-year period, the two squared off 17 times, including once in the 1979 Orange Bowl. Of those 17 historic matchups, the Sooners and Huskers were both ranked in the top 10 for 13 of them.

It was the Lakers vs. Celtics or the Yankees vs. Red Sox of college football. When Oklahoma and Nebraska met each year the day after Thanksgiving, the entire nation tuned in. What made the rivalry even more unique were the disparate personalities of Osborne and Switzer. Osborne was a very conservative-minded, Christian-valued coach; Switzer was flashy and liked to have fun. Yet the two developed a bond over the years.

Switzer held an all-time 12–5 record against Osborne, including a period from 1973 to 1980 where he won eight out of nine matchups. The only year the Huskers won during that period was in 1978, and the Sooners avenged the loss by beating NU later that season in the Orange Bowl.

When Switzer stepped down following the 1988 season, the Sooners only beat Osborne one time from 1989 to 1997. It was clear after Switzer left that the Oklahoma vs. Nebraska rivalry was never quite the same. "When Tom and I were coaching, Oklahoma and Nebraska were the best programs in the country," Switzer said during Osborne's retirement party in Omaha. "We were at the top of the heap. When I left I remember having a conversation with Tom. I was coaching the Cowboys actually and I asked Tom after he was hanging half hundred on Oklahoma and 60 or 70 points on everybody else. I asked him, 'What the hell has happened?' He

Despite squaring off as rivals during 17 contests over a 16-year period, former Oklahoma coach Barry Switzer and former Nebraska coach Tom Osborne hold each other in high regard.

said, 'It's not the same anymore,' and I said, 'I don't understand it. There's not the rivalry anymore?' He said, 'Barry, when you left, the rivalry left. It's not the same.'"

Even when Oklahoma was down and Osborne had some of his best teams, Switzer found a way to make it interesting. In 1983 Nebraska had their famous "Scoring Explosion Offense," but the unranked Sooners gave the top-ranked Huskers all they could handle as NU squeaked out a 28–21 victory in Norman, Oklahoma.

The 1987 Oklahoma-Nebraska game in Lincoln was probably the most legendary matchup between Switzer and Osborne as NU was ranked No. 1 and OU was No. 2. The winner would have a clear path to the national championship game to take on Miami in the Orange Bowl. Dubbed "The Game of the Century II," the Huskers jumped out 7–0 after a 25-yard touchdown run by running back Keith Jones. After that it was all Oklahoma. The

Sooners scored the next 17 points to defeat the Huskers 17–7. Switzer's defense completely shut down Osborne's offense, holding the Big Red to 235 total yards while OU's offense rushed for 419 yards on 70 carries.

Switzer would go on to coach only one more year at Oklahoma. He stepped down following the 1988 season after OU was placed on probation for committing numerous NCAA violations. Even though Switzer had the upper hand over Nebraska for most of his 16 seasons, he still considers Osborne the best coach in college football history. "What I want to say about Tom and what he accomplished in his career at Nebraska in 25 years is it's the greatest 25 years any football coach has ever had in college football," Switzer said. "He cast a shadow longer than anybody that's ever coached the game. You don't win like what he won and not be the best.

"His last nine years after I left were fabulous. I think he started doing a lot of things we did. He got athleticism at quarterback and he started to run the option and doing things to the perimeter of defenses we did to defenses. With the great north-south running game he had attacking people on the edges, no one slowed him down. If I was going to coach again today, I'd probably run his playbook. I wouldn't run a spread offense and all this. I'd be a great defense and a great running game and I'd run the option."

24 George Flippin

Running back George Flippin was not only considered Nebraska's first football star, but in 1892 the Stromsburg, Nebraska, native also became the first ever African American football player in program history. According to legendary tennis player Arthur Ashe's *A Hard Road to Glory*, at the time Flippin was just the fifth black football player at a predominantly white university.

Flippin was the son of freed slaves Charles and Mahala, and his father fought in the Civil War for the Union Army shortly after receiving his freedom. Flippin's mother passed away three years later, and George and his father moved to Kansas. Following his wife's death, Charles Flippin fulfilled his lifelong dream to become a doctor by attending Bennett College of Eclectic Medicine. Flippin's father remarried, and the family moved to Henderson, Nebraska.

After graduating from Henderson High School in 1891, Flippin made history by attending the University of Nebraska and becoming the first African American player to try out for the football team. At the time Nebraska was referred to as the "Old Gold Knights" and eventually became the "Bugeaters" after back-to-back successful seasons in 1890 and 1891. It was also during this time that Nebraska dropped their gold colors in favor of scarlet and cream.

During Flippin's first season—and maybe the moment in history he's most famous for at Nebraska—Missouri refused to play the Bugeaters in 1892 because they had a black player. Missouri instead chose to forfeit the game 1–0. That would be the only year Missouri didn't play Nebraska because of Flippin. Mizzou won both the 1893 and 1894 games that featured the 6'2", 200 pound Flippin, who displayed exceptional size, speed, and athleticism. Besides football, Flippin also took part in baseball, wrestling, and the shot put. Flippin's presence in athletics helped NU cross a major bridge for the school.

However, even Flippin had to fight off racist remarks from his own coach, Frank Crawford, after Flippin was voted a team captain. "It takes a man with brains to be a captain; all there is to Flippin is brute force...I don't take exception to him because he is colored, but it takes a head to be a football captain," Crawford said, according to a netnebraska.org article.

Flippin got the last laugh as the intelligent African American star graduated from the University of Nebraska in 1895 with a degree in medicine and began his medical career in Pine Bluff, Arkansas.

In 1907 Flippin and his wife, Georgia, moved back to Nebraska to Stromsburg, so he could be closer to his father. Flippin opened a small private practice and eventually helped found and build a new hospital in Stromsburg, which is now a bed and breakfast. The Flippins would become one of the wealthiest families in the area, and according to the University of Nebraska's website, George was a "respected physician and surgeon known across the county and state for his willingness to make house calls regardless of the distance or the ability of the family to pay."

Flippin passed away on May 15, 1929 and is still the only African American buried in the Stromsburg cemetery. In 1974 Flippin became the first black player inducted into the Nebraska Football Hall of Fame. When Nebraska takes the field now, Flippin is one of four players featured on the iron doors, which the team comes out of during the Tunnel Walk in Memorial Stadium.

The University of Nebraska also honors Flippin's legacy with a four-by-six-foot mural-style portrait of Flippin standing in a white sweater emblazoned with a red 'N.' The portrait is displayed in the Jackie Gaughan Multicultural Center.

25 Dave Rimington

A lot of Nebraska's program history has been defined by great offensive line play. No player embodies what it means to be a Husker offensive lineman more than Dave Rimington. The Omaha

South product defines greatness in every stretch of the imagination. Rimington won the Outland Trophy as a center in both 1981 and 1982 and he's the only two-time winner of the award given annually to college football's best down lineman.

Rimington was also a two-time Academic All-American (1981 to 1982), a three-time All-Big 8 selection (1980 to 1982), and he's the only offensive lineman ever to win the Big 8 Offensive Player of the Year award (1981). Rimington's legacy lives on as his name is attached to the Rimington Trophy—given to college football's top center—and the Rimington-Pace Award—named for him and stalwart Ohio State lineman Orlando Pace—given to the Big Ten's top offensive lineman.

What former offensive line coach Milt Tenopir remembers the most about Rimington was how physically advanced he was coming out of high school. When Rimington arrived to campus in 1978, the coaching staff knew he was potentially bound for greatness. "He was extremely strong," Tenopir said. "He had been lifting weights since he was a seventh grader. For as big and wide bodied as Dave was, he could move on the ground. There was only one player I can remember that neutralized him, and that was 'The Refrigerator' Perry when we played Clemson in the Orange Bowl. He'd just grab and tackle him at the line of scrimmage. Other than that Dave dominated most anybody that he played against."

What Tenopir also remembers about Rimington was he fired off the ball so fast it almost looked like he was offside. Rimington would be at the second level before you could even blink your eyes. "Dave anticipated the count several times," Tenopir said. "He was smarter than the defense in some cases. He'd quick snap it a few times, and I had pro coaches a few times ask me how our guys got off the ball so quick."

Retired strength coach Boyd Epley has had a lot of prized pupils over his illustrious career, but Rimington may have been one of Epley's best. By Rimington's senior year in 1982, people all over the country were coming in to watch him train. "Dave was already advanced coming out of high school. He could bench 340 pounds," Epley said. "We had another lineman that came in that same year named Tom Carlstrom that was drafted in the NFL, and he had to spend years just to get up to that. Rimington had quite an advantage because of his high school strength program. He came in the door ready to go, and I mean ready to go to the NFL. Because he won the Outland Trophy as a junior, he then got a lot of publicity as a senior. In fact, so much that almost every day his senior year, some film crew would come in and film him working out. We had to install color-balanced lighting in the weight room, so TV cameras would not have to set up lights every day. We were the first school in the country to have color balanced lights in the weight room, so they could come in and shoot and have the quality and the foot candles. We did all that just for Dave Rimington's publicity because people wanted to see him all the time."

Rimington credits Epley and NU's advancements in the weight room for his development at Nebraska. He said Epley came up with concepts like giving Lifter of the Year awards to create competition nobody else was doing back then. "Boyd Epley is a pioneer in the strength and conditioning coaching profession," Rimington said. "He was one of the first guys out there. There was a mix of science and a mix of motivation, and he had the perfect mix: *If we could do this, we'd get a more effective exercise.* There was always the motivation part where he motivated you to get you in the weight room and work. He seemed to have the ability to put people together where they would push each other. The offensive linemen worked together, and we always wanted to push each other to become the strongest out there."

When Rimington reflects on his career at Nebraska, his only regret is not winning a national championship. Many feel the 1982 Huskers are one of the greatest teams ever because they featured quarterback Turner Gill, running back Mike Rozier, offensive lineman Dean Steinkuhler, wide receiver Irving Fryar, running back Roger Craig, and Rimington. "That '82 team was a great team," Rimington said. "We had all the guys from that great '83 team plus all the guys in my class. It was a special team. We had a good enough team that we just kept playing after that Penn State loss, but it hurt at the end because we knew that this was a special team that probably should've won it all. In that era if you lost one, you lost the whole year."

A first-round pick in the legendary 1983 NFL Draft, Rimington played seven seasons in the NFL for the Cincinnati Bengals and Philadelphia Eagles.

26 Grant Wistrom

"He's the quintessential Blackshirt to me. If you had to pick one guy to represent what it means to be a Blackshirt, I would pick Grant Wistrom just because how he was as a teammate. We knew he loved us. We knew he was a great leader. He was great in academics, and his standard was so high."

—Ralph Brown

Nebraska's former All-American cornerback Ralph Brown may have described Grant Wistrom best. The defensive end from Webb City, Missouri, is the "quintessential Blackshirt." If there's a player who embodies every quality and trait you want to see in a Blackshirt, it's hard to find one better than Wistrom.

Not only was Wistrom a two-time All-American and Big 12 Defensive Player of the Year, he also captured the 1997 Lombardi

Award and ranks first all time in NU school history with 58½ tackles for loss and second with 26½ quarterback sacks. What puts Wistrom over the top, however, is that he was a two-time Academic All-American. In the history of Nebraska football, only 15 players have been selected as two-time, first-team Academic All-Americans.

Former NU defensive coordinator Charlie McBride said Wistrom has to be considered one of the best if not the best Blackshirt in program history. "He has to rate up there at the top. There's no question about that," McBride said. "I remember watching him in high school, and somebody told me I needed to look at him. I looked at him for about two minutes, and that was the end of that. You knew his motor was a million miles per hour. He was one of those special kids that—when you go through all those years of watching film—he was one that I can really remember. Those kinds of guys really jumped at you. His effort never changed. He was that way in pro ball. Until that whistle blew, he was going a million miles per hour.

"Then you look at the time he spent on academics. I remember hearing stories about players like him through the years, studying until 3 AM on a Thursday night, and we are playing on Saturday. You realize that—when time goes on—the effort some of these guys put into it. It's not just some passing thing. It's a big deal how much their education means…It's pretty good to see a guy like that do those things and then go on and have a good NFL career and do the right the things with his money and things like that. It makes you feel pretty good."

Over Wistrom's four-year career from 1994 to 1997, the Huskers compiled a 49–2 record and won three national championships. During that period Nebraska only lost to Arizona State and Texas—both during the 1996 season. Of his 47 games, Wistrom started 35. He was one of the rare true freshmen to play for McBride on defense. In 1996 Wistrom easily could've left early for the NFL and been a first-round pick, but both he and fellow All-American defensive tackle Jason Peter decided after NU's Orange Bowl victory against Virginia Tech that they were going to come back and try to win another national championship.

Brown, who was a freshman in 1996, credits Wistrom for laying the foundation and showing so many young players what it means to be a Blackshirt. "He was just the consummate football player," Brown said. "He embodied everything you wanted in a football player on your team or in a teammate. He had a motor that I hadn't seen before. It was nonstop. He loved his teammates, he gave 100 percent in the weight room, and he understood what it meant to be a Blackshirt and what it meant to be a Husker. He brought it every day in practice. He brought it every day outside of the football field in terms of the academics. He was on the honor roll for all of his years as a Husker...He was very hard on himself, and we all rallied around him. He was very intense. There's a lot that he has in him that I knew a lot of guys tried to emulate as they came up the ranks. They would want to be like him. I know Mike Rucker learned a lot from Grant throughout the years playing behind him. He was just an awesome guy."

Wistrom would go on to play nine seasons in the NFL with the St. Louis Rams and Seattle Seahawks, playing in 132 games and starting 118. Wistrom finished his career in the NFL with 411 tackles and 53 quarterback sacks. He was also a part of the Rams' Super Bowl-winning team in 1999.

27 Rich Glover

The 1971 Game of the Century will always be remembered for Heisman Trophy winner Johnny Rodgers' punt return, but one could argue Nebraska may not have won that day against Oklahoma without the play of defensive lineman Rich Glover. The 6'1", 235-pound Glover had 22 tackles for the Big Red, dominating up front to help lead the Huskers to a 35–31 victory against Oklahoma.

Glover and the Huskers would later go on to steamroll Alabama 38–6 in the 1972 Orange Bowl, their second national championship in a row. It was the worst loss ever at Alabama for legendary head coach Bear Bryant, who praised Glover's domination up front. "The only game going on for anyone to watch last Saturday night in Miami was between Nebraska's Johnny Rodgers and Rich Glover to see which one of them could do the most to make it the worst thing that ever happened to Bear Bryant," wrote *Sports Illustrated* writer Dan Jenkins.

It's hard to believe that the year before, in 1970, Glover played a very small role with only 19 total tackles. Glover played that season as reserve behind fellow All-American and Outland Trophy winner Larry Jacobson. It wasn't until defensive line coach Monte Kiffin and head coach Bob Devaney decided to move Glover from tackle to middle guard in 1971 when Glover's career really took off. The move was brilliant because it allowed Glover and Jacobson to be on the field together. "Rich Glover was the greatest defensive lineman I've ever seen," Devaney said in Don Bryant's *Tales from the Nebraska Sidelines*. "We took him for granted some of the time because he never had a bad game. He always played from great to super and forced other teams to do things they wouldn't ordinarily do."

Even to this day, Glover still has that same chip on his shoulder that made the undersized lineman one of the most decorated defensive players in school history. "They may say I was undersized. To me you're never undersized," Glover said while taking in some of Nebraska's 2013 Capital One Bowl practices from Orlando, Florida. "I had a big heart and I just wanted to play. For me that's all it was. You can say I'm undersized, but to me I'm going to say I'm not undersized. I relied on my quickness and my speed, but it was a lot of heart and desire. I liked playing the game, you know? Playing with toughness. That's what it was—toughness."

Glover would go on to be inducted into the College Football Hall of Fame in 1995. He was a consensus All-American in 1971 and 1972 and finished third in the Heisman Trophy voting in 1972. As a senior, Glover finished the season with 100 tackles, including nine tackles for loss, to earn Big 8 Defensive Player of the Year honors. He won both the Outland and Lombardi Trophies in 1972, and his No. 79 jersey was retired following that season.

He still bleeds Husker red and follows the program from his home in New Jersey. "You know what brings me by here: the Big Red," Glover said from NU's bowl practices in Orlando. "I want to see the practice, I want to see the coaches, I wanted to see some of the players that you see on TV, but I don't get an opportunity to meet them face to face and shake their hands and at least say 'Great job.'"

28 Bob Brown

Former Nebraska offensive lineman and linebacker Bob Brown (1961 to 1963) is just one of two players in school history to have his jersey number permanently retired by Nebraska. Nicknamed "Boomer," Brown was Bob Devaney's first All-American at NU and he was also the first black All-American in school history. Brown would later be inducted into both the College Football Hall of Fame (1993) and the Pro Football Hall of Fame (2004), and his No. 64 jersey was permanently retired in November 2004 by former athletic director Steve Pederson.

"We are proud to declare November 26 as Bob Brown Day," Pederson said to honor Brown's jersey retirement. "No other Nebraska football student-athlete has made such an impact at the collegiate and professional levels. As Bob Devaney's first All-American, he paved the way for future success of Nebraska student-athletes. As great as he was on the field, he was a student first, and we are honored to bring him home to this institution to share his football and life experiences with us."

Standing at 6'5", 260 pounds, Brown would be considered a specimen even in today's football standards. In addition to his imposing size, Brown had the versatility to play on the offensive line and at linebacker.

One of the more unique stories to come out of Brown's career happened against Auburn in the 1964 Orange Bowl. According to former media relations director Don Bryant, there was a concern going into the game against Auburn because the Tigers had never faced a team before that had black players. Devaney instructed Bryant to talk to Brown about what he might run into, but there wasn't much that intimidated the massive lineman from Cleveland. A man among boys, Brown was looking forward to knocking a few Tiger heads. "Relax, Mr. Bryant, I've had a deep-seeded animosity toward the great state of Alabama," Bryant recalled Brown telling him in his *Tales from the Nebraska Sidelines*.

It didn't take long for Brown to show his lack of fear. On the game's second play, Brown drove a Tigers defensive lineman 30 yards down the field, paving the way for Dennis Claridge's

68-yard touchdown run that put the Huskers up 7–0. NU ended up winning the game 13–7, giving the Huskers their first Orange Bowl victory in school history.

Brown would go on to become a first-round draft pick and the second overall selection by Philadelphia in 1964. He enjoyed a 10-year NFL career, including five years with the Eagles (1964 to 1968), two with the Los Angeles Rams (1969 to 1970) and three with the Oakland Raiders (1971 to 1973). Brown was known as one of the first professional football players to embrace weight training and year-round conditioning.

Brown battled knee injuries for most of his pro career, but he still earned NFL/NFC Offensive Lineman of the Year three times and he was selected to six Pro Bowls. Brown was named to the first-team, All-NFL team seven times over his career and he was named to the NFL's All-Decade team of the 1960's.

Brown's former coach, Hall of Famer George Allen of the Rams, summed up his career. "At his best, no one was better than big Bob Brown," Allen said. Another Hall of Famer from Brown's Rams days, defensive end Deacon Jones, also had some strong words to describe Brown's playing career. "He's a linebacker in an offensive lineman's body," said Jones, who died on June 3, 2013. "He had a cold-blooded mentality. He'd kill a mosquito with an ax."

29 Brook Berringer

When legendary coach Tom Osborne thinks about his career at Nebraska, it's hard not to talk about quarterback Brook Berringer (1992 to 1995). Even when speaking at the Nebraska Football Coaches Clinic in March of 2013, Osborne told the crowd of nearly 1,000 coaches from around the region about the impact Berringer had on him and his football team. Osborne called Berringer "the most influential player he has ever coached," referring to how Berringer handled losing the starting job to Tommie Frazier before the 1995 season.

In 1994 Berringer stepped in and started seven games in place of Frazier, who was out with blood clots. Frazier would go on to start the Orange Bowl against Miami, but Berringer came off the bench to help fuel the Huskers comeback, which gave Osborne his first national championship. To this day Osborne still remembers how difficult the decision was to name a starter for the 1995 season. "We could've started any one of those two and we probably still would've won the national title," Osborne said.

During the fall camp before the '95 season, Osborne and quarterbacks coach Turner Gill charted every single play and pass. Both players graded out extremely high, but the job went to Frazier. A single interception thrown by Berringer was the deciding factor. Amazingly, Frazier didn't throw a single pick during fall camp while Berringer threw just one.

The Huskers would go on to win the national championship in 1995, and Berringer played limited snaps while Frazier became a Husker legend. Never once, though, did Berringer get upset. He understood his role, and people respected him even more for that.

Then on April 18, 1996, something happened that would change Nebraska football forever. The 22-year-old Berringer died in a plane crash just outside of Lincoln. Berringer was flying the plane with his girlfriend's brother, Tobey Lake, who also died in the crash. The passing of Berringer sent shockwaves across the entire state of Nebraska. The accident happened just two days before NU's Red-White spring game, which turned into a memorial service for Berringer and the 48,659 fans in attendance. "I think his death probably had more impact on our football team than any one event I could remember," Osborne said on the Big Ten Network's special about the 1994 season. "Everybody respected him and admired him. I think a lot of people when they're young they think they're bulletproof, and they think they are going to live forever. A lot of our players realized if a guy like Brook could be taken from us that quickly, than maybe you ought to think about what your life is all about and what's really important in the long term."

All-American offensive lineman Aaron Graham was Berringer's roommate and considered the Kansas native one of his best friends. To this day he still thinks about Berringer and the impact he had on so many. "The news of him dying in a plane crash was just like a stab in the heart," Graham said on BTN. "Losing one of your best friends after everything we went through and collectively winning a championship the next year, it was a tremendous tragedy, but I'm just very thankful to have known Brook and I'm going to do everything I can to remember his legacy. As a matter of fact, my daughter's middle name is Brook after him."

Frazier said it's hard for him to think of any player more beloved in Nebraska history than Berringer. "You will never see at any other university where the backup quarterback is just as big in a given year as the starting quarterback," Frazier said. "The reason why is because of the way he played, the things that he did in the community, the type of teammate he was, and he was always encouraging. We knew that we had each other's back."

It remains a mystery what type of NFL career Berringer would've had, but the Denver Broncos said they planned on drafting him to be a backup to quarterback John Elway.

Every year during Nebraska's spring game, Berringer's legacy is honored. Each April before the Red-White game, the Brook Berringer Citizenship Team honors Husker players for their outstanding work in the community. Berringer's mother, Jan, is there each year to hand out the awards.

"A lot of Nebraskans saw in Brook Berringer a lot of what they'd like to see in themselves," historian Mike Babcock said on the Big Ten Network. "He was kind of a hard working Midwestern guy—just do the right thing and step up when the opportunity comes. Don't complain—just work hard. I think that's the way Nebraska people see themselves in that way. I think some of it was Brook Berringer represented what they felt was the best part of being in the Midwest."

30 Matt Davison's Miracle Catch

"If Davison, a freshman from Tecumseh, Neb., never catches another ball for the Cornhuskers, it won't matter. Last Saturday his diving retrieval of a deflected pass in the end zone with no time remaining in regulation allowed the Huskers to tie Missouri 38–38. When Nebraska won in overtime, 45–38, Davison forever won a place in the hearts of Husker fans."

—Ivan Maisel

Those were the words written by Maisel, the former *Sports Illustrated* and current ESPN.com writer to describe freshman wide receiver Matt Davison's miracle catch as time expired, allowing undefeated Nebraska to keep their national championship hopes alive in 1997 with a 45–38 overtime win at Missouri.

Every national championship season seems to have a moment like this—a moment where you get that one key break, or somebody makes an unexpected play down the stretch. For the Huskers it was a 6'1", 170-pound freshman wide receiver, who only had seven catches for 117 yards going into the Missouri game.

Trailing 38–31 with 1:02 left in the game, quarterback Scott Frost drove the Huskers 67 yards in 10 plays. Facing a third down from the 12-yard line and with seven seconds remaining, Frost found Davison for the game-tying touchdown. The pass was originally intended for receiver Shevin Wiggins, but the ball deflected off his foot, and a diving Davison made the catch as time expired. "I saw the ball get deflected off Shevin," Davison said. "It was floating like a punt, kind of end over end. It seemed like it took forever to get there. I dived and I guess the Lord was watching over me. I was in the right spot at the right time."

Little did Davison know at the time, but that catch would help him become a Husker legend. NU went on to win the national championship, and without Davison's heroics, Nebraska never would've had a chance to send head coach Tom Osborne out as a winner in his final season. "I'm hearing what everybody's saying," Davison said two days after the catch. "It doesn't seem as big to me as everybody else. If we go on to win the national championship, *then* it will be a bigger thing."

Davison would go on to become more than a one-catch wonder at NU as he caught 93 passes for 1,456 yards. His 167 yards receiving in the 1998 Texas A&M game still stands as a Nebraska school record. None of this, though, even comes close to overshadowing what he accomplished at Missouri that 1997 November afternoon. The "Miracle at Missouri" received the 1997 ESPY Award as both the college football and overall sports play of the year.

Davison currently resides in Lincoln and serves as the color commentator for both football and men's basketball on the Husker Sports Network. He also does television work for the Big Ten Network and runs his own foundation, Creating Captains, which helps young student-athletes build character both on and off the field. To this day Davison is revered and beloved around the state for his place in Husker history.

31 Suuuuuh!

After defensive tackle Ndamukong Suh's 12 tackle, four-and-a-half sack, seven tackle-for-loss performance against Texas in the 2009 Big 12 Championship Game, Husker defensive coordinator Carl Pelini was emotional and also in awe of what he had just seen. "If Suh didn't win the Heisman tonight it's a disgrace," Pelini said. "He's the best player in college football."

The Huskers may have lost that night, but Suh came out of that game the biggest winner. The Oregon native did not end up winning the Heisman Trophy, but he made it to New York, finishing fourth in the final voting. Suh also captured the Outland, Lombardi, and Bednarik Trophies along with the Associated Press Player of the Year award in 2009.

A Husker legend was born, and the Suh brand was officially known all across the football world. A Nebraska favorite, he would induce cheers of "Suuuuuh!" from Nebraska patrons.

The Bill Callahan recruit was part of NU's top five 2005 recruiting class and came to Nebraska in large part because of the recruiting efforts of John Blake. The connection to Blake started when Suh's older sister, Ngum, played soccer at Mississippi State while Blake was an assistant coach there. That early relationship helped the Huskers beat out several other top programs for his services.

When head coach Bo Pelini came to Nebraska in 2008, Suh seriously considered transferring to Oregon State. Because of an offseason surgery, Suh didn't even go through spring ball with Pelini in 2008 and he had a very sour taste in his mouth following the 2007 season under Callahan. What convinced Suh to stay was the job Bo Pelini did at LSU coaching several highly drafted NFL

Ndamukong Suh—an intimidating defender who won the Outland, Lombardi, and Bednarik Trophies—grapples with a lineman during a 17–3 victory against Kansas State in 2009.

defensive linemen, including 2007 Outland Trophy winner Glenn Dorsey. "I would probably be at Oregon State right now," Suh said in December of 2009. "That was my plan, but I obviously wanted to check out Bo Pelini and his staff and give them a chance and give them an opportunity to see what they had to offer me. If it didn't work out, I would've went back to Oregon State, but obviously I felt and still feel I made the best decision to stay in Lincoln and have that great staff, and Coach Carl and Bo helped me through this tremendous process of getting better as a player and a person on and off the field. It's definitely working out for the best in my opinion."

Suh was far and away the most talented player Bo Pelini inherited on the 2008 Huskers. Pelini, however, has long been known for his black and white approach and he set things pretty straight to Suh during their first meeting. Even Pelini probably didn't know truly how good Suh could be, but he clearly saw the potential, and that played a big part in motivating Suh to stay. "I remember my first ever meeting with Coach Pelini in his office," Suh said in 2009. "He basically told me I'm a very good raw talent, and he feels that I can play at a very high level. I just need to be refocused and taught some good technique, which is what they came in and did. What I've been doing the last two years is all because of them. Me being able to work hard and trying to play up to their excellent level of their expectations. That's all I'm trying to do, and it's really helped me to be the best. Even [in 2008] when I was thinking about coming out [for the draft], Coach didn't try to recruit me at all. He laid out the pros and cons for me and let me make the decision. I came back both times, and they've both been great decisions and I'm very happy."

During 2008 Suh didn't begin to come into his own until the final few games of the season. Against Colorado he returned an interception for a touchdown to solidify the win for the Huskers. In NU's upset victory against Clemson in the Gator Bowl, Suh had eight tackles, including two quarterback sacks and four tackles for loss. That was probably the moment when people started to realize his potential for the 2009 season. Experts said Suh would've been a mid to late first-round draft pick in 2008, but by coming back for his senior season in 2009, it allowed him to go No. 2 in the draft behind Oklahoma quarterback Sam Bradford. In his first NFL season with the Detroit Lions, Suh earned All-Pro and Defensive Rookie of the Year honors.

At Nebraska, Suh finished with 215 career tackles, 57 tackles for loss, 24 quarterback sacks, six blocked kicks, 15 pass breakups, and 38 quarterback hurries. He also scored three touchdowns—two on interceptions and one as a receiver on offense. Pelini credited Suh's

Suh's Generosity

Defensive tackle Ndamukong Suh will go down as one of the most decorated defensive players in college football history.

Maybe one of the most impressive things Suh did following his career at Nebraska, however, occurred off the field. He donated $2.6 million to NU just four months after his playing career ended in April of 2010. Of the donation $2 million went to the football program, and $600,000 went to the UNL College of Engineering where Suh was an undergraduate, earning his degree in construction management.

"I had a fantastic football career at Nebraska and thanks to my coaches and support staff, I have learned the value of hard work, teamwork, and life skills," Suh said. "These skills will help me tremendously as I prepare for my career in the NFL. As a thank you to everyone in Nebraska who has assisted me on my collegiate journey, I want to donate $2 million to the athletic department."

success over his career to his ability to continually stay grounded despite all the major accolades he earned. "To be one of the best, you have to be uncommon," Pelini said. "That means you have to never be satisfied. [Suh] understands that, but he also understands that it's not all about him. At the end of the day, that [philosophy] is going to make you a more complete player and a more complete representative of the organization you're in."

32 Hang Out With College Football's Classiest Fans

"The two best things to ever come out of Nebraska are Johnny Carson and sportsmanship. Nebraska sets the standard for how fans should act."

—Beano Cook

The late Cook may have described Nebraska and its fan base better than anyone. You'll be hard pressed to find a fan base as knowledgeable and classy. Whether it's giving a standing ovation every game for the opponent as the visitor exits the field or filling Memorial Stadium to near capacity for pregame warm-ups, Husker Saturdays in Lincoln are special.

ESPN College Football analyst Lee Corso recalls his former coaching days at Indiana. In 1975 Corso took the Hoosiers into Memorial Stadium and lost 45–0. As Corso and his team left the field, they were greeted with a standing ovation. "I never forgot that," Corso told the *Lincoln Journal Star* in 2007.

Even after Northwestern shockingly upset Nebraska in 2011, Memorial Stadium still gave the Wildcats a standing ovation as they left the field. "I went into the locker room at the end of the game, and the Nebraska fans were lining the walkway as the team went through and they were clapping," Northwestern President Morty Schapiro said. "Our coach [Pat Fitzgerald] looked at them, and I looked at them, and we just clapped back. I have never in my life seen anything like that. I am a Nebraska fan forever."

You almost have to experience Memorial Stadium firsthand to truly understand how good the hospitality is. If you are in Lincoln to watch your favorite team play Nebraska, don't be surprised if a stranger hands you a beer at Barry's or a group of Husker fans invite you to join their tailgate party to share a few stories.

Nebraska's ability to travel in large numbers also blows away opposing fan bases. In 2010 at Washington, more than 25,000 Husker fans filled Husky Stadium. There were so many fans in downtown Seattle that Friday night that many bars ran out of beer. The Hard Rock Cafe in downtown Seattle had the highest food and drink sales of any Hard Rock Cafe in the world that night.

In 2007 at Wake Forest, Huskers fans occupied nearly half of the Demon Deacons' 32,000-seat stadium in Winston-Salem, North Carolina. On the Friday night before that game, the Fox and

Hound Bar in Winston-Salem had their highest grossing sales night ever as Husker fans completely took over their bar.

Stories like this are endless. Nebraska fans continue to amaze people with their passion, class, and overall knowledge of college football. "The best college football fans in the nation are right here," Corso said, "because they respect the way the game of football should be played—not only by the Big Red—but by the opponent also."

33 NU's Greatest Upset Victory

Former Nebraska head coach Bill Jennings never had one winning season at NU from 1957 to 1961, but he did deliver arguably the greatest upset victory in school history. In 1959 No. 19 Oklahoma came to Lincoln with a 74-game conference unbeaten streak led by legendary coach Bud Wilkinson. The Huskers had lost their previous 16 games against the Sooners with the last victory coming under head coach Glenn Presnell in 1942. OU won the national championship under Wilkinson in 1950, 1955, and 1956.

Oklahoma had a 47-game winning streak from 1953 to 1957, which is still the longest in college football history. To go along with that, Wilkinson's squad won 13 consecutive conference championships from 1947 to 1959, compiling a 74–1–2 record during that time in conference play. Meanwhile the Huskers were not a winning program during that era under Jennings with records of 1–9 in 1957, 3–7 in 1958, and 4–6 in 1959.

That's why NU's 1959 victory against Oklahoma is still considered the greatest upset in program history when you compare where the two programs were at during that period. "It was the first time we'd beaten Oklahoma in 17 years, and the first time any team in the conference had beaten OU in 13 years, so it was a happy day for the whole Big 8 conference," former Husker quarterback Harry Tolly said in a Huskers.com feature, remembering the upset victory 50 years later.

Statistically, Oklahoma completely dominated the game in every area other than the scoreboard. OU had 19 first downs compared to NU's eight. The Sooners outrushed the Huskers 240 to 127 and outpassed them 100 to 34 for a total yardage difference of 340 to 161. It didn't matter, though, as the final scoreboard read 25–21 in favor of the Huskers. "It was a great victory, and this weekend will be a great reunion," said guard Lee Zentic when NU honored the team before the Oklahoma vs. Nebraska game in 2009. "It'll be fun for all of us to get back together and rehash some old times. The thing about our team was we could beat anybody, and we could lose to anybody."

The win against Oklahoma was so big that classes actually got called off the following Monday. "So we were all very popular people on campus," said fullback Don Fricke, one of the team's tri-captains with Pat Fischer and Ron McDole.

Don Bryant was the sports editor of the *Lincoln Star* in 1959 and he would eventually become Nebraska's media relations director. Bryant called the win "sensational" and said, "The town went crazy. The fans stormed the field, and down came the goal posts." Bryant told Huskers.com in 2009 that the Extra Point Club later tore up those historic goal posts and sold pieces of them as paper weights to make money for NU's first major football booster club.

34 Frank Solich

There's an old saying that you never want to be the person who follows a legend because no matter what you accomplish it probably won't be good enough. In 99 out of 100 programs, winning 58 games in six seasons would be considered great success. For Nebraska, however, it was considered average. Replacing legendary head coach Tom Osborne was never going to be an easy task for anyone. Under Osborne the Huskers won 255 games and three national championships over 25 seasons. In a lot of ways, Frank Solich was doomed from the start.

Right out of the gates in 1998, Solich's team was hit with a number of injuries, and the Big Red suffered their first four-loss season since 1968. Solich would rebound the following three years with 12, 10, and 11-win seasons. The Big Red won the conference championship in 1999, and the Huskers played for the national championship in 2001. But by 2002 the landscape started to change.

Heisman Trophy-winning quarterback Eric Crouch graduated, and first-year starter Jammal Lord suffered some early growing pains. The Huskers would go on the road early in 2002 and lose 40–7 at Penn State and then follow that up with a 36–14 loss at Iowa State two weeks later to fall out of the AP top 25 for the first time since 1981, which amounted to 348 consecutive weeks of being ranked.

The lumps kept on coming. NU lost 24–21 at Oklahoma State, 27–24 to Texas, 49–14 at Kansas State, 28–13 to Colorado, and 27–23 to Mississippi in the Independence Bowl. The Huskers finished the 2002 season 7–7. It was the first time Nebraska failed to win nine games since 1968—snapping an NCAA-record streak of 33 straight seasons of nine wins or more.

Before the bowl game in 2002, Solich made staff changes. During that same time, however, athletic director Bill Byrne left Nebraska for Texas A&M, and Steve Pederson was hired shortly after. Heading into the 2003 season, some people felt no matter what Solich did, Pederson had his mind made up that a coaching change would be made. Pederson and Solich were really never close, dating back to Pederson's days as Osborne's recruiting coordinator.

Solich's new coaching staff, though, won over the hearts of Husker Nation after newly named defensive coordinator Bo Pelini revitalized the Blackshirt defense. After a 31–22 win at Colorado, NU finished the 2003 regular season with a 9–3 record. But the week before the CU game, a report in the *Lincoln Journal Star* said Pederson planned to fire Solich after the Colorado game. Pederson dismissed the report, and most expected Solich to be retained after Nebraska's win in Boulder, Colorado.

The following day Pederson met with Solich on a Saturday night and fired him. It was a shocking development that no journalists around the program was prepared to cover. The news of Solich's firing became public after members of his family began phoning local media outlets. Former KMTV Channel 3 sports director Travis Justice broke into CBS' ice skating coverage to break the news. "The bottom line is Pederson wanted to hire his own coach," Solich's son-in-law Jon Dalton told the *Journal Star* on the night of Solich's firing. "I don't know how Pederson will announce this stuff. I know it'll be partially snake oil and mostly personal. But he'll make himself come out smelling like a rose. He doesn't like Frank and wanted to get rid of him from the beginning."

Former players also were upset with the news. "I don't know what we're looking for here," two-time Outland Trophy winner

Dave Rimington told the *Omaha World-Herald*. "Steve's a guy I have confidence in, and I'm sure his decision is going to work out. But you just hate to see people who have been in the program as long as [Solich], who paid the dues with blood, sweat, and tears get ousted like this. I just didn't like it. I didn't like it at all."

Solich came to Nebraska in 1962 and he was a part of Bob Devaney's first recruiting class. Solich was the first Nebraska player to be featured on the cover of *Sports Illustrated* and was an All-Big 8 fullback for the Big Red in 1965. After Solich enjoyed a short high school coaching career, Osborne hired him in 1979 and picked him as his successor following the 1997 national championship season.

From 1962 to 2003, Solich gave more than 40 years of his life to Nebraska football. He was allowed one last opportunity to meet with his team after Pederson's firing. Solich conducted himself in his typical classy manner and most importantly wanted his team to finish things the right way. "It was very hard," Solich told the *Journal Star*. "I appreciate the opportunity to get in front of the players one final time and let them know I appreciate what they're all about. I always felt they gave everything they had and stayed together no matter how much attention came from the outside."

With Pelini serving as the interim coach, the Huskers would go on to win the Alamo Bowl 17–3 against Michigan State to finish 2003 with a 10–3 record. An emotional Solich couldn't even bring himself to watch the game that night from his home in Lincoln. "The comment that he made to me that I'll always remember is it was hard for him to watch that game, and he just couldn't," said Steven M. Sipple, the *Journal Star* columnist, who had a tight relationship with Solich. "The firing really took its toll. It was a difficult time for Frank."

Immediately after being fired at Nebraska, Solich was offered the Army job in January of 2004 but turned it down a day after verbally accepting. A year later he accepted the Ohio job and has led the Bobcats to five bowl game appearances and 59 wins over eight seasons. Before Solich got to Ohio, the Bobcats had not appeared in a bowl game since 1968. Ohio's back-to-back bowl wins in 2011 and 2012 were the Bobcats' first bowl victories in school history.

35 Devaney's First Big Win

From 1918 to 2011, Nebraska and Michigan would only play one time during the regular season. The historic programs met before that in 1905, 1911, and 1917. Before NU joined the Big Ten in 2011, the only other regular season meeting between the Huskers and Wolverines came in 1962. Nebraska and Michigan did meet in the 1986 Fiesta Bowl and the 2005 Alamo Bowl, but for whatever reason, regular season matchups were far and few between.

That's why in 1962 newly named Husker head coach Bob Devaney saw the matchup with the Wolverines as an opportunity to give the program a signature win against one of the bluebloods of college football. For the previous five seasons under Bill Jennings, Nebraska fans didn't have much to be proud of as NU had a 15–34–1 record, one of the worst stretches in program history.

Going into the game, the *Detroit Free Press* referred to the matchup as an "opening-day breather" for the Wolverines. Devaney, who was a Michigan native, had different ideas when he took his team to Ann Arbor, Michigan. Ever since the day Devaney was hired, he pointed at the Michigan game as one that could jump-start the program.

Devaney knew the Wolverines had lost a lot of seniors from the year before and from coaching under Duffy Daugherty at Michigan

Nebraska Faces Michigan in the 2005 Alamo Bowl

One could argue at the time that Nebraska's 32–28 victory against Michigan in the 2005 Alamo Bowl had a similar feel to Devaney's 1962 win against the Wolverines. NU was in the second season of head coach Bill Callahan's tenure, and the Huskers entered the game as a two-touchdown underdog against Michigan.

The 2005 Michigan team was absolutely loaded with NFL talent as the Wolverines featured a roster with 18 future NFL draft picks. A year later that same Michigan team would fall one game short of playing for the national championship after an 11–1 regular season.

Callahan had a sound game plan, but midway through the fourth quarter Michigan built a 28–17 lead, and it looked like the game was over. However, led by quarterback Zac Taylor and running back Cory Ross, the Huskers found a way to win the game with a remarkable fourth-quarter comeback.

What many remember the game for, though, was Michigan's version of the "Stanford-Cal band play" where the Wolverines used a series of seven flea flickers and laterals to nearly run back a game-winning touchdown on a hook-and-ladder pass play.

While all of this was happening, players from both teams stormed the field, thinking the game was over, but the play was never blown dead. It wasn't until Nebraska defensive back Titus Brothers ran Michigan tight end Tyler Ecker out of bounds at the 13-yard line that the play was ruled dead. Some credit should also go to ESPN broadcasters Mike Tirico and Kirk Herbstreit for sticking with the call all the way to the end when even Nebraska and Michigan's players thought the game was over.

State he was well aware of Big Ten football. The Huskers went into the game as a 10-point underdog, but Devaney was still confident they could go to Ann Arbor and pull off the upset.

Devaney also knew that if a team from the Big 8 could beat a power from the Big Ten, it would be a program changer. "The Big Ten and Notre Dame were the two brands in college football," said Nebraska football historian Mike Babcock. "According to Bob they had picked that game out as one where if we can go up to Michigan and win that game, it will draw attention to the program and it'll also give the players confidence."

The week before Devaney's Huskers had routed South Dakota 53–0, and they were clicking on all cylinders. Nebraska came into Ann Arbor and beat Michigan 25–13 as All-American lineman Bob Brown helped the Huskers dominate up front on both offense and defense. The same Michigan newspapers that were calling for a blowout sang a different tune the next day after the Huskers' thorough beating of the Wolverines. The *Detroit Free Press* wrote, "An itinerant band of Cornhuskers paid their first visit to Michigan in 45 years, looking for work. They found a fertile field, ready for shucking. And, man, how they shucked it." *The Detroit News* wrote, "The Cornhuskers of Nebraska chugged along like a well-oiled threshing machine."

And during that threshing machine-like performance, a 25-year-old named Tom Osborne roamed the sideline as a young graduate assistant.

Michigan would go on to have a 2–7 season in 1962, but the victory still made a statement, which helped propel the Huskers to a 9–2 record during Devaney's first year at Nebraska. "I don't think that was maybe one of Michigan's better teams," Osborne told the Associated Press in 2011, "but still going to win at Michigan was a big deal. Every win that year was a big deal."

The victory marked the beginning of the modern era of Nebraska football as we know it. Devaney would go on to win two national championships, and Osborne would win three. Many to this day still regard that victory in Ann Arbor as the start of it all. "It was the beginning of a real dynasty," said Nebraska running back Dennis Stuewe, who ran for a team-high 60 yards and a touchdown against the Wolverines.

36 Will Shields

In the 1980s Nebraska offensive line coach Milt Tenopir ran into Lawton (Oklahoma) High head coach Clarence Madden, who was speaking at a coaches clinic that winter in San Antonio. Several years later Madden reached out to Tenopir to see if he'd have any interest in coming down to Oklahoma for a few days in the spring to help them install the I-formation offense.

As a former high school head coach, Tenopir was always generous with his time when it came to helping other coaches. Tenopir got in his car and drove to Lawton and spent four days with Madden and his staff. By the end of the trip, Lawton had learned NU's entire offense from Tenopir. His team knew the play calls and most importantly how to make the proper reads at the line of scrimmage. That fall Lawton would go on to capture the state championship in Oklahoma.

Later that summer Lawton repaid the favor back to Tenopir by sending nearly their entire team to Nebraska's football camp. This was the first time Tenopir ever laid eyes on offensive lineman Will Shields. Little did Tenopir know that the relationship he struck up with the Lawton coaching staff would help him land one of the best offensive linemen we've ever seen play the game of football.

The 6'1", 305-pound Shields would eventually commit to Nebraska and by his freshman year in 1989 he immediately made an impact, which was helped in large part because he ran NU's exact same offense in high school. "When Will got here, we had the first three or four days with just freshmen in the room," Tenopir said. "The first couple of days, we were pretty generic with what we ran and then we'd add another defense where they would have to make some offensive line calls. Will was spouting out the offensive line calls in the back of the room, and the other guys in the room were looking around wondering how the heck he knew that? Well, that's what he did in high school. Will had a little bit of an edge on people as far as the mental part of the game and Will was one of a few kids that played for me as a true freshman."

The one area where Shields wasn't developed as a true freshman was in the weight room. Both Tenopir and defensive coordinator Charlie McBride remember Shields being self-conscious because he was so far behind in the weight room. Thankfully the Huskers had a world-class strength staff led by Boyd Epley. "The offensive linemen would go in there, and [Shields] was embarrassed because he couldn't lift as much as they could," McBride said. "They got him in there and said, 'Hey, look, so what?' It made him a different person. They were behind him and helped him.

"Shields had a great lower body, but he was almost embarrassed to lift weights in the weight room because of his lack of upper body strength," Tenopir said. "I know I heard from some other guys that one of the strength coaches would take him over to the rec center to lift."

Even being behind physically in the weight room, Shields' knowledge of the offense got him on the field immediately for Tenopir, playing in nine games. By his second season, he became just the second sophomore since Dave Rimington to be named first team All-Big 8. During his junior season, Shields would once again be named All-Big 8 along with second team All-American. As a senior in 1992, Shields would go on to win the Outland Trophy—the fifth Husker at the time to take home the prestigious award.

It was arguably the most impressive offensive line career any player had put up at Nebraska since Rimington captured back-to-back Outland Trophies in 1981 and 1982. Not bad for a guy who didn't know how to bench press four years earlier. "[Shields] was special in what he meant to the football team and what he meant to youth," Tenopir said. "He was one of the first mentors that Tom [Osborne] had when they started Teammates [a mentoring program to inspires students]. Will was just an exceptional young man."

As an NFL player, Shields played 14 seasons with the Kansas City Chiefs. From 1993 to 2006, Shields started 231 straight games for KC and was named to 12 Pro Bowls along with being named All-Pro eight times. In 2011 Shields was inducted into the College Football Hall of Fame. And the guy who was initially behind the rest of his Nebraska teammates in lifting weights now owns and operates 68 Inside Sports, a fitness and sports center in Overland Park, Kansas.

Tenopir said to this day he's never seen a player with the type of durability of Shields. "I had the opportunity to go to the last Pro Bowl he ever played in. He took my wife and I over to Hawaii, and we got to watch him play," Tenopir said. "Just watching him even then, I thought he could continue to play forever. He played well in that game, and I said something to him about that after the game. Then he said, 'Coach, you don't see me in the morning. It takes me an hour to get to walking right.'"

Shields' son, Shavon, would follow in his father's footsteps and attend Nebraska. Shavon impressively averaged 8.6 points as a freshman on the 2012–2013 Husker basketball team.

37 The Fumblerooski and the Bouncerooski

Over the years Nebraska head coach Tom Osborne became known as an offensive genius. Some of the more memorable moments of his play-calling career were his ability to not only create trick plays, but to also call them at the right time. Two of Osborne's more memorable trick plays were the "fumblerooski" and the "bouncerooski."

According to Husker historian Mike Babcock, NU ran the "fumblerooski" four times before the NCAA outlawed it in 1992, and it also ran the "bouncerooski" and the "Bummerooski" once under Osborne.

Of these six legendary trick play calls, three stand out. In the 1982 Oklahoma-Nebraska game, Osborne called the bouncerooski. The play consisted of a backward lateral pass that skipped across the turf like a bounce pass in basketball. Husker quarterback Turner Gill nonchalantly lateraled a bounce pass to wide receiver Irving Fryar, who in turn threw the ball downfield to receiver Mitch Krenk for a 37-yard gain. NU would eventually score a touchdown on that drive, and the play helped lead the No. 3 Huskers to a 28–24 victory against the No. 11 Sooners.

The Bummerooski

Tom Osborne also ran the "Bummerooski," named after former coach Bum Phillips—who used the trick play in the NFL—one time in a 1975 game at Missouri. The Tigers had beaten Osborne each of the last two seasons, so there was a lot of pressure on him to win the game.

Leading 10–0 with 1:46 remaining before halftime, Osborne faced a fourth down at Mizzou's 40-yard line. NU sent punter Randy Lessman on the field with three running backs in front of him, and they lined up in a triangle near the line of scrimmage.

Running back Tony Davis was directly behind the center with Monte Anthony and John O'Leary right in front of him. Davis took the snap, pushed the ball from behind through O'Leary's legs and pretended to hand it to Anthony, who was running to his right. The play looked like it was a reverse as all of NU's players ran to the right. O'Leary held the ball, delayed for a split second, and then ran to his left untouched for a 40-yard touchdown. Nebraska won the game 30–7, and the first of six rooski plays called by Osborne was born.

Dean Steinkuhler, one of many in a long history of great Nebraska offensive linemen, rumbles for a 19-yard touchdown on a fumblerooski play during the 1984 Orange Bowl.

In the 1984 Orange Bowl against Miami, Osborne called the legendary fumblerooski play, but he actually dialed it up before—twice in the same 1979 game against Oklahoma. The play consisted of the quarterback pretending to take the snap and running one direction, but he actually dropped the football on the turf and allowed the guard to pick it up and run the other way. Senior left guard John Havekost ran the first ever fumblerooski for an 11-yard gain. Then later in that same game, junior right guard Randy Schleusener took his fumblerooski for a 15-yard touchdown, but it wasn't enough as the Huskers lost to the Sooners 17–14.

Trailing 17–0 to Miami in the 1984 Orange Bowl, Osborne brought out the fumblerooski for a third time. Being behind by such a deficit was unfamiliar territory for Nebraska's 1983 Scoring Explosion Offense as it had outscored opponents 624–186 in its previous 12 games. Osborne turned to Outland Trophy winner Dean Steinkuhler for a spark in the second quarter, and the right guard from Burr, Nebraska, delivered.

The 6'3", 270-pound Steinkuhler boasted a 4.87 in the 40-yard dash and he showed his nimbleness as he raced past the Hurricanes' speedy defense for a 19-yard touchdown. In 2009 ESPN ranked Steinkuhler's fumblerooski touchdown as the No. 28 all-time greatest play in college football during the last 30 years. "The funny thing was every time we ran that play in practice it never worked," center Dave Rimington joked.

Osborne would call the fumblerooski one final time in 1992 before the NCAA officially outlawed the play the following season. On Halloween night against No. 8 Colorado, Osborne called the fumblerooski on a third-and-4 at the Colorado 21-yard line. NU led the game 17–7 as the first half was coming to a close. Freshman quarterback Tommie Frazier put the ball on the turf after taking a snap from center Jim Scott, and Outland Trophy-winning right guard Will Shields scooped it up for a 16-yard gain to the 5-yard line. Three plays later running back Calvin Jones scored, and the Huskers would go on to rout the Buffaloes 52–7.

According to Babcock the NCAA outlawed the fumblerooski because it was too difficult to officiate. "They always say one of the attributes of a great coach is when they cause rules changes," wide receiver Mitch Krenk said.

38 10 Great Huskers Quarterbacks

Quarterbacks like Tommie Frazier, Eric Crouch, and Turner Gill are well known among Nebraska fans for their career accomplishments. But here's a list of 10 other quarterbacks that all Husker fans should know.

Bob Churchich (1964-1966)—Churchich was Bob Devaney's first All-Conference quarterback and was inducted into the NU Hall of Fame in 1989.

Jerry Tagge (1969–1971)—Nebraska's two-time national champion quarterback, Tagge was an All-American in 1971 and MVP of the January 1, 1971 Orange Bowl. Tagge's 63.03 completion percentage in 1970 was a NU school record all the way up until 2008.

Dave Humm (1972–1974)—The 1974 All-American held the NU single-season (2,074) and career passing marks (5,035) up until Zac Taylor broke both records in 2005 and 2006.

Vince Ferragamo (1975–1976)—If you count Ferragamo's two years at Cal along with his two years at Nebraska, he passed for 5,061 yards and 46 touchdowns in four seasons. Ferragamo's 20 touchdown passes in 1976 was an NU school record until 2006. Ferragamo, a 1976 All-American, is the only Husker quarterback to start in a Super Bowl when he started for the Los Angeles Rams in Super Bowl XIV.

Steve Taylor (1985–1988)—A two-time All-Big 8 selection and a 1987 All-American, Taylor finished his career in 1988 as NU's most prolific rushing quarterback. Taylor had 2,125 career rushing yards and 32 rushing touchdowns. He also threw for five touchdowns against No. 3 UCLA in 1987, which was a school record at the time.

Gerry Gdowski (1989)—Playing behind Taylor, the Fremont, Nebraska, native only started for one season but was still named the Big 8's 1989 Co-Offensive Player of the Year. Gdowski broke Taylor's single-season quarterback rushing mark by running for 925 yards and 13 touchdowns to go along with 1,326 yards passing and 19 touchdowns through the air. Gdowski averaged 7.91 yards-per-carry, which was a school record at the time.

Scott Frost (1996–1997)—The Wood River, Nebraska, native, Frost started his career at Stanford with Bill Walsh before transferring to Nebraska in 1995. He led the Huskers to the 1997 national championship by becoming the first quarterback in school history to rush and throw for 1,000 yards in the same season. Frost finished his career with a 24–2 record as a starter.

Zac Taylor (2005–2006)—The son of former Oklahoma captain Sherwood Taylor, Zac Taylor came to Nebraska via El Dorado Kansas' Butler Community College. The Norman, Oklahoma, native was the 2006 Big 12 Offensive Player of the Year and finished his career with 5,850 yards passing and 45 touchdowns—both school records at the time.

Joe Ganz (2007–2008)—In his first start against Kansas State in 2007, Ganz threw for a school record 510 yards and seven touchdowns while stepping in for the injured Sam Keller. In 2008 he helped first-year head coach Bo Pelini to a nine-win season by throwing for a school-record 3,568 yards and 25 touchdowns. Ganz finished his career with 27 NU school records.

Taylor Martinez (2010–2013)—Martinez is the only quarterback in school history to start an opener as a freshman. (Frazier didn't start until midseason his freshman year.) When Martinez's career is finished at Nebraska, he almost certainly will hold every single quarterback passing and rushing record in school history.

39 1994 Colorado at Nebraska

Before the 1994 Colorado game in Lincoln, many national experts did not realize just how good Nebraska really was. It would be the fourth game NU played without quarterback Tommie Frazier, who was out because of blood clots.

Backup Brook Berringer took over the starting job in Frazier's place but suffered collapsed lungs in his first start against Wyoming, a Huskers 42–32 victory. At No. 16 Kansas State the following week, Nebraska started walk-on Matt Turman and squeaked out a 17–6 victory in Manhattan, Kansas. Berringer would return the next week at Missouri, and NU cruised to a 42–7 win.

None of these three opponents, though, were close to the caliber of Nebraska's next opponent—Colorado. The Buffaloes had a No. 2 ranking and a perfect 7–0 record. They already owned victories over nationally ranked Michigan, Wisconsin, Texas, Kansas State, and Oklahoma. They were led by the trio of quarterback Kordell Stewart, Heisman Trophy-winning running back Rashaan Salaam, and wide receiver Michael Westbrook on offense. In all the 1994 Colorado team had nine players picked in the NFL Draft that season, including seven in the first three rounds.

The game in Lincoln was also Nebraska's 200th consecutive sellout, and a national television audience tuned into ABC to see if the Huskers were contenders or pretenders. The winner of this game was going to put itself in the driver's seat to play for a national championship in January. "This game was huge," wide receiver Abdul Muhammad told the Big Ten Network. "That's all we talked about. It's all the fans talked about. It's all the students talked about in class—are you going to beat Colorado?"

"It was kind of the clash of the titans type of thing," offensive lineman Zach Wiegert said. "We had one of our most talented teams, and they had one of their most talented teams. It was probably two of the most talented teams both schools ever had."

From the get-go Nebraska took the field with a focus and determination unlike ever seen before. NU entered the game as

The Pipe Cutters

During the Big Ten Network's feature on the 1994 Nebraska team, it told a unique story from within the Colorado game that offensive lineman Rob Zatechka still laughs about to this day.

Zatechka said he told the entire starting offensive line before kickoff that CU's defensive linemen were carrying "pipe cutters" off the plane, signifying how they were going to "tear apart the Huskers famed pipeline" up front.

"I told that to our offensive line, and a lot of the guys got awfully fired up about it," Zatechka said, smiling. "The best part about it, though, was walking through the locker room after the game when the press interviews were wrapping up, and I still heard two or three offensive linemen talking about [how] 'their defensive line carrying a pipe cutter off of the plane—it was really something that motivated them to go out and really just put this absolutely dominating performance on Colorado that day.'

"It was a completely made-up story."

a 1-point underdog, which was the only time the Big Red didn't enter as favorites all season.

The Huskers got on the scoreboard first thanks to a 14-yard touchdown run by fullback Cory Schlesinger with 5:47 left to go in the first quarter. A Tom Sieler field goal and a Clinton Childs touchdown with 36 seconds remaining in the second quarter gave Nebraska a 17–0 lead at halftime. Any hopes of a Colorado comeback in the second half ended pretty fast when Berringer found tight end Eric Alford for a 30-yard touchdown to make it 24–0 with 10:42 left in the third quarter. "Colorado had no chance," former talk radio host Jim Rose said on BTN. "It was the 200th consecutive sellout at Memorial Stadium. It was a beautiful fall day with a national TV audience. Yes, the Buffaloes had great talent and spectacular talent on defense, but this was a game where Brook Berringer played his very best game, and the defense played a spectacular game."

Berringer would go on to finish 12-of-17 for 142 yards and a touchdown. "Before the Colorado game [CU head coach] Bill

McCartney said he wasn't sure that Brook Berringer could handle the pressure of a game like that," Husker historian Mike Babcock said on BTN's special about the 1994 Nebraska team. "Those were his famous last words, and [Berringer] handled it pretty well."

Running back Lawrence Phillips led the Huskers on the ground with 103 yards on 24 carries. There was nothing really fancy about the victory for the Big Red. They were the team that came out and seemed to want it more. "From an emotional standpoint, we were even more ready to play that game than we were to play Miami for the national title," offensive lineman Rob Zatechka said. "I think it showed on the field."

It was one of the most memorable games of a very memorable season. "Other than the championship game, it was my favorite game I ever had an opportunity to play in," offensive lineman Aaron Graham said. "I think at one point in time that Colorado defense had 10 guys that started in the NFL."

The win against Colorado helped propel the Huskers from No. 3 to No. 1 in the polls over Penn State. In 1994 the Big Ten champion was locked in to the Rose Bowl, so there was no way NU and PSU could meet in a bowl game. That meant whoever was in the No. 1 spot at the end of the regular season would have a significant advantage in taking home a national championship by winning the bowl game. Penn State would struggle in close wins against both Indiana and Illinois, which was enough to keep the Huskers in the No. 1 spot heading into the Orange Bowl against No. 3 Miami. "Winning the [Colorado] game wasn't going to be enough," Zatechka told BTN. "We had to make a statement. We knew that, the fans knew that, the media knew that. So Brook did what he always did. He had a good completion percentage. He always ran the ball well. He always made incredibly good decisions. He got out there and did it on that day. He did it against one of the best defenses in the country."

40 Herbie Husker, Lil' Red, and the Bugeaters

Believe it or not, Nebraska can thank the Iowa Hawkeyes for the name "Cornhuskers." Long before Nebraska took on the Cornhusker mascot name with the Scarlet and Cream colors, NU was referred to as the Old Gold Knights, Antelopes, and the Rattlesnake Boys in the late 1800s.

Beginning in 1892 Nebraska adopted the Scarlet and Cream colors and took on the nickname the "Bugeaters." The Bugeater name was derived from the insect-devouring bull bats that hovered over the plains, and the early Nebraska teams had great success in the 1890s with the Bugeater nickname.

In 1899 Nebraska suffered their first losing season in a decade, which led to yet another mascot change. Charles "Cy" Sherman, who wrote for the *Nebraska State Journal* at the time but would later go on to become the sports editor of the *Lincoln Star* gets credit for the Cornhusker nickname. He adopted the name for Nebraska after the University of Iowa dropped the Cornhuskers nickname. Iowa fans preferred to be called the Hawkeyes over the Cornhuskers. Sherman was tired of calling Nebraska the Bugeaters, and the Cornhusker nickname caught on like wildfire, and it would eventually become the nickname for the entire state of Nebraska.

The official mascot "Herbie Husker," which is used today for Nebraska, did not evolve until the 1974 Cotton Bowl in Dallas when Nebraska played Texas to end the 1973 season. According to Huskers.com, artist Dirk West of Lubbock, Texas, designed a Cornhuskers cartoon for the Cotton Bowl media headquarters that caught the eye of former NU media relations director Don Bryant. Eventually Bryant contacted West for permission to use the cartoon.

West was commissioned by Nebraska to draw an original Cornhusker cartoon character to serve as the mascot for all of Husker athletics. Herbie Husker would be portrayed as a "burly, rugged, and confident fellow who is proud of both the athletic and agriculture traditions" at Nebraska.

In 1995 former athletic director Bill Byrne forced the controversial retirement of Herbie Husker because he felt like it didn't market or portray Nebraska Athletics in the most favorable light. "We've worked and worked with Herbie," Byrne said at the time. "No matter what we do, he doesn't seem to be very appealing to our fans." The perception was Herbie portrayed Nebraskans as hicks, and he was fat or ugly.

Byrne had already created the inflatable Lil' Red mascot, who appeared to be the next successor as the Nebraska mascot, but Husker fans weren't ready to let go of Herbie. A fan uproar in 1995 caused Bryne to surrender, and Herbie was back on the field by September of that season. However, apparel companies like Nike, Adidas, and Starter wanted nothing to do with Herbie. Instead of seeing Herbie on shirts and jackets, they chose to go with a big "N" and "Huskers" scrolled across it.

In 2003 former athletic director Steve Pederson released a plan to revive the image of Herbie Husker. Pederson put together a spoof press campaign where former strength coach Boyd Epley and his staff put Herbie through a workout regimen to get him slim and trim. The athletic department held a press conference to announce this, and Huskers.com would post monthly updates during the entire offseason on Herbie's progress with Epley's strength staff. "Herbie has now lost 70 pounds of fat, and his physical appearance is noticeably better," Epley said in a 2003 press release put out by Huskers.com. "In fact Herbie is feeling so much better that he wanted to get a trim and start working on other areas of his outward appearance."

Mascots Herbie Husker (front) and Lil' Red (back) pump up the Memorial Stadium crowd before a 2007 contest.

Another release said Herbie had lost so much weight that he was forced to go out and buy new clothes. Eventually Pederson would release his slim and trim Herbie Husker at the start of the 2003 season. Lil' Red also remains active as a mascot at all sporting events, but Herbie is still universally recognized as the face of Nebraska athletics.

In recent years there's been a strong demand for vintage style T-shirts that feature the original Herbie Husker. Things have almost gone full circle back to 1974, and it appears Nebraska fans embrace Herbie for who he is.

41 Turner Gill

December 3, 2004 was a watershed mark—the official ending of an era that started in 1962. It was exactly one week after Nebraska finished a 5–6 regular season under first-year head coach Bill Callahan. On that Friday afternoon, former Husker quarterback Turner Gill announced he'd be resigning from his coaching position at NU.

Gill was the last link in the football program to former head coaches Tom Osborne and Bob Devaney. The news was so significant that multiple local television stations carried Gill's press conference live that afternoon. In most cases when an assistant coach resigns, a simple press release or statement is all you'll see. In Gill's case this day needed much more than an emailed statement from media relations. Athletic director Steve Pederson realized it and so did Callahan.

"I have been called to take a leap of faith, and I plan to pursue full-time my career goal of being a head football coach," said Gill, a Husker quarterback coach for 12 years before taking over as receivers coach. "For the past few years, I have been working on my vision of what I believe coaching should be about and where I believe our responsibility and passion should lie. While I have always remained true to my vision, it is now time I give it wings and see where it takes me."

In a lot of ways, Gill took one for the team by staying at Nebraska in 2004. He clearly wasn't a fit in Callahan's West Coast offense as a receivers coach, nor was he accustomed to the 6 AM to midnight hours Callahan's assistant coaches became known to work. Gill was an Osborne man. He was not only extremely loyal to Osborne, but also to former head coach Frank Solich. Most importantly Gill was loyal to Nebraska, and that's why he chose to stay on another season in 2004. "Well, Nebraska's been unusual in that you had roughly 42 years where you always had a strain of continuity, and that's pretty well gone now," Osborne said following Gill's resignation. "Basically from 1962 on, a player could come back to campus and always find somebody they could relate to. When that changes it's always kind of painful."

Solich, who was fired by Pederson the previous season, also understood the significance of Gill's resignation in 2004. "My feeling is that it's a huge loss—not only to the program, but to the entire state—because he's been such a great ambassador," Solich told the *Lincoln Journal Star*. "Plus the thing about Turner is he cares about those players on and off the field, and his caring is genuine."

During his time in Lincoln, Gill helped develop the skills of some of the finest quarterbacks in Husker history, including 2001 Heisman Trophy and Davey O'Brien award winner Eric Crouch and 1995 Johnny Unitas Golden Arm award winner Tommie Frazier. Frazier led the Huskers to two national championships with Gill on the sidelines while another star, NU quarterback Scott Frost, added a third national title.

Gill also saw great success on the field as a player. Nebraska's starting quarterback from 1981 to 1983, Gill led one of the most explosive offensive attacks in college football history as NU averaged 546.7 yards of total offense and 52 points per game in 1983.

Gill went on to take a player development position with the Green Bay Packers in 2005 before becoming Buffalo's head coach from 2006 to 2009 where he led the Bulls to a MAC Conference title in 2008. In 2010 Gill took over at Kansas for the fired Mark Mangino but was let go following the 2011 season. Gill is now the head coach at Liberty, which plays in the Big South Conference at the FCS Level. In both 2004 and 2007, Gill interviewed for the head coaching job at Nebraska. Osborne said he chose Bo Pelini over Gill following the 2007 season because the Huskers greatly needed a defensive-minded head coach.

42 Texas: The Big 12's Villain

When the Big 12 first formed in 1996, Nebraska and Texas were on opposite ends of the spectrum. The Huskers were the class of college football, winning national championships in 1994, 1995, and 1997 while the Longhorns were a very inconsistent program that had five losing seasons from 1986 to 1997.

Even though the Huskers were the king of college football in 1995, they had very little pull in some of the initial key decisions of the Big 12 conference that merged Texas, Texas A&M, Baylor, and Texas Tech with the Big 8 in 1996.

In a lot of ways there was jealously within the Big 8 of NU's remarkable run over the 1990s, and you saw the rest of the league go against Nebraska and side with Texas in some of the initial voting. NU was shot down 11–1 on having a conference title game. Nebraska was the only program that wasn't for the game because—in head coach Tom Osborne's eyes—an extra game like this would cost the league a chance to play for a national title in some years. Osborne was right. In 1996 and 1998, both Nebraska and Kansas State lost in the Big 12 title game and were knocked out of the national championship race.

The Big 12 also disallowed schools to take partial qualifiers—players, who didn't initially qualify academically out of high school but were given their first year of college at a four-year school to see if they could make the grade to get eligible. With the state of Nebraska's limited population base, this was a big blow to NU's recruiting because the Huskers had a lot of success over the years signing partial qualifiers and getting them eligible to add to the available talent pool. This rule greatly helped schools like Texas because of their large in-state recruiting base.

The Big 12 offices would also eventually move from Kansas City to Dallas, giving the league an even more slanted feel toward Texas in the eyes of many Nebraskans.

The Nebraska-Texas rivalry got going against this backdrop, and things really intensified after the Longhorns beat the Huskers 37–27 in the inaugural Big 12 championship game, which cost NU a chance to win a third consecutive national championship in 1996.

The rivalry would only intensify when Texas hired Mack Brown from North Carolina in 1998. Before Brown's hiring the Longhorns were 77–60–2 from 1986 to 1997. In Brown's first 12 seasons at UT, the Longhorns would own a 128–27 record and win no less than nine games from 1998 to 2009.

Most notably Brown always seemed to have Nebraska's number —even in 1998 when an underdog Longhorns team snapped the Huskers' 47-game home winning streak with a 20–16 victory. The win helped catapult Texas running back Ricky Williams to the Heisman Trophy as it was NU's first home loss since September 21, 1991 against national champion Washington. Brown immediately captured the hearts of Longhorn fans with his 9–3 record and that upset of the Huskers in Lincoln.

Even in 1999 Brown figured out a way to spoil the Huskers season. Most considered the 1999 Nebraska team one of the best squads in school history that didn't win a national championship. The Huskers traveled to Austin and lost to UT 24–20 in what was dubbed "the Fumble Game." NU had three costly fumbles, including one at the goal line by running back Correll Buckhalter in the fourth quarter in what would've been the go-ahead touchdown. The Huskers would go on to beat Texas 22–6 in the Big 12 championship later that season but still were denied an opportunity to play for the national title with an 11–1 record.

Texas was the only team that beat the Huskers three times in the 1990s, and two of the losses cost Nebraska a chance to play for a national title. The third snapped the nation's longest home winning streak. "We couldn't understand why Texas had our number," former Husker All-American cornerback Ralph Brown said. "They broke our home winning streak, and then we go back up there and they beat us again. They just had our number. I don't know why we couldn't beat them. I was just so glad we beat them most my senior year when it counted, but they did have our number, and we just couldn't figure it out. We were more talented than they were, but the ball ended up bouncing their way when the game was on the line. That's something that angers me to this day because that's what they have over us. They just had our number."

The Longhorns would go on to beat Nebraska in 2002, 2003, 2006, 2007, 2009, and 2010. From 1996 to 2010, the Huskers were 1–9 against the team they hated most. Even in the final meeting between these schools in 2010, Nebraska was a 10-point favorite at home against a UT squad that would go 5–7. After a controversial defeat to Texas in the 2009 Big 12 title game, there was mounting pressure to not only beat Texas in 2010, but also run them out of the stadium in what would be the final Big 12 meeting between these two schools.

The Huskers once again fell flat and lost 20–13, giving Texas the last laugh as the Big Red moved to the Big Ten. What Ralph Brown remembers about all those Texas teams was—no matter what their record was, they were never intimidated by Nebraska, and it showed with their 9–1 record. "Mack Brown had those guys playing on all cylinders," Ralph Brown said. "They had a confidence about them that no other team had when they would play us.

In 1996 when we played in the Big 12 championship game, those guys felt like they were better than us on the football field. They had some good talent on that 1996 team with James Brown and Ricky Williams and Priest Holmes. Every time we played Texas, we could tell by the look in their eyes that they felt they were better than us. There wasn't another team that we played throughout my four years that felt that way. They ended up winning mostly every time. The time we felt we owed them and wanted a little payback was my senior year and we dominated them. They just felt like they were better than us on the football field every time we played."

Texas' politicking and bullying in 2010 led Nebraska to approach the Big Ten about possible membership. The Huskers would leave in June of 2010, and Colorado, Texas A&M, and Missouri would follow them by going to the Pac-12 and SEC.

The original Big 12 changed forever, and many great rivalries like Nebraska vs. Oklahoma, Nebraska vs. Colorado, Texas A&M vs. Texas, and Missouri vs. Kansas were lost forever. Many people still point the finger at Texas and their financial greed of starting the Longhorn Network with ESPN as to why the original Big 12 broke apart. In the eyes of Texas, a multi-year Longhorn Network television contract with ESPN—valued at $247.5 million over 20 years—was worth more than playing traditional rivals like Texas A&M.

The 1983 Scoring Explosion Offense

Not even the no-huddle, spread option attacks of today's pass-happy game can touch the output of Nebraska's 1983 Scoring Explosion Offense. Led by quarterback Turner Gill, Heisman

Trophy running back Mike Rozier, and wide receiver Irving Fryar, NU's 1983 offense still holds several team and individual scoring records at Nebraska. They are considered the best offense in school history and one of the best in NCAA history.

Counting the 1984 Orange Bowl, Nebraska scored 654 points and 93 touchdowns in the 1983 season. Both marks remain school records at NU. In the Huskers' 84–13 win at Minnesota, NU had 595 yards rushing on 55 carries for a school record nine touchdowns. In its win against Colorado in 1983, Nebraska scored 48 points in the third quarter, including a span of 9:10 where it put up 41 points. The list goes on and on. The Huskers averaged 401.7 yards rushing per game and had 4,820 rushing yards. They had 66 rushing touchdowns, averaged 7.16 yards-per-carry on the season, and put up 6,560 yards of total offense. All of these marks still remain Nebraska school records.

Rozier also rewrote the record books in 1983, rushing for 2,148 yards and 29 touchdowns to finish his career with 4,780 yards and 49 touchdowns. He ran for 200 yards or more in Nebraska's final four games during the regular season. In a 67–13 win against Kansas, Rozier had 230 yards by halftime and finished with 285 yards rushing—a school record at the time. Fryar finished the 1983 season with 780 yards receiving, which was second at the time to 1972 Heisman Trophy winner Johnny Rodgers.

The 1983 Scoring Explosion Offense had just about every individual and team offensive accolade one could imagine. The only thing that kept the 1983 Huskers from being considered one of the all-time great teams in college football history was their 31–30 loss to Miami in the Orange Bowl for the national title.

The buzz about Nebraska's Scoring Explosion Offense began before that season when former athletic director and football recruiting coordinator Steve Pederson created a poster of Gill, Rozier, and Fryar exploding through the large scoreboard that formerly rose above the north end of Memorial Stadium. Several flying footballs also filled the sky in the poster along with the 1983 schedule. Pederson designed the poster for recruiting reasons, but it became a popular piece of memorabilia that all Nebraska fans wanted to have.

During the 2005 Red-White spring game, Pederson honored the Scoring Explosion Offense with a special tribute to Gill, Rozier, and Fryar along with a remake of the poster. "The days of the Scoring Explosion at Nebraska were exciting times," Pederson said. "Mike, Turner, and Irving brought so much to Nebraska, and we are grateful. It is our pleasure to be able to bring these men back to Nebraska as a group for the first time since they have all completed their playing career. They are a big part of Husker football history."

44 Defensive Coordinator Charlie McBride

Charlie McBride remembers the day like it was yesterday. The year was 1976, and he had just finished a 5–6 season under John Jardine at Wisconsin. It was Thanksgiving when McBride was watching the Nebraska vs. Oklahoma game on television with his wife, and something just jumped out to him about the Huskers. "I came in the house, and Oklahoma had run the hook-and-ladder and won the game with it," McBride said. "I went out to the kitchen, and my wife was cooking, and we had a house full of people. It was crazy. I just had mentioned to my wife that I would really like to work for Coach Osborne, which was kind of off the top of my head. She remembers it, though, and I remember saying it, and that was kind of it."

Other than those words, McBride had zero connections to Osborne or the Big Red, but the former Colorado Buffalo was

Two More Years

It wasn't publicized much, but Charlie McBride actually wanted to ride off into the sunset and retire from Nebraska with Tom Osborne following the 1997 season.

Osborne, however, convinced him to stay and help Frank Solich with the transition to a new regime in 1998, and a group of senior players led by defensive backs Mike and Ralph Brown convinced McBride to finish out the 1999 season with them as well.

"I was having some physical problems and I said, 'Well, I'll stay one more year [in 1998].' Then as it ended up, Ralph and Mike came into the office and heard I was going to retire and said, 'We're going to be seniors. Would you consider staying one more year until we graduated?' There were some other guys, too," McBride said. "We were building a house in Arizona, and it wasn't going to be ready. I decided I'll go one more year then all these guys will be gone except for Loran Kaiser was the one guy playing a lot on the defensive line that had another year. He was mad as hell I didn't stay with him for his senior season, but he's the first one to always still call me today."

Said Ralph Brown: "We didn't want to lose essentially two fathers that we looked up to, so we told Charlie, 'We need you here. We have to have you here throughout our senior year.' We begged him. Eventually he came back and spoke to the team and said, 'I'm going to stay until '99.' It felt so good to know that we helped change his mind as a defensive coordinator because he really cared about Mike and myself and some other guys on the team and he wanted to go out with us. I thought that was an amazing thing that he did to support us and our college career."

well connected across college football to names like Frank Kush at Arizona State and Buck Nystrom at CU. Following the 1976 season at Wisconsin, Jardine told McBride that it may be in his best interest to explore his options because Jardine was having some medical issues that were probably going to force him to resign in Madison, Wisconsin.

During the 1977 AFCA Coach's Convention in Miami, McBride remembers getting a phone call to his room that he thought was one of his friends playing a joke on him. "Tom on the phone is so soft spoken that you don't know for sure that when he says 'This is Tom Osborne' you kind of go, *yeah right*. Well, that's what I did," McBride said, laughing. "What happened was we were both in the same hotel. I was in 315, and he was in room 215. I got a phone call in my room, and Osborne called, and I actually said, 'No, really, who is this?' I thought it was some of my friends pulling my chain. Then he said, 'I'm in the room down below you. I was wondering if you could come down for about 15 minutes. I'm in between appointments. I'd like to talk to you.' Then I said, 'No, really, who is this?' Then when he said it a second time, I believed him. It was kind of like I wasn't really sure what was going on, so I went down there to talk to him, and he invited us out to dinner."

McBride and his wife still joke today that Osborne didn't exactly take them out to a five-star Miami restaurant. "When I tell the story, I always laugh because I like to say, 'Tom really likes to live high on the hog and he took me to this great place to have dinner. It's called Denny's.' My wife still says to this day, 'Did we have anything to eat because all you guys did was draw circles on napkins?' Then he offered me the job," McBride said.

From that point on, McBride became Osborne's right-hand man, helping him build and reconstruct the Blackshirt defense into one of the most dominant forces in college football. But it wasn't until Nebraska made the switch from the 5-2 to the attacking 4-3 defense in 1993 that McBride saw the fruits of his labor.

From 1993 to 1999, McBride's defenses pitched nine shut-outs and held opponents to seven points or less 28 times. Former All-American cornerback Ralph Brown said McBride had an unbelievable ability to motivate, and several defensive players looked up to him like a father figure. "What I really respected about McBride is he was such a hard ass in practice. He was one of the worst guys in practice to hear yell," Brown said. "You didn't want to hear McBride yelling or screaming about any plays you messed up on or mistakes you made. On gameday he was all positive. He never yelled at us and he was always supportive. He was totally different. His mentality was we were going to make practice so tough and so hard that he was going to beat us until the beginning of practice until the end of practice that once we got into the game on Saturday it was going to be easy."

McBride's final defense at Nebraska in 1999 would go on to be one of his best. NU ranked in the top six nationally in four major defensive categories, including second in pass efficiency (87.9 rating), third in scoring defense (12.5 points per game), fourth in total defense (252.3 yards per game), and sixth in rushing defense (77.1 yards per game). It was the third time in McBride's final six seasons at Nebraska that the Huskers were in the top 10 of all four major defensive categories. That 1999 defense also holds the school record with 54 quarterback sacks in a season for a loss of 403 yards. During McBride's career at NU, 17 different defensive players were named All-Americans, and seven different players were named either the Big 8 or Big 12 Defensive Player of the Year.

45 I-Back High

From 1967 to 2002, Omaha Central High took on the nickname of "Nebraska's I-Back High." During that period the Eagles had nine different running backs sign with the Huskers, including a span from 1986 to 1997 where all but one year (1994) an Omaha Central running back either started or played heavy snaps in head coach Tom Osborne's backfield. There was even a period in the early 1990s where three Omaha Central running backs started for different Big 8 teams at one time. Eagles running backs Keith

Ahman Green, one of many successful Huskers running backs to come out of Omaha Central High, churns out yardage during Nebraska's 55–14 win against Michigan State in 1996. (Getty Images)

Jones, Leodis Flowers, Calvin Jones, and Ahman Green combined for 11,156 yards and scored 132 total touchdowns for the Huskers.

When you talk about the history of Central's running backs, though, it really starts with the one that got away. In 1961 future Pro Football Hall of Fame running back Gale Sayers picked Kansas over Nebraska—in large part because NU head coach Bill Jennings mismanaged his recruitment. 1961 was Jennings' final season at

Nebraska as he was fired with a 15–34–1 record, and at the time KU was considered a better football program than NU. Sayers would go on to become one of the all-time great running backs to ever play the game. In Bob Devaney's second season at Nebraska in 1963, Sayers set an NCAA record by rushing for a 99-yard touchdown run against the Huskers. Sayers finished his career in Lawrence with 3,917 all-purpose yards.

After Sayer's success at Kansas, Nebraska vowed to never let another Omaha Central running back slip through the cracks. From 1967 to 1970, Eagles running back Joe Orduna rushed for 1,968 yards and 26 touchdowns for Nebraska, including a team-high 897 yards during the Huskers' 1970 national championship season. Orduna would go on to play in the NFL for the New York Giants and Baltimore Colts.

After Orduna, Pernell Gatson (1984) came to Nebraska out of Omaha Central. Gatson was an athlete who played wingback. Former Eagles head coach Joe McMenamin started out at Central as an assistant coach in 1978 and was their head coach from 1990 to 2006. He still recalls Houston head coach Bill Yeoman coming into Central and offering both Gatson and linebacker Larry Station scholarships in 1981. Yeoman told McMenamin that Gatson and Station were the first two players the Cougars had offered outside the state of Texas in more than five years. Station would end up going to Iowa where he would become an All-American linebacker and the Hawkeyes' all-time leading tackler.

Following Gatson the Eagles went on their special run of I-backs. Keith Jones was an All-Big 8 running back for two seasons, rushing for 2,488 yards and 26 touchdowns and starting for the Huskers in both 1986 and 1987. Flowers would step in after Jones and rush for 1,635 yards and 18 touchdowns from 1988 to 1990. Calvin Jones would follow Flowers and rush for 3,153 yards and 40 touchdowns from 1991 to 1993. After Calvin Jones came arguably the best running back the state of Nebraska's ever produced since Sayers.

Ahman Green moved to Omaha from Los Angeles after the eighth grade but didn't actually attend Central until his junior season. Green went to Omaha North as a freshman but played for the North Omaha Bears Club team in 1991 and then he played for the Omaha North Vikings as a sophomore in 1992. Before his junior season, Green's father phoned McMenamin about transferring to Central. In 1992 the Eagles already had an All-State sophomore running back in Damion Morrow, but the Green family did not care. Green's father wanted him to be a Central running back. "Ahman's dad stepped in after that season and said, 'We are transferring Ahman to Central,' and I said, 'Really? We've got an All-State running back,' and his dad said, 'Yep, we know.' He just really wanted Ahman to go to Central," McMenamin recalled. "The people at North really did their best to get him to stay, but he still came. They had to move into the attendance area for Ahman to go to Central and they did that during the winter semester. Him and Damion started together as juniors and seniors. They were both All-State. Ahman was No. 1 in the state in rushing, and Damion was No. 3."

Green would go on to be ranked the No. 1 high school running back in the country and a *Parade* All-American for the Eagles in 1994. He didn't commit to Nebraska until January of his senior year. Michigan, led by the recruiting efforts of assistant coach Les Miles, nearly got Green, but at the end of the day he decided to stay home. "Ahman committed right after New Year's," McMenamin said. "I was at the coaches clinic in Orlando, and he called me and said, "Coach, I want to commit. It's just too much pressure, and there are too many people.' I asked him if he talked to his family and then I said, 'Go ahead.' He committed there in January."

Even with a loaded backfield that featured Lawrence Phillips, Damon Benning, Clinton Childs, and Jay Simms, Green managed

The One that Got Away

In 1961 Nebraska obviously lost out of running back Gale Sayers to Kansas. In 2004 the Huskers would lose out on another NFL running back from their own backyard.

North Platte native Danny Woodhead will be entering his sixth season in the NFL in 2013 with the San Diego Chargers. Before that he was one of Tom Brady's main backfield mates in New England. Woodhead came out of high school in a bizarre year because in 2003 former head coach Frank Solich was under an intense amount of pressure to win, and he would eventually be fired in November after a 9–3 record. NU went 40 days without a head coach, so Woodhead fell between the cracks.

Scott Downing was the recruiting coordinator for both Solich in 2003 and newly named head coach Bill Callahan in 2004. Downing said if Solich would not have been fired in November of 2003 there was a good chance Woodhead was going to get a scholarship offer following the season. "I really think under Frank's staff we were going to find a place for [Woodhead] to play," Downing said. "Obviously a lot depends on how the scholarships play out, but I really believe that Frank wanted him to come to Nebraska. We felt like he'd be a guy that could contribute at a high level at some point in his career."

Nebraska elected to sign Brandon Jackson in 2004, who ended up being a second-round NFL draft pick. Aside from Jackson, NU also had Cory Ross, Marlon Lucky, Cody Glenn, and Kenny Wilson as highly recruited running backs on their roster during Woodhead's career.

Downing feels Woodhead probably made the best decision to attend Division II Chadron State because it allowed him to play immediately. Woodhead won the Division II equivalent of the Heisman Trophy in both 2006 and 2007 and finished his career with an NCAA record 7,441 yards.

to find his way onto the field as a true freshman in 1995. Suspensions and injuries played a factor in this, but Green took advantage of his opportunity and rushed for a Nebraska freshman-record 1,086 yards and 13 touchdowns.

At 6'0", 220 pounds Green had a rare combination of strength and speed that allowed him to excel immediately. Green helped the

Huskers win national championships in both 1995 and 1997 and finished with 3,880 yards and 42 touchdowns over three seasons, including an NU junior-record 1,877 yards and 22 touchdowns in 1997. "I knew he has the physical ability to play right away," McMenamin said. "In high school he was 220. He had the speed, the size, and strength. He was squatting 500 pounds and had all the physical stuff to play."

After Green two more Central running backs played for the Big Red—DeAnte Grixby (2000 to 2003) and David Horne (2002 to 2004). Both players showed flashes over their careers, but neither was able to put it together like the four previous Eagles running backs at NU.

If you walk into Omaha Central High School, you will find a Running Back Wall of Fame honoring the great players who played for the Eagles starting with Sayers. Young boys across Omaha during the '80s and '90s went to Central, hoping to be the next great Eagle I-back. "We put that up there, and it was mainly just for the running backs," McMenamin said. "It was put up there mainly to get attention for the football program. A lot of people would come up just to see that. Every kid in the building would see it when they walked down the hall, and it gave the football program and the players more notoriety."

46 Offensive Line Coach Milt Tenopir

When you recruit offensive lineman in today's football world, the first thing anybody looks for is measurables. Tackles are typically 6'6" with long arms, while guards and centers are ideally 6'3" to 6'5". When former Nebraska offensive line coach Milt Tenopir recruited players, he only looked for one thing, and it couldn't be measured by a ruler or a scale. "You can't measure a guy's heart by inches," Tenopir said. "I was always a strong believer you get a kid to perform rather than how pretty he looks in a uniform."

For example Aaron Taylor (1997) and Will Shields (1992) were both Outland Trophy winners for Tenopir and only 6'1". In the history of the Outland Trophy, the last time an offensive lineman shorter than 6'1" won the award was in 1960.

After serving as a high school coach in Kansas, Colorado, and Nebraska, Tenopir joined Tom Osborne's coaching staff in 1974. Little did Osborne know at the time that he was hiring perhaps the best offensive line coach in college football history. Osborne and Tenopir had a relationship that dated back to high school, which paved the way for him to join the staff in 1974. "[Osborne and I] ran track against each other. He was three years ahead of me, but we ran the hurdles against each other," Tenopir said. "When [Osborne] got the job, I called him and asked him if he'd consider hiring anyone out of the high school ranks. His answer was he didn't have anything open because most of Bob [Devaney]'s assistants stayed on. He said he would call back a year from now if something opened up. I thought I'd never hear from him, but I did."

Twenty-nine years later Tenopir helped coach 13 offensive lines that won NCAA rushing titles, three national championships, six Outland Trophies, and two Lombardi Awards from 1974 to 2002. NU also had 21 different All-Americans, 49 All-Conference offensive linemen, and 27 different O-linemen sign NFL contracts under Tenopir's guidance. From 1978 to 2002, Nebraska's offense ranked in the top four nationally in rushing yards in 24 out of 25 years. Osborne installed the option offense in the fall of 1979.

Tenopir created an offensive line culture that has yet to be matched by anyone today. On average Tenopir carried 32 to 34

Jake Young

When people talk about the late Jake Young, the word most used to describe the Midland, Texas, native was "competitor." From the minute offensive line coach Milt Tenopir recruited Young, he not only saw his talent but also his outstanding leadership skills. In 1986 Tenopir had enough confidence to immediately throw Young, a true freshman, right into fire, and he became the first ever true freshman to earn a letter on the offensive line since freshmen became eligible in 1972.

By 1987 Young was already in the starting lineup for the Big Red—the first true sophomore to start on the offensive line since Rick Bonness in 1973. Young would go on to earn second team All-Big 8 honors that season. By 1988 and 1989, Young would become a two-time first team All-American for the Huskers—joining Bonness, Aaron Taylor, and Dave Rimington as the only offensive linemen in school history to be named two-time All-Americans. Young was also named a second team Academic All-American in 1988 and a first team Academic All-American in 1989 for his outstanding work in the classroom. "Jake had an extra gear that most people didn't have," Tenipor said. "He was very competitive and a very tenacious guy. He was a good player—just a tremendous competitor. His first year he played guard for us. Then that spring I moved him to center and had a little bit more control over him once I had him for a year. He ended up starting three years for us at center and he was a very big reason why we had good football teams those years."

It was Young's worth ethic that really stood out to his teammates. "He was just a hardworking classic overachiever," said former Huskers tight end Tom Banderas, who played with Young in 1986 and

linemen on the roster each year. Under Osborne the Huskers would break practice up into stations. In order to do this properly, it was vital to have several walk-on players. There were four stations total in practice—two offensive and two defensive. Each Tuesday and Wednesday during the fall both the No. 1 and No. 2 offensive lines saw 110 snaps in practice. In 17 to 18-minute

1987. "He wasn't gifted with great speed or strength, but he had true grit. He was a grinder."

Young used that same work ethic to excel after football by earning his law degree from Nebraska in 1994. After practicing law in Kansas City, he took a job in Hong Kong. While in Hong Kong the 6'4" Young began playing rugby for a local club team. He eventually would accept another job in Kansas City by 2002, but before he moved back to the United States, Young chose to play with his rugby team one last time in a tournament in Bali, Indonesia.

The 34-year-old Young convinced his wife, Laura, to let him stay an extra couple of days to play in the tournament while she and their son, Wilson, flew back to Kansas City. After the tournament was over, he and his teammates went to a local Bali nightclub to celebrate. The nightclub would become the target of a terrorist bombing, killing more than 180 people. It took several days before officials could verify Young's death. The news sent shockwaves through Husker Nation as just six years earlier NU lost quarterback Brook Berringer to a tragic plane crash. Nobody took the news harder than Tenopir. "He was a kid that I probably took under the wing as much as anybody," Tenopir said. "It was tough, very tough."

2002 would end up being Tenopir's final season of coaching at Nebraska. A 7–7 season, along with the death of Young, made 2002 a very difficult year for Tenopir. "It was extremely tough for me because I was close to Jake, and I had a lot of respect for him and his parents," Tenopir said. "He was a good player and a good guy."

The Jake Young Memorial Endowed Scholarship was created in his honor and is awarded each year to a varsity football student-athlete who demonstrates a high level of athletic and academic achievement along with leadership skills.

periods, Tenopir said NU would run an average of 33 to 35 plays simultaneously with each unit. This allowed several more players the opportunity to develop, which made it easier to reload—rather than rebuild after a heavy graduation year.

In Tenopir's world it didn't matter if you were an NFL prospect or how many stars you had coming out of high school. One case in point came during the 1993 Orange Bowl against Florida State. "We had a scholarship eight-man football left tackle Lance Lundberg from Wausa, and our left guard was a walk-on named Kenny Mehlin from Humboldt. Jim Scott was our center and he was a walk-on. He transferred from Kearney and was from the small town of Ansley, Nebraska," Tenopir said proudly. "The entire left side of our line was made up of eight-man players, and only one of them was a scholarship guy."

Another great walk-on success story was 1997 guard Matt Hoskinson, who was from the small Nebraska town of Battle Creek. As a senior Hoskinson weighed between 255 and 260 pounds and started on a national championship offensive line. Most offensive line coaches would be scared to start a lineman that size, but Tenopir never showed any doubt. Tenopir's loyalty toward his players made him a very popular figure in the locker room. "Milt is the type of guy that rooted for the underdog," Hoskinson said. "He recruited people like me. He recruited people like Aaron Taylor. From a mentality standpoint, Milt loved guys that had a chip on their shoulder. Milt actually sought guys like us out. Who's the guy that's playing with a chip on his shoulder? Who's the guy that's playing with a high motor that's going to give you the maximum on every single snap every single time? I think that's what made him so brilliant. He surrounded people like [All-Americans] Zach Wiegert and Brenden Stai and some of the bigger time prototypical players with people like myself and some of these other guys."

Maybe one of Tenopir's favorite compliments he ever received came after the 1997 national championship season when the Huskers stomped Tennessee in the Orange Bowl. "After Peyton Manning's last year in 1997, [one of] Tennessee's coaches came up to us at the coaches convention, and I ran into them and he said, 'We looked over there in the fourth quarter, and I told Coach [Phillip] Fulmer—look at that sideline. We wouldn't even recruit those guys. They were all 6'1" and 6'2" guys.' That was a pretty good group of kids though," Tenopir said smiling.

47 Unsung Heroes: Nebraska Fullbacks

When you think about great positions in Nebraska's history, offensive linemen, running backs, or even quarterbacks immediately come to mind. However, the fullback position over the years at NU has produced several unsung heroes. These are the guys who do the dirty work behind the scenes but don't necessarily get the recognition of the other positions.

There is no award given to the nation's best fullback, and often times they aren't even recognized on All-Conference teams. When you look at the fullback tradition around college football, it's hard to find any school that matches Nebraska. Here's my list of the Huskers' 10 greatest fullbacks ranked from earliest to most recent.

Frank Solich (1963 to 1965): The Ohio native was part of Bob Devaney's first recruiting class at Nebraska and rushed for 1,024 yards and seven touchdowns in the 1964 and 1965 seasons. Against Air Force in 1965, Frank Solich rushed for 204 yards, which set an NU single-game rushing record at the time. Those 204 yards still stand as a Nebraska fullback record. Solich, who would eventually become Nebraska's head coach in 1998, is also the first Husker player ever featured on the cover of *Sports Illustrated*. Solich was an All-Big 8 selection in 1965 and a co-captain for the Big Red.

Dick Davis (1966 to 1968): Solich's successor was Dick Davis, who still holds fullback school records for rushing attempts in a season (162) and career (349) at Nebraska. Davis was a first team All-Big 8 selection in 1967.

Tony Davis (1973 to 1975): No relation to Dick, Tough Tony Davis out of Tecumseh, Nebraska, started his career in 1973 at running back where he rushed for 1,158 yards. In 1974 and 1975, Davis moved to fullback where he put up 1,331 yards. Davis was named MVP of Nebraska's 13–10 win against Florida in the 1975 Sugar Bowl with 126 yards on 17 carries. Davis finished his career in 1975 as NU's all-time leading rusher with 2,445 yards and went on to play six seasons in the NFL.

Andra Franklin (1977 to 1980): The Alabama native was a rare freshman letter winner for Tom Osborne. Andra Franklin holds the fullback record at NU with 1,738 rushing yards on 324 attempts for a 5.4 yards-per-carry average. He was a 1980 first team All-Big 8 selection and a second-round NFL draft pick by the Miami Dolphins.

Mark Schellen (1982 to 1983): The Waterloo, Nebraska, native was the forgotten fourth member of Nebraska's famed Scoring Explosion Offense. Everybody talked about quarterback Turner Gill, running back Mike Rozier, and wide receiver Irving Fryar, but Mark Schellen rushed for 450 yards and a fullback single-season record nine touchdowns. Schellen also was crucial in the blocking game opening up holes for Rozier and Gill.

Tom Rathman (1983 to 1985): The Grand Island, Nebraska, native is considered the best fullback in school history by many. Tom Rathman rushed for 1,425 yards and 12 touchdowns, including a Nebraska fullback-record 881 yards on 118 carries in 1985—good for a 7.5 yards-per-carry average. Rathman was adept at avoiding negative plays, too. In fact out of 220 carries, he amazingly only lost a total of four yards. The 1985 All-Big 8 and third team All-American selection played nine seasons in the NFL and was critical in helping the San Francisco 49ers win two Super Bowls, blocking for former Husker running back Roger Craig.

Cory Schlesinger (1992 to 1994): The Duncan, Nebraska, native became legendary by scoring two fourth-quarter touchdowns in the 1995 Orange Bowl victory against Miami, giving Nebraska its first national championship since 1971. Cory Schlesinger didn't put up the numbers of a Rathman or Franklin, but he averaged 7.2 yards-per-carry, rushing for 456 yards during the 1994 national championship season. Schlesinger played for 12 seasons with the Detroit Lions.

Jeff Makovicka (1992 to 1995): The first of four Makovicka brothers to play at Nebraska, Jeff Makovicka was a key part of Nebraska's 1995 national championship season, rushing for 371 yards on 63 carries. The Brainerd, Nebraska, native played a key role in lead blocking for quarterback Tommie Frazier and running backs Ahman Green, Lawrence Phillips, Damon Benning, and Clinton Childs.

Joel Makovicka (1995 to 1998): Carrying on the legacy of homegrown, in-state walk-on fullbacks, Joel Makovicka had a stellar career at NU and is one of only a handful of Huskers players to be a part of all three national championship teams. (He was a redshirt on the 1994 squad.) Makovicka finished his career with 1,447 yards and 11 touchdowns—highlighted by a 685-yard season in 1997. Makovicka was a fourth-round draft pick by the Arizona Cardinals and played four seasons in the NFL.

Judd Davies (2000 to 2003): Injuries limited the Millard North High product, Judd Davies, from having a huge career numbers wise, but he holds the school record for career touchdowns by a fullback with 14. In Nebraska's 2001 win at Baylor, Davies was one of four players to rush for 100 yards, which is the only time that's happened in school history.

48 The Four Food Groups: Runza, Valentino's, Fairbury, and Colby Ridge

Many different things make Nebraska's gameday experience at Memorial Stadium unique, and definitely one of them is the variety of local vendors that sell food on football Saturdays. Four in particular—Valentino's Pizza, Runza, Fairbury hot dogs and Colby Ridge Popcorn—make up what I call, "Nebraska football's four food groups."

For the last several years, many things have changed at Memorial Stadium, but the one constant has been that you can always get an individually boxed slice of Valentino's Pizza, a fresh Runza sandwich, a Fairbury hot dog, or a bag of Colby Ridge Popcorn. What's even more unique about the four food groups is they are all Nebraska-based companies with a strong statewide presence.

Runza opened in Lincoln in 1949 as a stand-alone franchise but now has more than 80 locations in Nebraska, Iowa, Kansas, and Colorado. If you aren't familiar with a Runza sandwich, it's a hot, fresh sandwich consisting of homemade dough stuffed with ground beef, onions, cabbage, and secret spices. On cold Huskers gamedays, a Runza sandwich in your pocket even serves as a good hand warmer when making your way to your seats, and it sells for $4 at all Nebraska sporting events. It truly is something you will only find in Nebraska.

In the 1970s and early 1980s, Don Everett Sr., founder of Runza Restaurants, and a team of employees sold sandwiches outside Memorial Stadium. Seeing their success the athletic department invited Runza into the stadium as the first outside vendor in 1984. The first contract with Runza ran from 1984 to 1994. After a short hiatus, Runza signed a new contract in 1999 and has been part of the Husker gameday experience ever since. "Our involvement with Husker athletics reinforces our Nebraska roots and provides fans from all over the country the opportunity to try a sandwich unique to the area," Runza marketing director Becky Perrett said. "Our fan base builds every time the Huskers play, and often we hear from the newly initiated Runzatics via Facebook and Twitter. Our online store statistics show many orders each year from Texas, California, Kansas, Colorado, and Iowa. Husker fans provide the best recommendation and description of what a Runza sandwich is with an ending comment like, 'You have to try one!' The Huskers are Nebraska's team, and we are proud of our long-standing relationship."

Valentino's, started in Lincoln in 1957 by Val and Zena Weiler, now consists of more than 30 different restaurants in Nebraska, Iowa, Kansas, Minnesota, and South Dakota. On Husker game-days you can purchase a slice of traditional Valentino's hamburger pizza for $4. As you walk into Memorial Stadium, young children often line up along the concourse, selling containers full of Val's Pizza and Runza sandwiches.

The other major staple at Husker football games is Fairbury red hot dogs, which is associated with Wimmer's Meats in West Point—also a Nebraska-based company—since 1934. One of the gameday traditions with Fairbury hot dogs in the stadium is the Der Viener Schlinger, an air-powered cannon that fires foil-wrapped hot dogs into the stands. (The cannon is powerful enough to reach the upper deck.) You'll often see coaches from other Nebraska sports or local celebrities firing Der Viener Schlinger into the stands.

The final local Nebraska staple in Memorial Stadium is Colby Ridge Popcorn, which is a Lincoln-based company that formed in 1985 and now serves and distributes popcorn around the country. Colby Ridge makes just about every flavor of popcorn imaginable, including cinnamon-flavored popcorn, which is obviously Husker Red in color.

So if you are going to Memorial Stadium for the first time, you are encouraged to try a Runza sandwich, a slice of Valentino's hamburger pizza, a Fairbury hot dog, and a bag of delicious Colby Ridge popcorn. Then you'll definitely leave with a taste of Nebraska favorites.

49 2001 Nebraska at Colorado

It was November 23, 2001. No. 2 Nebraska was 11–0, heading into their regular season finale at No. 14 Colorado. The Buffaloes had an 8–2 record after setbacks earlier in the year to Fresno State and Texas. The Huskers already owned a big win against defending national champion Oklahoma, and all that stood in their way for an appearance in the Big 12 championship game was the Buffaloes. The Huskers entered the game as a nine-point favorite on the road, and they were expected to roll through CU and move one step closer to the BCS national championship game.

However, what happened that day in Boulder, Colorado, changed Nebraska football forever. Never before in the modern Bob Devaney-Tom Osborne-Frank Solich era had anything ever happened to Nebraska like what occurred at Folsom Field. The Buffaloes scored 62 points on the Huskers, the most by an opponent at the time in NU's glorious history. Colorado scored touchdowns on five of its first six possessions, rushing for an astounding 380 yards to go along with 202 yards passing. The final score read 62–36, but it wasn't even that close. It was a beatdown unlike any Husker fans were accustomed to seeing.

Colorado running back Chris Brown rushed for 198 yards and a school-record six touchdowns while backfield mate Bobby

Purify added 154 yards of his own along with a touchdown. CU quarterback Bobby Pesavento, who at the start of the season was a backup, wasn't sacked or intercepted by the Huskers. "This is a terrible feeling because we had played so well for 11 games," Nebraska defensive tackle Jeremy Slechta said. "We had given up so few points all year and to give up 62—it's disappointing. They played great, and we played like crap."

Husker quarterback Eric Crouch was one of the lone bright spots for Nebraska as he put up 360 yards of total offense, which at the time was a school record. "This is pretty much a nightmare for us," Crouch said. "They played a great game offensively and defensively. They really put it to us. Colorado took care of the football and didn't make mistakes. We made some mistakes that really hurt us. This is a big shock. It's tough to talk about because this never happens to us. I can't remember the last time someone put up that many points against us."

While meeting with the press after the game, a confident Brown said he felt that no team had tried to challenge the Huskers with a physical running attack all season. He said that was their game plan going in, and the Buffaloes executed it to perfection. "It was easy," Brown said. "The holes were huge. The first guy I'd usually run into was a safety. And their safeties were scared to come straight up and tackle me. Definitely they didn't expect us to come out and play the way we did. I think they were overconfident. They're used to coming in here and whipping us every year, but it was a different story today."

That game represented a watershed mark for the Nebraska program. Since that 2001 loss to Colorado, the Huskers have only been ranked in the top five for one week from 2002 to 2012. From 1993 to 2001, NU was ranked in the top 10 or top 5 all but a handful of weeks. Despite losing to Colorado, the Huskers still played in the Rose Bowl against Miami for the national title and Crouch captured the Heisman Trophy.

The Hurricanes embarrassed Nebraska 37–14, and NU would go on to have a 7–7 record in 2002. Head coach Frank Solich made staff changes after that season, but it wasn't enough to keep his job, and he was out following the 2003 season.

50 Kenny Walker

It's hard to think of a more emotional moment in Memorial Stadium than on November 3, 1990 when No. 3 Nebraska took on No. 9 Colorado. It was Senior Day at Memorial Stadium, but what made this event unique was Kenny Walker. The defensive lineman from Texas was deaf since the age of two when he contracted spinal meningitis. Husker fans have long been known as the classiest in college football and they wanted to figure out a way to pay tribute to Walker, who was named an All-American in 1990 and the Big 8's Defensive Player of the Year.

A week before the Buffaloes and Huskers played, a group of people secretly organized a campaign that was picked up by the media and learned by the NU cheerleaders. The group wanted to pay tribute to Walker by having all of Memorial Stadium make the sign language signal for "clapping." The campaign went viral, and when Walker took the field for his Senior Day introduction, 76,464 people had their arms up like a referee signaling a touchdown and their wrists rotating counterclockwise. The entire crowd chanted "Walker."

An emotional Walker responded back with his arms raised in the air and his hands making the universal symbol for "I love you." Walker's sign language interpreter, Mimi Mann, fought back the tears as she watched Memorial Stadium pay tribute to her student.

Mann worked with Walker all five years of his Husker career to help him learn the different defensive signals each week from defensive coordinator Charlie McBride.

Walker could read lips, so teammates made sure they had their mouthpiece out when making an audible, or they created ways to communicate with him on the field by tapping on his leg. "Here's the thing people don't understand—there are no signs for football terminology," McBride said. "The hard part was when Mimi and Kenny had to make their own sign language up. Think about that with just all the blitzes and things we had. One time [Mann] told me the blitz call sounded like a dog taking a dump, and they had no word for blitz or all of those things. Kenny had to learn the terminology on everything. When I corrected him during a meeting, I had to look at him straight in the face because he had to read my lips. There were a lot of things that went into it, and a lot of the players really helped him a lot because when he was on the field I couldn't look at him for every second. He depended on the guys to help him, and that's what they did. It was a challenge, but Mimi was the key to the whole thing."

Walker, who would play two seasons for the Denver Broncos, finished his senior season at Nebraska with 12 quarterback sacks and 23 tackles for loss. In a 2010 interview with Huskers.com's Randy York, Walker said he remains extremely grateful to Nebraska because it was the only school in the recruiting process that was open to his handicap. "Most of the schools I looked at it didn't accept my deafness," Walker said. "This was before the Americans with Disabilities Act of 1990, so it was hard to find a school that would be open to the deaf. When I had my interview with Nebraska, I learned about the different programs they had to offer me and I was sold."

Even to this day, McBride said coaching Walker and developing him into an All-American ranks as his single greatest accomplishment. McBride still remembers when he first told Walker the that he had been named an All-American. "If I was to take one thing from my whole coaching career—even above the national championships—it's coaching Kenny Walker, and he being the first ever deaf All-American there was in college football," McBride said. "I remember telling him and both of us were just crying. He was so excited. The fact that [Walker] was able to be an All-American and do all he did will probably be something I'll never forget. The national championships were great, but the kids were the ones that won the national championships."

51 The First Family: The Swanson-Ruuds

There are a lot of families that have strong connections to Nebraska football, but there is one that stands out over the others. The Swanson-Ruud family has a lineage the spans throughout multiple generations of the program.

Clarence Swanson began his Husker football career in 1918. An All-American end for the Huskers in 1921, he would eventually be inducted into both the College Football (1973) and Nebraska football (1974) Hall of Fames. Swanson still shares the record for most touchdown catches in a game at three. It's a record that he set in 1921, and no player matched it until Heisman Trophy winner Johnny Rodgers tied it in 1971 against Minnesota.

Swanson would eventually become a successful area businessman and NU regent who played an instrumental role in hiring Bob Devaney in 1962. "He was the one that met Bob at the plane and was instrumental in getting Bob here," said Tom Ruud, who married Swanson's granddaughter, Jaime. "The stories that are passed on from Jaime's aunt, who tells the story, said Clarence and a couple of other people involved in the search were very instrumental in

The Fischer Family

After the Swanson-Ruud family, the Fischer family deserves mention as one of Nebraska football's first families. Brothers Cletus (1945 to 1948), Ken (1948 to 1949), Rex (1955), and Pat Fischer (1958 to 1960) all had standout careers in the Husker football program.

Pat Fischer had the most notable career of the family as he played 213 games in 17 seasons in the NFL for the St. Louis Cardinals and the Washington Redskins. He enjoyed a great career, making three Pro Bowls and collecting 56 interceptions. After his playing days were over, he also coached at NU for one season in 1979.

The late Cletus Fischer lettered all four years at Nebraska and later would serve as an offensive line coach from 1959 to 1985 for the Big Red. He had three sons who played and lettered at Nebraska as well—Dan (1980), Pat (1972 to 1973), and Tim (1976 to 1978). His daughters, Carrie (softball) and Kathleen (golf), also earned letters at NU.

Kenneth Fischer lettered at Nebraska for two seasons and would later go on to coach football in the Nebraska towns of Oakland and Grand Island where his teams won state championships in 1951 and 1978. He finished his career with a 214–69–9 record and was later inducted into the Nebraska High School Sports Hall of Fame.

Rex Fischer lettered for one season at Nebraska and he was the only one of the four Fischer brothers not to get into coaching. After his playing days, he moved to Kansas and became a dentist.

wanting him and convincing Bob Devaney that this would be a good place for him and a good place to have some fun."

In 1972 the university honored his contributions and years of service to Nebraska by creating the Clarence E. Swanson Memorial Award "for outstanding contributions to the University of Nebraska and the Husker athletic department through personal service, personal support of athletic department programs, and dedication to the Husker football program and intercollegiate athletics."

Two of Swanson's granddaughters—Jaime and Sheri Swanson—would eventually marry Husker football players. The late Jaime Swanson married All-Big 8 linebacker Tom

Linebacker Bo Ruud, readying himself for action during a 2006 game against Texas, has deep Husker bloodlines.
(Getty Images)

Ruud (1972 to 1974) while her sister Sheri Swanson married All-American and All-Big 8 defensive end Bob Martin (1973 to 1975).

Bob Martin's son, Jay Martin, of Waverly, Nebraska, walked on to Nebraska as a tight end and played in 21 games over his career (2008 to 2011) primarily on special teams.

Ruud was originally from Minnesota and picked Nebraska after taking visits to eight different Division I schools. His brother, John Ruud, would follow him to Lincoln and is best known for the crushing hit he put on Kelly Phelps in the 1978 Oklahoma game. Tom Ruud would eventually have two sons play for Nebraska to carry on the lineage Clarence Swanson started in 1918. Linebackers Barrett (2001 to 2004) and Bo Ruud (2004 to 2007) of Lincoln Southeast High were both All-Big 12 selections for the Huskers.

Barrett Ruud set the school record for career tackles at 432 and he also holds the school records for solo tackles in a season (86) and a career (218) along with assisted tackles in a career (214). He is regarded as one of the best linebackers in school history.

"I obviously was excited and proud of them that they wanted to pursue it," Tom Ruud said. "Probably more than anything early on, they understood that when they competed they gave it everything they had, and I think that's what they did when they played. It was a lot of fun to have them play and play here because of the history of the family and being close by. They both played at a high level. They both scored touchdowns—which I never did. There was a game where they were on the field at the same time in 2004. I thought that was pretty special. They were playing defense on the field together at the same time. I thought that was a pretty neat deal."

52 Bo Pelini

A year after playing for the national championship in 2001, the Nebraska football program suffered its first seven-loss season since 1958. Following that 7–7 season, former head coach Frank Solich went on a mission to find a defensive coordinator who could put the confidence and swagger back into the Blackshirt defense.

Solich knew this hire was probably going to come outside of the Husker family, so who better to turn to for advice than

Monte Kiffin? The former Nebraska native, player, and assistant coach was in the midst of a Super Bowl-winning season, calling the defense for Jon Gruden in Tampa Bay. Kiffin was the hottest defensive name in football and knew of several young coaching prospects.

After Solich phoned Kiffin, the defensive guru turned to USC head coach Pete Carroll, for whom Kiffin's son and future USC head coach, Lane, worked. "I said, 'Pete, who's out there right now in college football that would be a really, really good coordinator at Nebraska?'" Kiffin said. "I told him, 'I'm trying to help out Frankie Solich.' And he told me, 'There are a lot of good college coaches out there, but I'll give you a guy that might just go back to college football and that's Bo Pelini [who was the Green Bay Packers linebacker coach at the time but previously had worked for Carroll].' Pete said, 'Let me call Bo and see if he'd have some interest.' Pete called Bo, and Bo called Pete back, and they talked, and then Pete called me back, and then I called Bo and then I called Frank. That's how one thing led to another."

Five years later Pelini became Nebraska's new head coach in 2008 after Bill Callahan failed to get it done in his four-year stint following Solich. Carroll said he knew all along Pelini—who has what Carroll calls a "tremendous" defensive mind—would be a great fit in the college game and he was excited to see him get his first head coaching job at a place like Nebraska. "We've been together a long time, and I watched him kind of grow up in coaching," Carroll said. "He's got a great sense for what's happening and he's a very bright, tough guy. He's a really demanding coach that's innovative. He's really got all the right stuff and he's a great competitor, and that comes through in his style of coaching."

When he originally was hired by Nebraska, Pelini had spent just one year as a college coach—as a graduate assistant at Iowa in 1991. He was a high school assistant at Youngstown (Ohio) Cardinal Mooney in 1993 then was hired by George Seifert and the San Francisco 49ers in 1994 to be a scouting assistant. But a few months later, he was named secondary coach, a position he held for three seasons until 1996. He then moved on to become the New England Patriots linebackers coach under Carroll for three seasons and then coached linebackers for Green Bay from 2000 until Solich and the Huskers called. He was Nebraska's defensive coordinator in 2003 and then held the same position at Oklahoma (2004) and LSU (2005 to 2007) before going back to Nebraska as head coach.

It's amazing to think how much impact Solich's call to Kiffin ultimately had on the history of Nebraska football. Pelini would begin to win over Husker Nation with his no-nonsense approach off the field mixed with his fire and passion on the field. In just one year, Pelini took Nebraska's struggling defense from being ranked 55th nationally in 2002 to leading the nation in turnover margin and being ranked 11th in 2003. Before coming back to Nebraska in 2008, Pelini helped lead LSU to the national championship in 2007 as the Tigers were ranked third nationally in total defense.

By his second season as Nebraska's head coach, Pelini had NU's defense completely turned around after its worst statistical season in school history under Kevin Cosgrove in 2007. The Huskers led the nation in scoring defense at 10.4 points per game, ranked seventh in total defense, first in passing efficiency defense, and ninth in rushing defense in 2009. Just two seasons earlier, the Huskers ranked 114th in scoring defense at 37.9 points per game, 112th in total defense, 75th in passing efficiency defense, and gave up 232 yards per game on the ground.

53 Lawrence Phillips

If you were to talk about pure physical ability, there aren't very many players in Nebraska's history better than running back Lawrence Phillips. The West Covina, California, native came to NU in 1993 as a top 100 recruit and the top overall running back in the state of California, according to multiple recruiting services. His play at Baldwin Park High was legendary.

Future 1999 Husker All-American cornerback Ralph Brown also grew up in Southern California and said Phillips' decision to go to Nebraska directly affected his a few years later. "I had known Lawrence Phillips since I was 10 or 12 years old," Brown said. "He was the man in Baldwin Park, and I was like the second coming for athletes coming out of that town. He went to Nebraska, and that put me on notice. I watched Nebraska for all those four years Lawrence played there and played in big bowl games and won national titles. That kind of kept me interested. I wanted to also go to Nebraska just so I could play with [Phillips]."

Phillips came to Nebraska and immediately contributed as a true freshman in 1993, rushing for 508 yards on 92 carries, including 96 yards in NU's 18–16 Orange Bowl loss to Florida State. As a sophomore he tied a school record by rushing for 100 yards or more in 11 straight games. His 1,722 yards rushing was a Nebraska sophomore record, and his 286 carries still represents a school record.

None of Phillips' early success at Nebraska came as a surprise to anyone back home in California. "Just his sheer size, his legs, his back, his arms…I mean he was a man amongst boys in high school," Brown said. "He was a beast. We would go to his games and watch him play on Friday nights, and everybody would want to be like [Phillips]. Everybody wanted to run like him, and everybody wanted to be as cool as him. He was the man. We all wanted to emulate him and run like him and walk like him and do everything that he did. He was like Superman to us."

Every Superman has his kryptonite, though, and Phillips couldn't control his temper and off-the-field behavior. After rushing for 206 yards and four touchdowns in Nebraska's 50–10 victory at Michigan State in 1995, Phillips was arrested that night for assaulting his ex-girlfriend, Kate McEwen, in her Lincoln apartment. Phillips was suspended for six games by head coach Tom Osborne, and many felt he deserved more. Osborne's reasoning for bringing him back after six games was—without football Phillips had nothing else in his life. The football program at least gave him a structured environment with rules and discipline to keep him in line.

Before the suspension Phillips was considered the front-runner for the Heisman Trophy. Phillips' former teammates still talk about his greatness and what could've been. "To me, it's really not even a question who was the best player. It was Lawrence Phillips. He was just a special, special player," backup quarterback Matt Turman said. "I know he got into some trouble outside of the football field, but once he stepped inside those lines, he was the best player that I played with, and I know a lot of my teammates say the same thing. I really think that if he wouldn't have gotten into some outside trouble in 1995, he would've won the Heisman Trophy over Eddie George and Tommie [Frazier]."

It remains a mystery what type of numbers Phillips would've produced if he had played the entire 1995 season. Many speculate he would've challenged Mike Rozier's 1983 school record of 2,148 yards. In NU's first two games before Phillips suspension, he had 359 yards and seven touchdowns. "He's the greatest talent this program has ever had at that position—pound for pound," former Husker play-by-play voice and talk show host Jim Rose told the Big

Ten Network. "He was that unique combination of speed, power, size, and agility. He was a 1990s version of Gale Sayers, a 1990s version of Herschel Walker."

Even after his suspension, Phillips was able to make an impact and help NU capture its second consecutive national title. In three games leading up to the Fiesta Bowl against Florida, Phillips shook off the rust from his suspension by rushing for 188 yards on 37 carries and two touchdowns in victories against Iowa State, Kansas, and Oklahoma.

With a month to prepare for the Fiesta Bowl, Phillips regained his old form and arguably displayed some of the best skills shown by a Husker running back in a bowl game. Phillips rushed for 165 yards on 25 carries and scored three touchdowns in NU's 62–24 blowout win against the Gators. Phillips' 42-yard touchdown run in the second quarter started a 36–0 scoring run. "Lawrence was a cut above of everybody else that was around in the country," running back Clinton Childs told the Big Ten Network. "Everyone noticed that when he came here in 1993 that Lawrence was very talented, and as hard as this might sound to some people, Lawrence and I are still great friends to this day. He's probably the best running back I've seen with my own two eyes."

Despite Phillips' problems the St. Louis Rams still drafted him with the No. 6 overall pick in the first round in 1996. Off-the-field problems and behavior issues once again plagued Phillips in the NFL, and he only played a total of four seasons with the Rams, Miami Dolphins, and San Francisco 49ers, rushing for just 1,453 yards and 14 touchdowns.

Unfortunately most will never remember Phillips for the great player that he was as his transgressions far outweighed anything he ever accomplished in his football career. "His off-the-field trials have been well documented, and it will unfortunately be a stain on the Nebraska football program for many, many years to come,"

Rose said. "If you separate Lawrence's behavior off the field from his immeasurable skill on it, there is no doubt he is one of the very best ever here and would probably be considered one of the very best college backs of his generation."

54 The Oklahoma-Nebraska Rematch

Heading into the 1978 season, Nebraska had lost to Oklahoma six consecutive years, and Tom Osborne was 0–5 against the Sooners after taking over for Bob Devaney in 1973. When Osborne beat the No. 1 Sooners for the first time in 1978, a large weight was lifted off his shoulders—or at least he thought.

When NU beat the top-ranked Sooners on November 11, the victory sent shockwaves across the state, and people immediately began considering Osborne a worthy successor to Devaney. The Huskers won nine straight, following a season-opening 20–3 loss to No. 1 Alabama, and rose all the way up to No. 2 in the polls. The only roadblock in front of them and a possible chance at a national title was unranked Missouri in the regular season finale.

The Tigers were led by former Husker player and assistant coach Warren Powers. The previous season Powers was at Washington State and beat Nebraska 19–10 in the season opener.

There was a little bit of a tiff between Osborne and Powers in 1977 before the Washington State game. When Powers departed for WSU, Osborne wanted to exchange film of each team's spring game to prepare for the season opener. Being a first-year head coach who had the element of surprise on his side, Powers chose not to exchange film with Osborne. The fact Powers knew everything about Nebraska and had the element of surprise on his side helped the Cougars pull off the upset.

Then a year later in 1978, Powers did it again and stunned the Huskers 35–31 in Columbia, Missouri, making NU's 17–14 win against Oklahoma the week before meaningless. The loss to the Tigers caused more damage to Osborne and his team than anyone could've ever imagined. Instead of going to the Orange Bowl and playing for the national championship against Penn State, the Huskers reward was a rematch game against Oklahoma.

In former Nebraska media relations director Don Bryant's *Tales from the Nebraska Sidelines*, he recalls the news being relayed to Osborne that the Huskers were going to play Oklahoma again in the Orange Bowl. "We moved into the locker room and found Osborne, dejected by the loss to Missouri, and he received the news with the enthusiasm of an innocent man getting a death sentence," Bryant wrote.

Osborne's reaction to the news said it all: "You can't be serious. That's a terrible decision. We're not happy about the whole replay idea. We shouldn't have to play a team we've already beaten."

What should've been a reward for winning the Big 8 conference instead turned into a punishment. The trip to the Orange Bowl was Nebraska's first since 1972. NU's players, coaches, and fans were not excited about their rematch against the Sooners. It's very hard to beat an elite team and your rival once in a season—let alone twice.

The Sooners would go on to win the rematch game 31–24, but Alabama and USC ended up splitting the national title in 1978. Osborne would never lose to Missouri again in his career, and the Huskers would win 23 straight games against the Tigers before finally losing to them in 2003.

55 Nebraska Switches to a 4-3 Defense

Nebraska football had hit a wall. In 1990 the Huskers lost to eventual national champion Georgia Tech 45–21 in the Citrus Bowl. In 1991 eventual national champion Miami beat Nebraska in the Orange Bowl 22–0. The following season NU went back to the Orange Bowl and lost to Florida State 27–14. The Huskers also struggled those years against elite programs like Washington and Colorado. Something about Nebraska's approach had to change. Head coach Tom Osborne knew it, defensive coordinator Charlie McBride knew it, and countless Huskers fans, who had grown tired of bowl game beatings by teams like Miami and Florida State, knew it, too.

Throughout Tom Osborne's coaching career, scoring points on offense was never a problem. In the big games, it was NU's lack of speed on defense that ended up hurting them more often than not. The biggest thing those countless Orange Bowl losses taught Osborne was that NU needed to restructure their out-of-date 5-2 defensive scheme and upgrade to an attack-style 4-3. The 5-2 defense was very much a bend-but-don't-break zone defensive scheme. It was very hard for NU to create any kind of a pass rush. The coverage ability of NU's cornerbacks was also very suspect. With the 5-2, Osborne put very little emphasis on cornerback recruiting. According to McBride, Brian Washington was the only cornerback he can ever remember Osborne putting on scholarship in the 1970s and 1980s. Before the 1990s, all of the cornerbacks used in NU's 5-2 defensive scheme were walk-on players—predominantly from Nebraska.

When it came time to play athletic offenses from the South, the Huskers lack of speed on defense showed up in big ways. "You could put no pressure on anybody, and a lot of the corners couldn't cover," McBride said when talking about NU's 5-2 defensive scheme. "You'd hang them out to dry. They couldn't keep up with the receivers, and about 95 percent of the corners were walk-ons. Good kids that were tough—there wasn't any problem with that part of it. Speed was the problem."

By moving to the 4-3 defense, NU put an emphasis on recruiting speed and finding defensive backs who could cover in man-to-man situations. "We started moving guys that were normally corners to safety, safeties to linebacker, linebackers to defensive end, and we got extremely fast," safety Mike Minter told the Big Ten Network.

"A lot of those guys were normally 4.4 and 4.5 guys [in the 40] that would normally play in the secondary," Osborne said on BTN's special about the 1994 national championship season. "We got more speed on the field and more pass rushers rushing the passer all the time instead of half the time, and I think it made us a better defense."

McBride wanted a defense with interchangeable parts. He wanted to have a defense where everybody could run. That way you didn't have to substitute to match up when offenses went with three and four-wide receiver sets. "One year we had Jamel Williams, and he was a strong safety and a running back. Eric Johnson was a running back, and they were both under 10.6 100-meter guys. Jamel ran a 10.4 down in Florida in high school, and they were playing linebacker for us," McBride said. "That kind of stuff paid off because you didn't have to have a lot of switching of personnel when teams went to no back or something. We might have to switch one guy. Now you see teams switching and subbing, and they can't get them lined up. Even in pro ball, it's a joke. They have a team for this and that, and we didn't have to do that because we had guys that could run on the field."

The transition to the 4-3 was not an instant success as there were some growing pains in the early stages. By 1993, however,

NU had all the pieces in place in their new defensive scheme. Guys like Trev Alberts, Donta Jones, Terry Connealy, Barron Miles, Toby Wright, and Kevin Ramaekers were some of the key players on that 1993 defense who laid the foundation of McBride's switch to the 4-3, and you saw the fruits of his labor from 1994 to 1999. "We turned into a pressure defense, and that's what I wanted to do," McBride said. "That was a lot more fun than standing around and getting your socks knocked off when you can blitz somebody and get after them and have some fun with it, and that's where I was coming from. We went out and we recruited speed. We turned guys down because they couldn't run—some good football players and a lot of them went to good schools—but they couldn't run there either."

56 The 1994 Orange Bowl

In a lot of ways, Nebraska's 18–16 loss to Florida State in the 1994 Orange Bowl on New Year's night was the start of something special. Yes, the Huskers lost their seventh consecutive bowl game under Tom Osborne and held a 1–8 record during their last nine bowl games. The loss to the Seminoles in the Orange Bowl, however, was different than the previous blowout defeats. The average margin of defeat in the past six bowl game losses was 16.7 points. The only one in which NU was even competitive was the 1988 Fiesta Bowl—also against Florida State—and Nebraska lost 31–28.

When NU (11–0) traveled to Miami to play FSU (11–1), the Huskers entered the game as a 17½-point underdog. Nebraska is rarely a double-digit underdog, but past bowl game history against top Florida programs led the oddsmakers to believe this would be another lopsided contest. With 1:16 left in the game, the Huskers took a 16–15 lead against Florida State despite some controversial calls in the game that hurt NU. A Corey Dixon 71-yard punt return for a touchdown was called back after a phantom block in the back penalty.

FSU's only touchdown of the game also came with controversy as replays showed running back William Floyd fumbling the ball before he crossed the goal line, but it was still ruled a touchdown. Instant replay in college football didn't exist until the 2006 season, so calls on the field could not be overturned. "We knew that we were the better team, and there's no way that anybody could tell me on that night that Florida State was better than us," Husker quarterback Tommie Frazier told the Big Ten Network.

"We outplayed Florida State," future Outland Trophy winner Zach Wiegert told BTN. "We had a punt return called back that nobody could really figure out why. There was a fumble in the end zone that was counted as a touchdown."

Even with these two controversial calls, NU's players still felt like they had the game won, but a late hit out of bounds by Nebraska gave FSU Heisman Trophy-winning quarterback Charlie Ward an additional boost to set up freshman kicker Scott Bentley's 22-yard field goal with 21 seconds left.

Even then the Huskers didn't give up. Frazier completed a pass over the middle to tight end Trumane Bell for 29 yards to the FSU 28-yard line. This set up a 45-yard field goal attempt with one second left for Byron Bennett, who earlier in the fourth quarter kicked a 27-yard field goal with 1:16 left to put the Huskers up 16–15. Bennett thought he had already kicked the game winner, so mentally he wasn't as prepared. His kick sailed wide left, and Bobby Bowden captured his first national title. "We still gave ourselves a chance after that," Frazier told BTN. "We drove down the field and had an opportunity for a field goal. I've always told people that the last thing you want to do is put the faith of a game on the leg of a kicker because anything can happen."

"The thing that stands out in my mind about that Florida State national championship game—with 1:16 left it's over. This game was in the bag," offensive lineman Aaron Graham told BTN. "I personally was celebrating on the sidelines."

Even though the Huskers lost that night in Miami, in the long run Osborne's team won. His players finally showed they could keep up and play with an elite Florida State program, and the loss to FSU gave Nebraska the extra motivation it needed to fuel their offseason and begin its string of three national championships in four years. "It was a very devastating loss against a very good Florida State team," offensive lineman Rob Zatechka said during BTN's *Big Ten Elite* special on the 1994 Nebraska team. "When we look back at it, that '93 Florida State team was literally a who's who of the next year's NFL draft. We came one second and a missed field goal away from beating an incredibly talented team in Florida State. We should've defeated them and won a national title in '93."

57 Trev Alberts

When you talk about all-time great defensive players in Nebraska's history, Trev Alberts (1990 to 1993) has to be included in the conversation. The 6'4", 245-pound defensive end from Cedar Falls, Iowa, is the NU all-time sacks leader with 29½, and his 15 sacks in 1993 are tied with Jim Skow for a school record as well. He also had 96 tackles, including 21 for loss, that season.

That 1993 senior campaign earned him All-American honors and the Big 8 Defensive Player of the Year award, and Alberts became Nebraska's first Butkus Award winner. In the 1993 regular season finale against Oklahoma, Alberts dislocated his right elbow but still strapped it up against Florida State in the Orange Bowl and wore a protective cast. Even though the Huskers lost to the Seminoles 18–16, Alberts had a memorable performance with six tackles, three sacks, and three hurries against Heisman Trophy-winning quarterback Charlie Ward.

Alberts would go on to be picked fifth overall in the 1994 NFL Draft by the Indianapolis Colts. A series of shoulder and elbow injuries, however, forced Alberts to hang up his football career after just three seasons.

When former defensive coordinator Charlie McBride looks at Alberts career, he compares him to another great Husker defensive player, defensive end Grant Wistrom. The only difference was Wistrom had a very successful pro career while Alberts never got to showcase his abilities at the next level because of injuries. "He was a lot like Grant," McBride said. "They were both smart, they could both run, and they were really good football players. People looked up to him because of how he played and because he knew the defenses, and players leaned on him for that. Sometimes kids are afraid to ask the coach because he'll think, *I'll be really stupid if I ask him.* Those are things you try to get out of him. That's why if you are a good coach, you better be a good listener because some of them might know more than you do."

And just like Wistrom, Alberts was not only an All-American on the field, but he was also an Academic All-American in the classroom. To this day McBride still refers to Alberts as one of the smartest players he ever coached. "You could tell [Alberts] once, and he got it," McBride said. "He was a guy that learned right now. Once you talk to him about a technique or something, he knew it. Some guys it took a year of repetitions and work, but with Trev he was kind of a leader mentally. He was coaching on the field almost.

When coaches aren't looking or aren't around, the other guys might have questions, and [Alberts] was just one of those guys that picked up stuff and had good, I mean, really good football intelligence."

Now Alberts uses that intelligence to run the University of Nebraska-Omaha's athletic department where he's served as the Mavericks' athletic director since 2009. Alberts came to UNO with zero athletic administration experience, but he has done several great things for UNO, including moving the Mavs to Division I in all sports, hiring nationally known hockey coach Dean Blais, and leading the efforts to get UNO their own $76.3 million on-campus arena.

58 Listen to Mr. Football's Classic Call

Joe Wylie in to kick. Wylie stands at his own 24, waits for the snap. Rodgers deep for Nebraska. Here's Wylie's kick. It's high. It holds up there. Rodgers takes the ball at the 30. He's hit and got away. Back up field to the 35, to the 40. He's to the 45! He's to the 50! To the 45! To the 40! To the 35! To the 20! To the 10!

He's all the way home! Holy moly! Man, woman, and child, did that put 'em in the aisles! Johnny "the Jet" Rodgers just tore 'em loose from their shoes!

Those were the words that became legendary in Nebraska football history. It was a radio call made by Lyell Bremser in The Game of the Century. On perhaps the biggest stage of his career, the late Bremser delivered a perfect call, capturing the moment of Johnny Rodgers' first-quarter punt return against Oklahoma in 1971.

"Man, Woman, and Child!"

Lyell Bremser's signature phrase as a broadcaster was "man, woman, and child," and there's been a lot of question over the years how he came up with those classic words.

   Al Mackiewicz married Bremser's daughter, Sue, and worked with his father-in-law as a spotter and statistician on the KFAB broadcast team for several years. Mackiewicz explained that Bremser's phrase "man, woman, and child" actually came from his days as a kid working at his family's grocery store in Dow City, Iowa. "Lyell had an uncle that worked for his father at the grocery store," Mackiewicz said. "Any time he thought he was going to use curse words, he would substitute 'man, woman, and child.' Lyell worked at his father's grocery store and heard his uncle saying this over and over again, and the uncle told him it was better than using the other [curse] words he'd otherwise be using."

Over his 45-year career of calling Nebraska football games for 1110 KFAB in Omaha, Bremser brought that same magic from 1939 all the way up to his final call in the 1983 Oklahoma game. (In those days local radio stations did not have the rights to broadcast bowl games.) During his 45 years calling Husker football games, Bremser watched 10 different head coaches roam the Nebraska sidelines and he was a part of 478 different games dating back to his first call on September 30, 1939 against Indiana.

When Bremser retired in 1984, the *Omaha World-Herald* dubbed him as Nebraska's "Mr. Football." "He had a certain flair, a flair for the moment, for everything," current KFAB program director Gary Sadlemyer told the *World-Herald* in 2012 when Bremser was inducted into the Omaha Sports Hall of Fame. "We know him for all of these great phrases, but I remember some advice he once gave. He said, 'Remember, every at-bat doesn't have to be a home run. In fact most of the time, you hit singles.'"

Former Husker football play-by-play man Kent Pavelka replaced Bremser in the booth in 1984, and Sadlemyer would move up to the color analyst role. Pavelka told the *World-Herald* in 2012 that when working around Bremser you could always feel his passion.

"I was 24 years old when I first went into the booth with him," said Pavelka, who began working with Bremser in 1974. "I was intimidated for a long time. He didn't say much, but when he did, he had everyone's attention. He really did it all. He studied the teams and the game every week, but he also had that flair for saying the right thing at the right time and in a way that stayed with you."

And even though Bremser may have had the flare for the dramatic behind the microphone, Pavelka described his personality away from the booth as much different. "He was a quiet guy—not a loudmouth or show off," Pavelka said. "He was a great guy and he could loosen up on the road as we all do. But once he got in that booth, there was a palpable tension. It was serious business."

Jim Rose, who called Husker games from 2002 to 2007 and worked on the radio network in multiple different capacities, grew up idolizing Bremser. With a certain star quality about him and respected by everyone, Bremser was Nebraska's Jack Buck or Vin Scully. "He had a charisma about him," Rose told the *World-Herald.* "There's only one other person in Nebraska I've seen that had his charisma, and that's [former Senator and Governor] Bob Kerrey. Whenever Lyell walked into a room, all eyes were immediately on him. It was a feeling that somebody very important was here. He had that kind of respect."

Bremser died in 1990, but one of the things all Nebraska fans should do is listen to his classic recording of the Rodgers return. Huskermax.com has an MP3 audio file, and you can find his call on other websites by doing a quick Google search.

59 The Peter Brothers

The 1990s national championship teams at Nebraska had a distinctive edge on defense, and a lot of that had to do large in part to brothers Christian and Jason Peter. Both Christian (1993 to 1995) and Jason (1994 to 1997) were standout defensive tackles out of New Jersey, and they brought a passion and toughness that set the tone for the Blackshirts during the national championship seasons. Christian was a second team All-Big 8 selection in 1994 and a first team selection in 1995 while Jason was first team All-Big 8 in both 1996 and 1997 along with being named a first team All-American in 1997.

Former Huskers defensive coordinator Charlie McBride said the intensity level the Peter brothers played with each and every day made his job as a coach pretty easy. "Christian was a leader," McBride said. "He was a grab-you-by-the-throat leader. Christian was maybe more so like that, but both of them were like that. Both deep down they were going to do everything possible to win. I remember when we played Missouri in 1997 and went into overtime, and we scored and we have to stop them. I'm standing on the sideline…I'm going to give a speech and I turn around and I'm looking right at [Grant] Wistrom and Jason Peter. They ran right by me, and their eyeballs were as big as silver dollars. I was like, *And I'm going to give them some speech?* I just shut my mouth and let them go. The next thing you know they were sacking the quarterback twice. There was no way they were going to beat us —absolutely none."

When the Peter brothers walked into a room, people took notice. Former NU All-American cornerback Ralph Brown recalls going into the weight room for the very first time as a true freshman in 1996. "You could just hear this yelling and screaming and grunting," Brown said. "I'm talking *loud* screaming and yelling. I was just 17 and was trying to bulk up a little bit and I'm just hearing all this screaming. I was a little nervous, but at the same time, I'm excited because those guys are my teammates. They were intimidating because they let you know from Day One: 'You are a Husker, and this is how you are going to practice and this is how things are done around here.' Coach Osborne didn't have to say anything to new guys. All the guys, that were juniors and seniors that knew the standard, they put the finger in your faces saying, 'This is how we practice' and 'You are going to bust your butt' and 'You are going to make sure you give it all every day in the weight room and on the football field.' That was something that stuck with me that I remember vividly from Day One dealing with those guys."

McBride said he can't think of one moment where Christian or Jason Peter took a play off in practice, and it was that standard of excellence that helped NU become so dominant up front during the national championship years. "When we used to have NFL coaches come in and watch practice in half pads, they thought we were scrimmaging because we were going so hard," McBride said. "I can remember one time Tom [Osborne] came over and asked me to slow down [the Peter brothers] a little bit because they were going so hard. And I just laughed. That's just the way those guys were. It was a good thing. It wasn't a deal where you had to get them motivated or anything like that."

And luckily for McBride, his worst fear with Christian and Jason Peter never happened…at least not on the football field. "I was really worried about—and I mean *really* worried—that they would get into a fight in the game on the field and blame one another for making a mistake," McBride said. "I remember one time in the back of a car they got into a fight, and Jason punched Christian and broke his nose, and they laugh about it. These guys were scary because they were so competitive. Even in games when somebody gained a yard, they would get mad at one another. I thought they'd get into a fight on the field. They'd be yelling at each other in between plays and stuff like that."

Later on a third Peter brother, Damian, would join the football program after a neck injury ended his career at Notre Dame before it even started. Damian Peter worked with McBride as a student coach, so he could be alongside his brothers in Lincoln. McBride joked that Damian didn't sign with Nebraska out of high school because he didn't want Christian and Jason "beating the snot out of him every day."

McBride had Damian go out for preseason camp one year, even though medically he wasn't fit to play. Though originally a lineman, Damian was on the roster as a backup kicker. Because after he was cut at the end of camp, his status on the roster meant it was within NCAA rules for him to join NU as a student coach. "He helped me and helped on stuff up in the office," McBride said. "He wanted to be with his brothers every single day, and it made it even better."

To this day it's hard for McBride to think of anybody who had the impact on the program like the Peter brothers had in the '90s. "They are the kind of people that will do anything for you," McBride said. "If there was something needed, they'd get it done. That's just the way they played. They were guys you can't replace. There isn't any better attitude than those guys had in terms of going hard and things like that."

60 Bill Callahan

It was December 2, 2006. More than 60,000 Nebraska fans piled into Arrowhead Stadium to watch Bill Callahan's 9–3 Nebraska team take on 10–2 Oklahoma for the Big 12 championship. Earlier that season when defending national champ Texas squeaked out of Memorial Stadium with a 22–20 victory, Longhorns head coach Mack Brown proclaimed, "Nebraska's back" in his postgame press conference.

Just a few years removed from taking the Oakland Raiders to the 2003 Super Bowl, Callahan had Nebraska rolling. The Huskers had the Big 12 Offensive Player of the Year in quarterback Zac Taylor, and they had a loaded offense featuring running backs Brandon Jackson and Marlon Lucky along with wide receivers Maurice Purify, Nate Swift, Terrence Nunn, and Frantz Hardy.

The Huskers had a Big 12 South team playing in frigid northern conditions with 75 percent of the stadium wearing Husker red. The stage was set. Nebraska was in a position to win its first conference championship since 1999.

Then reality hit. On the game's opening play from scrimmage, Purify fumbled a bubble screen on the 2-yard line. Within 48 seconds of the opening kickoff, Oklahoma was up 7–0. The Sooners marched down again later that quarter to make it 14–0. The game was over, and the Huskers fell flat on the big stage, losing 21–7. Oklahoma won the game using converted wide receiver Paul Thompson at quarterback, and many considered the Sooners one of the more flawed Big 12 championship teams in league history.

Callahan was a wreck. He did his weekly coach's television show the next day with host Jim Rose on no sleep. He was extremely emotional, knowing the opportunity he let slip through his hands. Little did anyone know that this was the beginning of the end for Callahan. The Huskers dropped their bowl game to No. 10 Auburn 17–14 to finish 2006 a disappointing 9–5 when they easily could've had a 12-win season after disappointing losses to Oklahoma State, Texas, and OU.

In the summer of 2007, athletic director Steve Pederson gave Callahan a three-year contract extension despite the fact he only had a 22–15 record over his first three seasons. "In terms of what he's done for the program, he has certainly met or exceeded my expectations at this juncture," Pederson said in a statement following NU's season-opening 52–10 win against Nevada. At the time of the contract extension, NU had a top five nationally ranked recruiting class that featured future NFL first-round draft picks like quarterback Blaine Gabbert and offensive tackle Riley Reiff. The previous three seasons NU had recruiting classes ranked 13th, 20th, and fifth nationally.

After a win at Wake Forest in 2007, the Huskers sat at 2–0 and were ranked No. 14 in the country. Arizona State transfer quarterback Sam Keller was starting to find his rhythm, and top-ranked USC was making its way to Lincoln. This was *the game*. It was the game Callahan had been circling for quite some time because it would allow the Huskers to get that signature win they had been searching for to put them back in college football's elite. Twenty high-profile recruits were in Lincoln for either official or unofficial visits. ESPN's *College GameDay* was in Lincoln for the first time since 2001. ABC televised the game in primetime.

Then on USC's first possession, it gashed Kevin Cosgrove's defense for 96 yards on four plays. On the Trojans' first two plays from scrimmage, they raced for runs of 50 and 40 yards on the ground. The holes were so big you could drive semitrucks through them. Callahan's team was shell shocked. Memorial Stadium was at a loss for words, and USC had a 42–10 lead by the start of the fourth quarter before Pete Carroll called off the dogs, and the Trojans won the game 49–31. USC rushed for 313 yards on the ground and averaged 8.2 yards-per-carry.

The next week Ball State would put up 610 yards on Nebraska, Missouri would rack up 606, Oklahoma State 551, Texas A&M 459, Texas 545, Kansas 572, and Colorado 518. The athletic department was in shambles. The sellout streak was at risk. Chancellor Harvey Perlman fired Pederson, following a 45–14 home loss to Oklahoma State, and Tom Osborne stepped in the next week. Otherwise many predicted there could've been several thousand empty seats against Texas A&M.

Osborne wanted to give Callahan a fair shake, but in all reality, it was never going to work. Callahan was fired after a 5–7 season in 2007. Over his four-year coaching tenure at Nebraska, there were several things he did right, but some of his mistakes were just too much to overcome. Callahan was not a "Nebraska man," and it was never realistic to expect him to run the program like Osborne or Bob Devaney.

Callahan attempted to change Nebraska's option-based system into an NFL West Coast Offense overnight. He nearly succeeded, but the bigger problem was defensive coordinator Kevin Cosgrove's inability to scheme against Big 12 spread offenses with his Big Ten roots. Former Husker players also felt alienated under Callahan, which made it very difficult for him to succeed without their support.

Osborne called Callahan a seasoned coach and a hard worker. "I wish him well in the future," he said. "He gave this program his best effort, but I believe we need to go in a different direction. I know this is not an easy place to be a head football coach."

61 Watch HuskerVision

When athletic director Bill Byrne announced in 1994 he was going to add two big-screen boards to the southeast and northwest corners of Memorial Stadium, there was concern at the time that video replay boards could hurt the gameday atmosphere and bring too much of a corporate presence. No other non-professional football stadium in the country featured big-screen replay boards in 1994. Nebraska chose to go with two 17-foot wide by 23-foot high Mitsubishi Diamond Vision boards over the more popular Sony JumboTron boards.

Former KOLN-TV sports director Jeff Schmahl was the man Byrne put in charge of structuring and managing Nebraska's new in-house big-screen boards. Before the big screens were put in, Schmahl was hired by Nebraska to do in-house production on various different projects. Little did Schmahl know he was stepping into a position that ultimately would have a major impact on the entire landscape of stadium big screens. "I don't think there was any doubt in Bill's mind that that's what he wanted to do," Schmahl said. "There may have been a little bit of a debate in terms of should it be done. Really Bill had pretty much made up his mind that this was what we were going to do. Once he had made up his mind, there really wasn't any more discussion. Then we went through a bid process."

The bid process was what led Nebraska to Mitsubishi. The next step for Byrne and Schmahl was figuring out how to brand Nebraska's new big-screen boards. NFL teams all referred to theirs as "JumboTrons." The only problem was these weren't Sony JumboTrons. Mitsubishi's first name recommendation to Nebraska was to call them "Diamond Vision" screens. Schmahl had a different idea. "I want to brand everything with our own name. We were kicking around names, and I had already called Mitsubishi and asked, 'What if we call our screen HuskerVision? Instead of Diamond Vision, we would call it HuskerVision,'" Schmahl said. "Mitsubishi took it up to their corporate headquarters, and they said, 'That would be fine. It's better than calling it a JumboTron.'...We can call everything that we do HuskerVision. That's what our control room is. That's what our TV shows are. It's HuskerVision. It was one of those things that once you said it, people said, 'That's perfect.'

"Over the summer we created the HuskerVision graphic, and that was another thing that just took off immediately. Nebraska is one place where you will never hear somebody call the screen a JumboTron. They call it HuskerVision, and everybody knows what you are talking about. Now you have SoonerVision or Buff Vision. Every screen around now is practically called Vision. It gave it its branding, and people liked it. It was ours. People like the uniqueness that: Hey, we are the first and we are the only ones. There weren't very many things that set us apart from a cutting edge standpoint, but this really did. This set us apart, and all of a sudden everybody was trying to copy Nebraska."

What HuskerVision also allowed Nebraska to do was be the first school to bring all of their coaches television shows in-house. In the early years of HuskerVision, Schmahl's team of predominantly student-workers produced the weekly football, men's and women's basketball, volleyball, and baseball coaches shows along with a Friday night football kickoff show and a Husker show that featured the different Olympic sports.

Schmahl created a competitive environment where anywhere from 80 to 100 NU students applied each year to work in HuskerVision for six to 10 spots that would open up. Several of those early HuskerVision workers now run and manage different stadium big-screen boards around the country, including Brandon

Meier at Oklahoma and Andrew Young at Illinois. "We also got a reputation that if you were trained in HuskerVision you were seen as somebody that knew the business," Schmahl said. "That helped a number of people get a head start of where they are now running screens at a number of schools across the country. That's been really satisfying for me in all honesty to see a number of those people surpass what I was doing at HuskerVision at the time."

Even after all the success NU has had with HuskerVision, Schmahl still flashes back to that first moment in 1994 before the UCLA game where many Nebraska fans had their doubts about the new big-screen boards. "We had the unveiling of the screen the night before the UCLA game that Friday night, and Bill Byrne spoke, and he got booed," Schmahl said. "In fact he came into the control room afterward and said, 'Jeff, I just got booed out there.'...There was a real pressure of like, *Geez, I hope they don't want to take these things down before we ever even start.*"

However, that UCLA game wasn't very far along before Byrne and Schmahl realized they had something pretty special. "There was a play in the second quarter of the UCLA game, and it was one of those plays that you were like, *Can you believe that?*" Schmahl said. "We put the replay of that play on, and you could hear the crowd explode for the touchdown. When we put the replay of that play on, the crowd exploded even louder. It was at that point I even went, *You know what? I think this is going to work. They really liked that.* Then we showed another angle of that replay, and there was another explosion, and it was just kind of like, *Oh my gosh, this is really cool. We get to see the replays.*"

In 2006 Nebraska added a 117-foot by 33-foot HuskerVision board in North Stadium, which was roughly five times the width of the original screens. Approximately 10 of the old replay boards would fit inside Nebraska's new screen. At the time it was the largest stadium big-screen board in the country, only to be surpassed that same year by you guessed it—Texas. NU also replaced the two original screens with similar-sized HuskerVision boards on the southeast and southwest corners of the stadium. The two new screens in the south are slightly larger than the originals, measuring 24-feet wide by 21-feet high.

Schmahl left HuskerVision in 2002 to follow Byrne to Texas A&M in an athletic department administration role while both Kirk Hartman and Shot Kleen still currently run and manage all the day-to-day operations. Byrne retired in May of 2012 from A&M, and Schmahl resigned from his position at A&M in January of 2013 to pursue a new business opportunity.

62 JUCO Recruiting Success

Nebraska never wants to be a school that solely relies on junior college talent to build their program, but because of the state's low population numbers, it's a recruiting resource that's paid off in big ways for the Huskers over the years. NU has been able to find a Heisman Trophy winner and multiple All-Americans and All-Conference players from the junior college ranks during the last 30 years.

The most notable junior college recruit for Nebraska is running back Mike Rozier. The New Jersey native came to NU after attending Coffeyville Community College in Kansas. In nine games as a freshman, Rozier had 1,157 yards and 10 touchdowns at Coffeyville, including a 7.4 yards-per-carry average. Rozier would go on to win the 1983 Heisman Trophy, rushing for 2,148 yards and 29 touchdowns. Rozier is still the only NU running back to rush for more than 2,000 yards in a season and he's the all-time leading rusher in school history with 4,780 yards. Rozier's 29 touchdowns in 1983 also remains an NU school record. Rozier would go on to be the No. 2 pick of the 1984 NFL supplemental draft by the Houston Oilers and the No. 1 pick in the USFL Draft by the Pittsburgh Maulers.

Former head coach Tom Osborne landed another top player out of Coffeyville: cornerback Bruce Pickens. The Kansas City, Missouri, native was the 1988 Big 8 Newcomer of the Year and a first team All-Big 8 selection in 1989 and 1990. The Atlanta Falcons selected Pickens with the No. 3 pick of the 1991 NFL Draft, but he would never go on to have a successful NFL career and was labeled one of the bigger draft busts of the 1990s. Until Ndamukong Suh was drafted No. 2 by the Detroit Lions in 2010, Pickens remained the highest drafted Husker since defensive end Neil Smith, who went No. 2 to the Kansas City Chiefs in 1988.

One of the most talented junior college recruits at Nebraska who never materialized because of off-field issues was linebacker Terrell Farley. The 6'1", 195-pound Farley came to NU from Independence (Kansas) Community College, but he was originally from Georgia and signed with Arkansas State out of high school. In his final season at Independence, Farley was named the Jayhawk Conference Linebacker of the Year after registering 116 tackles, 12 sacks, and 15 blocked kicks. In one playoff game against Coffeyville, he scored two touchdowns off fumble recoveries. As a freshman he blocked seven kicks and totaled 95 tackles.

Farley made an instant impact at Nebraska as the Huskers went on to win their second consecutive national championship in 1995. He started five regular season games but played in all 11. He finished the regular season as the team's leading tackler with 62 stops. He also totaled five sacks, three interceptions, and two blocked kicks. He led the team in tackles and sacks in the 1996 Fiesta Bowl against Florida as the Huskers rolled to a 62–24 victory.

Farley was the nation's Defensive Newcomer of the Year in 1995, first team All-Conference, and a second team All-American. In 1996 Farley had 43 total tackles, 10 for loss, three sacks, one blocked kick, and a fumble recovery for a touchdown. He didn't finish the 1996 season after being suspended in November of that year. Farley's absence in the Big 12 title game against Texas was a big reason why the Huskers lost that game and were not able to defend their national championship. "Coach Osborne said some time after that game that if we had Terrell Farley we would've won that game," former Husker All-American cornerback Ralph Brown said. "I honestly believe him. I had a chance to watch Terrell Farley play and his impact on the field and what he did as a player. I never would've thought Coach Osborne would say that about one player. Just for him to say that about Terrell Farley showed you the capability and the impact he had on games throughout his career."

Another top junior college linebacker who came after Farley was Lavonte David. The Miami native came to NU via Fort Scott (Kansas) Community College where he was the No. 1 JUCO linebacker in the country, according to Rivals.com. David's JUCO team lost to future Heisman Trophy winner Cam Netwon's Blinn (Texas) squad in the 2009 National Championship Game. However, according to former Rivals.com expert and now ESPN.com executive vice president of recruiting, Jeremy Crabtree, David was "all over the field" that day. "A series late in the third quarter showed why David is one of the most coveted junior college players in the nation and a four-star prospect," Crabtree wrote. "On first down he ran down Newton after he scrambled to the right and brought him down with a great open-field tackle. Then on the next play, David blitzed through the line and forced Newton to get rid of the pass before his receiver was ready. He followed that up with a tackle on Newton for a 5-yard loss on third down."

David would go on to show that exact same skill set at Nebraska, shattering both the single season and two-year career tackling records at NU. David had a school-record 152 tackles in 2010, and his 133 tackles in 2011 rank No. 5 on the school's all-time regular season tackle chart. His 285 career tackles are good for fourth all time at NU only behind Barrett Ruud (432), Jerry Murtaugh (342), and Mike Brown (287). Both Ruud and Brown had four years to play, though, and Murtaugh achieved his mark in three seasons. David would go on to be named the Big 12 Defensive Newcomer of the Year in 2010, first team All-Conference in both 2010 and 2011, the Big Ten Linebacker of the Year in 2011, and first team All-American in 2011.

Other top junior college players at Nebraska in recent years were quarterback Zac Taylor (2005 to 2006), wide receiver Maurice Purify (2006 to 2007), and offensive lineman Carl Nicks (2006 to 2007). Taylor was the Big 12 Offensive Player of the Year in 2006, leading NU to the Big 12 championship game, throwing for 3,197 yards and a school-record 26 touchdowns. The Butler Community College (El Dorado, Kansas) signal caller was one of only a few bright spots to come out of the Bill Callahan era at NU from 2004 to 2007.

Purify caught 91 passes for 1,444 yards and 16 touchdowns, earning him second team All-Big 12 honors in 2006. The San Francisco City College product's 57 receptions in 2007 rank fourth all time in school history. There haven't been very many receivers at Nebraska who could match the physical skills of the 6'4", 220-pound Purify, and his last-second touchdown catch from Taylor at Texas A&M in 2006 remains one of the more clutch plays in program history.

Nicks came to Nebraska in 2006 with a ton of hype out of Hartnell (California) Salinas College but never was able to consistently put it together for the Huskers in either 2006 or 2007. Nicks would actually go on to become a better pro, playing a crucial role on the offensive line for the New Orleans Saints during their 2009 Super Bowl championship season. Nicks was named to the Pro Bowl in 2010 and 2011 and he was an All-Pro selection in 2011. In 2012 he signed a five-year, $47.5 million contract with the Tampa Bay Buccaneers, making him the highest-paid guard in the NFL.

63 Black 41 Flash Reverse Pass

It was October of 2001, and true freshman Mike Stuntz was walking off the practice field on Wednesday of Oklahoma week. The Council Bluffs, Iowa, native was recruited by Nebraska as quarterback, but he spent his first season in Lincoln as a wide receiver. When Stuntz first made the move to wide receiver, he joked that there might be a special passing play for him in the playbook.

When Stuntz walked out of practice that Wednesday, he was loosening up his arm, acting as if he had just finished throwing passes. I joked with Stuntz and said, "We're going to see that pass this week, aren't we?"

"That's classified," Stuntz said, smiling as he continued loosening his arm.

Little did Stuntz know that the one throw he would make that Saturday would have as much impact as any in school history.

The week before against Texas Tech, Stuntz didn't see a single snap—almost as if head coach Frank Solich was saving him for the Oklahoma game. The name of the play was called "black 41 flash reverse pass." It was set up by Solich two times during the Oklahoma game on previous plays where quarterback Eric Crouch handed the ball on a reverse to running back Thunder Collins around the right side.

Off a fourth-quarter trick play, quarterback Eric Crouch catches a pass and races in for a 63-yard touchdown, a signature moment in Nebraska's 2001 win against rival Oklahoma and Crouch's Heisman Trophy campaign.

With the Huskers leading the game 13–10 late in the fourth quarter, Solich dialed up the legendary play call on a first down from NU's own 37-yard line. The timing of the call was genius because OU's defense had already seen the reverse two other times, which made their safeties cheat up to the line when they saw Crouch hand off the ball to Collins. Little did OU know that Stuntz was coming around the other side, and Collins tossed the ball to him in stride. Then the left-handed former quarterback executed a perfect throw downfield to a wide open Crouch. The ball sailed 25 yards in the air, and Crouch outran two Oklahoma defenders for a 63-yard touchdown to put NU up 20–10 and give Solich a win against the defending national champion Sooners.

The ironic thing was Oklahoma head coach Bob Stoops called a similar reverse pass play during the game with wide receiver Mark Clayton, but wide open quarterback Nate Hybl lost his footing and fell harmlessly to the turf. When Stuntz executed the perfect throwback to Crouch, all Stoops could do was shake his head and smile. "I had to half chuckle to myself," Stoops said. "I said, 'I'll be a son of a gun. Theirs worked, and ours didn't.'"

That throw by Stuntz also gave Crouch the signature moment he needed to win the Heisman Trophy despite the fact that the Huskers were beat in the regular season finale 62–36 by Colorado. As for Stuntz he never made another play of significance in his career. He moved back to quarterback in 2002 as a sophomore, but after Jammal Lord won the job, he redshirted the 2003 season. Bill Callahan used Stuntz on special teams in 2004, and during his final season, he played limited snaps at safety.

After a strong start to his career in 2001, things obviously didn't finish quite the same for the Council Bluffs native. Stuntz, however, never complained about his role and was the perfect teammate all five years of his career. In fact Stuntz still embraces his moment in Husker history. "There have been a lot of people that have been in my situation, and good things happen to people who have patience, and I really just think I should stick with it," Stuntz told me in 2004 when rumors circulated that he might hang it up. "But you know, maybe it won't happen and if it doesn't then fine. I tried. It didn't work out, and that's the way it goes. But if I'm here and it's my turn, I'm going to be ready."

Stuntz's patience and persistence paid off in life as he's currently finishing his degree in medicine at Ohio State University. Stuntz's wife, Natalie, who starred as rocker Tommy Lee's attractive tutor in the NBC reality show, *Tommy Lee Goes to College*, is also a doctor in Columbus, Ohio.

64 Neil Smith and Broderick Thomas

Although most Husker fans remember the 1980s for great offensive players like running back Mike Rozier, quarterback Turner Gill, and offensive lineman Dave Rimington, that decade at Nebraska actually produced two of the better defensive players in school history. Both Broderick Thomas and Neil Smith were All-American and All-Big 8 selections. Thomas would go on to become the No. 6 overall pick of the 1989 NFL Draft by the Tampa Bay Buccaneers, and the Kansas City Chiefs made Smith the No. 2 overall pick in 1988.

According to former defensive coordinator Charlie McBride both defensive lineman Smith (1984–1987) and outside linebacker Thomas (1985–1988) were as talented as any defensive players ever to come through the program. "Those guys meant as much to the defense as any of the great guys we had on the offense during that time," McBride said. "They are as good a players as we've ever had. You can't say which guy is the best when talking about history, because it was different times and defensive systems. What I can say is Neil Smith—he's the best athlete I've ever coached as far as a defensive line guy."

Thomas is the nephew of former Chicago Bears great Mike Singletary. The Pro Football Hall of Famer made multiple visits to Lincoln throughout his career to visit his nephew. Thomas, who was nicknamed "the Sandman," was best known for his legendary smack talk throughout his Husker career. During the 1987 season, Thomas coined the phrase "Keys to the House" when talking about opponents coming into Memorial Stadium. He kept a plastic set of children's keys on the sidelines and would wave them in the air throughout the game to intimidate opponents, letting them know who held the "Keys to the House" in Memorial Stadium. "[Thomas] was a great player. He backed up whatever he said," McBride said. "He talked a lot and did a lot and sometimes made the coaches nervous because it was all bulletin board stuff, but he backed up what he said. He was a very goal-oriented guy. When we didn't reach our goals, he got upset. He was a competitor. I'll tell you that. A lot of times the press would make up something the other team said, and that would set him off. I think they kind of boxed him in a little bit. As he got older, he got a little quieter, but he stood up for what he thought."

Smith came to Nebraska from New Orleans. McBride said he can still remember seeing the gangly defensive lineman in high school and watching him turn into an athletic specimen by the time his career was over at Nebraska. "[Assistant coach] Jack Pierce recruited him out of New Orleans and he wanted me to look at some guy playing defensive tackle," McBride said. "I was looking at the film and I said, 'Wait a minute. Who's this guy playing defensive end? The kid that I'm supposed to be looking at is not in the game, and they moved [Smith] from defensive end to defensive tackle.' He just tore the joint up. You talk about athletic. He was the best athlete of the kids that I had, and I mean of all of them. He had 4.6 speed, and when the pros timed him, they might have even had a 4.5 or 4.4 on him. He could run, I mean really run. When he came here he was about 6'3½" to 6'4" and 215 pounds. He had over a seven-foot wing span. He was huge. He really got on the weights and worked hard at it. By the time he graduated, he weighed in at the NFL Combine at 262 pounds and could run like a deer."

Smith had a 13-year NFL career where he was a six-time Pro Bowl selection, finishing with 624 tackles and 104½ quarterback sacks. Thomas would go on to play nine seasons in the NFL and finish his career with 47½ sacks. The two Husker defensive greats from the 1980s still maintain a close friendship to this day.

65 Coach Jumbo Stiehm

Imagine in today's football world how crazy it would be if Nebraska turned down an invitation to the Rose Bowl because the university thought the trip was too expensive. That's exactly what happened to Nebraska in 1915.

Head coach Ewald O. "Jumbo" Stiehm had just led Nebraska to its third consecutive unbeaten season as his team took on the nickname "the Stiehm rollers." From 1913 to 1915, NU went 23–0–1 under Stiehm. After a convincing 52–7 victory against Iowa to end the 1915 season, an offer to play in the Rose Bowl was on the table.

That Rose Bowl trip didn't happen, though, and Stiehm never coached another game at Nebraska. At the time bowl games and investing extra money into football wasn't as big a priority for NU, and the trip to Pasadena for the Rose Bowl made little financial sense for Nebraska.

Following the 1915 season, Stiehm left Nebraska. According to Husker historian Mike Babcock, Stiehm made $3,500 as NU's head coach in 1915. Indiana came in and offered him $4,500 to leave after Nebraska's 8–0 season in 1915. A raise of $1,000 was considered hefty in those times. A group of boosters got together and came up with another $750 to get Stiehm up to $4,250 per year, but the faculty at the university shot down the boosters and wouldn't let Stiehm accept his new contract because there was concern that too much emphasis was being placed on athletics.

Stiehm would go on to coach Indiana and he never had another unbeaten season or conference championship again. In six seasons with the Hoosiers, Stiehm compiled a 20–18–1 record with his best season coming in 1920 with a 5–2 record and a 3–1 mark in the Big Ten. Stiehm still remains the only coach to leave Indiana with a winning record.

Stiehm was also Nebraska's first full-time, year-round head coach. Besides football Stiehm was the men's basketball coach, and he was the only coach in conference history to win both a football and basketball league title in the same academic year. Stiehm was even Indiana's basketball coach for one season.

One of Stiehm's most impressive wins at Nebraska came against powerhouse Minnesota in 1913, helping NU to its first ever unbeaten season in 1913. Nebraska beat the Gophers 7–0 in Lincoln. It was NU's first win against Minnesota since 1902. From 1900 to 1960, Nebraska only defeated Minnesota seven times in 37 games.

The 1915 Husker team coached by Stiehm still remains one of the most dominant in school history, outscoring their opponents by a margin of 282–39. Stiehm's 1915 squad was led by Guy "the Champ" Chamberlain who later became the first Husker player to be inducted in both the College and Pro Football Hall of Fame. Chamberlain helped Nebraska beat Notre Dame 20–19 in Lincoln as the Fighting Irish were the only team to play NU within three touchdowns that season.

Stiehm preferred smaller, quicker athletes who weighed an average of 160 pounds, according to his official university bio on Huskers.com. His style of play featured "fake passes and handoffs, precision timing, and intricately choreographed plays." After a long bout with stomach cancer, Stiehm passed away in 1923 at the age of 37 in Bloomington, Indiana.

66 Don "Fox" Bryant

When you walk into the office of retired sports information director and assistant athletic director Don Bryant in West Stadium, one of the first things you'll see is a houndstooth hat worn by Paul "Bear" Bryant. The legendary Alabama coach gave it to Bryant after a game against Nebraska. Then behind that you'll find a sketch from the Cotton Bowl of what eventually became known as Herbie Husker. Bryant helped create Herbie Husker with artist Dirk West after Bryant saw a cartoon that decorated the press room at the 1974 Cotton Bowl in Dallas.

Filled with countless pieces of Husker history, Bryant's office in Memorial Stadium feels like a museum. The walls are adorned with artifacts as I sat and talked with the legendary sports information director after whom Memorial Stadium's press box is named.

Bryant took on the nickname "Fox" while in high school at Lincoln High in the 1940s. Anyone who knows Bryant just refers to him as "Fox." "I was over in Council Bluffs, [Iowa,] for a big track meet and I anchored a two-mile relay race. We won, and I broke the tape," Bryant said. "We had a big lead when I got the baton. One of the girls that was holding the string was a cheerleader. She walked me down to the judges because we had broken the record, and they wanted a picture. She was cute, and we both kind of hit it off and went up and sat in the grandstand to watch the rest of the meet...We went back to Lincoln, and I never saw her again. I don't know what she did and I never asked. One of the guys on the team was hollering, 'Look at Bryant up there with a fox! What's Bryant doing up there with that fox?' So all the guys starting calling me 'Foxy,' and it went on from that to the Marine Corps, and now I'm stuck with it."

The 5'7" Bryant then went on to play football at Nebraska in 1948 after his military tour in World War II with the Marines. He quickly learned that there wasn't much of a future for a center of that stature. That's when he was first approached about getting into media work by somebody at the *Lincoln Star*. "[The sports editor] leaned over to me in a class and said, 'Fox, you aren't worth a darn as a center in football. Why don't you come to work for me as a sportswriter?'" Bryant said. "I said, 'You've got a deal.'"

From there Bryant worked at the *Lincoln Star* before going back into the Marines for the Korean War in 1950. He rejoined the *Lincoln Star* after his tour was complete and eventually became the sports editor from 1954 to 1963. It was in 1963 when Bryant was first approached by the university to become Nebraska's media relations director. He welcomed the career change because the hours were much better, and the university also offered a much better retirement package. Bryant became NU's media relations director in 1963 and worked all the way up until 1997 before moving into an emeritus role.

Besides being a part of every Nebraska game since the 1950s, Bryant was a member of the 1980, 1984, and 1988 U.S. Winter Olympic teams, serving as media liaison at Lake Placid, New York; Sarajevo, Yugoslavia (now Bosnia-Herzegovina); and Calgary, Canada. When the United States hockey team beat the Soviet Union in Lake Placid, Bryant was right in the middle of the Miracle on Ice. "I got them off the ice into the locker room," Bryant said. "They took the SIDs to work these events. There was a whole crew of us."

Bryant also served as a media relations director at the Final Four for 20 straight years along with the 1979 IAAF World Cup in Montreal and the 1987 Pan American Games in Indianapolis. Another claim to fame for Bryant was in 1971 head football coach

Bob Devaney had him put together a full-color media guide to send to recruits. At this time nobody put together anything like that, but Devaney thought it would help lure recruits to Nebraska. "It was expensive, but Devaney wanted them, and I put them together for him," Bryant said.

Bryant became one of Devaney's closest confidants, and the two became inseparable over the years. Another close friend of Bryant's is legendary college football announcer Keith Jackson. To this day Jackson and Bryant talk regularly.

When Nebraska built their new press box in 1999, one of the things Jackson suggested was NU put a private bathroom in the play-by-play booth to allow announcers to be able to relieve themselves during a broadcast. Not only did Nebraska listen to the idea, Bryant got NU to name the bathroom after Jackson. When Nebraska opened their new press box in 1999 against California, Jackson was there for the game. "He was so excited that he got a toilet in the broadcast booth he came in and saluted me for getting him a toilet, and we named it after him," Bryant said laughing. "It was always a problem for guys calling the games because they never had time to go during the game. They had to get out and make their way around with everybody else."

For more great stories from Bryant, check out his *Tales from the Nebraska Sidelines*, a great historical read for any Husker fan.

67 Alvarez, Kiffin, and Other Coaching Legends With Husker Roots

Everyone is obviously familiar with coaching names like Bob Devaney and Tom Osborne at Nebraska, but one thing unique about Nebraska is that several other former Huskers have also made big names in the coaching business. The two names that immediately jump out as former Huskers who have gone on to become legendary coaches are Monte Kiffin and Barry Alvarez. Both learned and modeled a lot of their coaching philosophies from their time at Nebraska under Devaney.

Kiffin played and coached under Devaney at NU and would eventually go on to be recognized as one of the premier defensive minds in all of football—pro or college. Currently the defensive coordinator for the Dallas Cowboys, he has been a head coach, coordinator, or position coach for eight different NFL teams and four different college programs since leaving Nebraska following the 1976 season. The pinnacle of Kiffin's career was in 2002 when he served as Jon Gruden's defensive coordinator in Tampa, leading the Buccaneers to a Super Bowl. Kiffin's Tampa 2 defensive scheme is regarded as one of the most successful in all of football, and several different coaches emulate his scheme and coaching philosophies each year. Even current Nebraska head coach Bo Pelini uses some of Kiffin's concepts in his approach to defense as Pelini learned under current Seattle Seahawks head coach Pete Carroll, and Carroll worked under Kiffin.

Alvarez never actually coached at Nebraska, but he played for Devaney from 1965 to 1967. After helping Notre Dame capture the 1989 national title as Lou Holtz's defensive coordinator, Alvarez resurrected Wisconsin's program into a Big Ten power. From 1990 to 2005, Alvarez won 118 games at Wisconsin, three Big Ten titles, and had a perfect 3–0 record in Rose Bowls over that period. Alvarez saw his perfect Rose Bowl record end, though, in 2013 when he coached the Badgers in an interim role against Stanford.

Some might call Alvarez a "modern day Devaney" as he built and structured his program just like his former head coach. Alvarez emphasized in-state recruiting, building a strong walk-on program, and physical offensive line play. He also built a dream team coaching staff of several different assistants who went on to take big-time jobs. "I stole the walk-on program from Nebraska. Having been the one Division I school in the state, as Nebraska is, I really felt that there were a lot of players that were borderline," Alvarez said in 2011 before the Nebraska vs. Wisconsin game, "guys that you're not quite ready to pull the trigger on that we would actively recruit. Quite frankly, they've been our savior. I call them our erasers. They make up for any mistakes you make in recruiting. That is definitely something I took from Nebraska. My background, and what I believe in, in football was established at the University of Nebraska. I felt fortunate to play for a great coach in Bob Devaney. He had a tremendous staff. As far as fundamentals, physical play, sound play—all those things are things I took with me and brought to this program."

Another great coach who left Nebraska was Warren Powers. Like Kiffin, Powers was also a Devaney player and assistant. Powers was one of three Osborne assistants to leave following the 1976 season, joining Kiffin and Bill Myles. The next season Powers took over Washington State, and coincidently the Cougars opened with No. 15 Nebraska in Memorial Stadium. Powers' coaching staff was full of Husker flavor, featuring names like John Faiman, Jim Walden, and Zaven Yaralian. The unranked Cougars pulled off a shocking upset as Powers took down his former boss 19–10.

The story gets even better, though, as in 1978 Powers and his Husker-connected coaching staff moved over to Missouri and beat No. 2 NU in Memorial Stadium for a second straight season, spoiling Nebraska's chances of playing for a national title. The Tigers didn't defeat Nebraska again for 25 years.

Husker assistant coaches have also gone on to have success at the FCS level, winning five national championships from 2005 to 2012. Former Osborne assistant coach and offensive coordinator Jerry Moore won three consecutive national championships at Appalachian State from 2005 to 2007. His team also pulled off one

Defensive guru Monte Kiffin, who played and coached under Bob Devaney at Nebraska, guides the Tampa Bay Buccaneers defense during a 2008 playoff game.

of the biggest upsets in college football history when it knocked off No. 5 Michigan in Ann Arbor, Michigan, 34–32.

Former Husker linebacker and defensive coordinator Craig Bohl is another coach who has gone on to have major success at the FCS level. He won back-to-back national championships at North Dakota State in 2011 and 2012. Bohl has been the head coach at NDSU ever since 2003 when former Nebraska head coach Frank Solich fired him as his defensive coordinator following the 2002 season.

And—speaking of Solich—after getting fired at Nebraska, he's helped build Ohio into a MAC power, winning back-to-back bowl games in 2011 and 2012. Before Solich got to Athens, Ohio, the Bobcats had never won a bowl game before.

Former Nebraska quarterback and assistant coach Turner Gill helped lead Buffalo to the MAC title in 2008. Before Gill got to Buffalo, it was considered one of the doormats of Division I football. Gill became a hot coaching prospect but would have much less success during his next two years as Kansas head coach. After KU got rid of him, he became the head coach at Liberty University in Lynchburg, Virginia.

Former head coach Bill Callahan has rebounded since being fired at Nebraska as have several of his assistant coaches. Callahan is now the offensive coordinator of the Cowboys and considered one of the top offensive line coaches in the NFL. Former Callahan assistants Jay Norvell (Oklahoma), Shawn Watson (Louisville), and Joe Rudolph (Pittsburgh) are now successful coordinators at major BCS programs.

Another former Husker player on the rise as a coach is Scott Frost. The legendary Nebraska quarterback became the offensive coordinator for Oregon's dynamic offense after Chip Kelly left to coach the Philadelphia Eagles. Zac Taylor, also a former NU quarterback, is the quarterbacks coach for the Miami Dolphins.

68 Mr. Nebraska Football

From 1923 to 1925, only one player and one team managed to get in the way of Notre Dame's famed Four Horsemen. The Fighting Irish played an annual series with Nebraska from 1915 to 1925, and during the 1920s, they dominated college football. From 1923 to 1925, the legendary Four Horsemen led by head coach Knute

Rockne only lost three games. During the 1923 and 1925 seasons, Nebraska beat the Irish 14–7 and 17–0 largely due in part to the play of tackle Ed Weir.

The Superior, Nebraska, native would eventually go on to earn the nickname "Mr. Nebraska Football," and *Lincoln Journal Star* sports editor Cy Sherman referred to him as Nebraska's "all-time All-American."

During 1924 after the Four Horsemen's only win against Nebraska, Rockne made sure he found his way to the Husker locker room to commend Weir on his play. "Weir," Rockne said, "I want to say to your face that you're the greatest tackle and the cleanest player I've ever watched." Those were strong words from Rockne, who was considered the brightest football mind in the game.

As a train brought fans from Superior to Lincoln to cheer on their hometown hero against the Irish, the 1925 Notre Dame vs. Nebraska game may have been Weir's finest. He played a flawless game, blocking a punt that set up Nebraska's first touchdown. On defense he made several tackles; on offense he carried the ball and caught a pass. To go along with that, Weir kicked a 25-yard field goal and two extra points to lead the Huskers to a 17–0 victory against the Four Horsemen.

In Nebraska football historian Mike Babcock's *Nebraska Football Legacy*, he described Weir's dominance in that 1925 Notre Dame game: "Weir recalled that late in the game he looked over at the Notre Dame bench," Babcock wrote. "Rockne broke into his contagious grin and gave Weir a big wink. No one else knew what the gesture meant. 'But I understood,' said Weir. Rockne often repeated that Weir was the finest tackle he ever saw."

Weir was also a track standout at Nebraska, winning the 120-yard high hurdles in 1926 to help the Huskers capture the Missouri Valley Conference championship. Weir was a charter member of the College Football Hall of Fame in 1950, and in 1970 the

Football Writers Association named him to the All-Star lineup of the best players from the 1920s.

Besides NU's victories over the Four Horsemen, Weir said one of the other great moments in his career was keeping legendary Illinois running back Red Grange out of the end zone. It was the only game the "Galloping Ghost" did not score a touchdown in his entire career.

After a three-year professional career, Weir would go back and coach both football and track at Nebraska. Weir was NU's head track coach from 1939 to 1955, capturing 10 conference championships during that period. After stepping down as the track coach in 1955, Weir served as Nebraska's assistant athletic director until 1968. In 1974 Nebraska dedicated the Ed Weir Track and Field/ Soccer Stadium in his honor at the conference outdoor championships in Lincoln. Weir passed away in Lincoln in 1991 at the age of 88. He still has family that resides in Imperial, Nebraska.

The 1941 Rose Bowl

In 1940 Nebraska was one game away from being in contention for the national championship. Led by head coach "Biff" Jones, Nebraska finished the regular season 8–1 with its only loss coming to eventual national champion Minnesota 13–7. The reward for the 1940 Nebraska football team was an invitation to the 1941 Rose Bowl. The bowl game invite was special for many reasons, but mainly because it would be the first bowl game the Huskers would ever play in.

In 1940 there weren't 35 bowl games like there are today. To be exact there were just six—the Rose, Sugar, Cotton, Orange,

The Largest Crowds to See Nebraska Play

The 1941 Rose Bowl remains one of the five biggest crowds to ever see a Nebraska game. Here's a listing of the top 10 largest crowds to witness a Husker game through the 2012 season.

	Opponent	Date	Attendance
1.	at Michigan	November 19, 2011	113,718
2.	at Penn State	September 14, 2002	110,753
3.	at Penn State	November 12, 2011	107,903
4.	at Ohio State	October 6, 2012	106,102
5.	Miami (Rose Bowl)	January 3, 2002	93,781
6.	Stanford (Rose Bowl)	January 1, 1941	92,000
7.	at Texas A&M	November 20, 2010	90,079
8.	Louisiana-Lafayette	September 26, 2009	86,304
9.	Michigan	October 27, 2012	86,160
10.	Oklahoma	November 7, 2009	86,115

Sun, and Pineapple. Bowl trips were expensive and nothing like we see in today's college football world. During the 1915 season, the Huskers also had a chance to play in the Rose Bowl but turned down the invite for financial reasons.

When Nebraska received an invite from the Rose Bowl to play Stanford on New Year's Day in 1941, Rube Samuelson of the *Pasadena-Star News* said the Cornhuskers went "mildly insane" upon learning they had been invited to play in their first bowl game in school history.

The special thing about that 1940 team was that 38 of their 39 players came from the state of Nebraska. Fullback Vike Francis was the only non-Nebraskan on the roster, but he attended high school in Nebraska, living in the Kansas-Nebraska border town of Oberlin.

NU was only the third Big Six team to ever play in a postseason bowl game as the homegrown Cornhuskers took a train ride out west to play Clark Shaughnessy's Stanford Indians. According to the *Star News*, Nebraska was an 8–to–5 underdog in the game, but the Huskers gave the Indians a battle, falling short 21–13 in front of a capacity crowd of 92,000. Up until the 2002 season, the 1941 Rose Bowl ranked as the largest crowd to ever see Nebraska play in a game. The capacity of Memorial Stadium in 1940 was just 31,000.

Probably the most memorable thing to come out of that 1941 Rose Bowl, according to Samuelson, was it allowed more of the country to check out Stanford's famous T-formation on offense, which featured great deception with multiple ball carriers. "The T formation's craze," Samuelson wrote, "ignited by Stanford's Rose Bowl triumph, spread like a prairie fire to every nook and cranny of the land."

Nebraska wouldn't play in another bowl game until the 1955 Orange Bowl.

70 Mr. Touchdown

At the start of the 1950 season, running back Bobby Reynolds may not have been a nationally known name around the country, but people within the state of Nebraska were more than aware of the homegrown talent. The Grand Island, Nebraska, native came to NU after one of the most historic high school careers in state history. Reynolds led the Islanders to state championships (as determined by the local newspapers since the playoffs didn't exist yet) in football in 1947 and 1948, two state championships in basketball, and he was a pro prospect in baseball.

After sitting out his freshman season in 1949, Reynolds burst on the scene in 1950 and put together one of the best seasons ever in Nebraska football history. In just nine games, Reynolds scored

157 total points (22 touchdowns and 25 extra points) for a 17.4 point per game average. That mark still ranks No. 1 as no other player has ever averaged that many points in school history. It also ranks second all time only behind Oklahoma State running back Barry Sanders, who averaged 21.27 points per game in 1988.

Reynolds put up 1,631 all-purpose yards, a single-season total which still sits in the top 10 in school history. He ran for 100 yards in eight consecutive games, and his 187-yard performance against Indiana in 1950 stood as the Nebraska record for 154 games. (The record would eventually be broken by Frank Solich in 1965.)

It didn't take long for the rest of the nation to catch on to the Grand Island native as he was a first team All-American in 1950, and he finished fifth in the Heisman Trophy voting as a sophomore.

In 1951 Reynolds' picture was on the cover of the *Official NCAA Football Gu*ide, the annual rules and record book published by the National Collegiate Athletic Bureau. Reynolds also took on the nickname "Mr. Touchdown" after his big season in 1950. The stage was set for Reynolds to become the school's first Heisman Trophy winner, but a series of injuries limited him during his final two seasons, and Husker fans never again got to see the player who dominated the 1950 college football season. Reynolds separated his shoulder during fall camp in 1951 in addition to breaking his leg and suffering lime-in-the-eye infection, a condition caused when field chalk kicks up into the eye. The series of tragic injuries made Reynolds a shell of the player he formerly was.

Arguably the most memorable play in Reynolds' career came in 1950 when he covered more than 100 yards, running sideline-to-sideline on a 33-yard touchdown run to help Nebraska beat Missouri 40–34 during NU's homecoming game.

Even with just one healthy year in the program, Reynolds more than left his mark on Nebraska football. His 211 career points was a school record for 22 years, and his 2,196 yards also was a school record for 21 years. His single-season rushing mark of 1,342 yards in 1950 would hold up as a school record for 32 years, and his mark of 22 touchdowns in a season would hold up another 33 years. Both the rushing and touchdown records would eventually be broken by Heisman Trophy running back Mike Rozier.

Reynolds was inducted into the Nebraska Football Hall of Fame in 1972 and the College Football Hall of Fame in 1984. Reynolds passed away in 1985.

71 Road Trippin' Through the Big Ten

When Nebraska officially left the Big 12 for the Big Ten Conference in June of 2011, it was completely new territory for Husker fans. A new league meant learning new teams and road destinations. Instead of day trips to Ames, Iowa; Lawrence, Kansas; and Manhattan, Kansas, Husker fans traded them in for stops in places like Ann Arbor, Michigan; State College, Pennsylvania; and Madison, Wisconsin.

Here is a quick summary of what you need to know about each new Big Ten city. (We won't worry about Maryland and Rutgers just quite yet. They are joining the Big Ten in 2014.)

Illinois: Champaign is an eight-hour car ride from Lincoln or just two and a half hours south of Chicago. Your best food options are The Ribeye, Black Dog Smoke and Ale, and Papa Del's. Some of the more popular places to grab a drink are Kam's, Murphy's Pub, and the Blind Pig.

Indiana: Bloomington is about an hour from Indianapolis or about an 11-hour car ride from Lincoln. Some great places to eat include Janko's Little Zagreb, FARMmarket & Cafe, Uptown café, and Lennie's & the Bloomington Brewing Company. Grab a drink at either Nick's English Hut or Kilroys.

Iowa: Iowa City is easily the closest Big Ten city to Lincoln. It's just a 300-mile drive across Interstate 80. Make sure you grab a bite to eat at Iowa River Power Co., Hamburg #2, and the Motley Cow. Iowa City features a great bar district as well. Some of the better places to hit up are Joe's Place, Sanctuary Pub, and The Airliner Bar. Backpocket Brewing in nearby Coralville is also worth a stop.

Michigan: Your best bet to get to Michigan is flying to Detroit. Ann Arbor is about 45 minutes from the Detroit airport. From Lincoln it's about 12 to 13 hours in a car. Some good places at which to grab a bite are: The Chop House, Zingerman's Deli, The Real Seafood Company, and Jolly Pumpkin Cafe and Brewery. Some of the better bars to hit up in Ann Arbor are Ashley's (great food, too), Arbor Brewing Company, and Conor O'Neill's. I also highly recommend checking out a Wolverines hockey game in Yost Ice Arena if Michigan is at home that weekend.

Michigan State: East Lansing is about a 90-minute drive from Detroit or you can fly directly into Lansing with an easy connection in either Minneapolis or Chicago. Some of the most popular places to eat are Crunchy's, State Room, and Enso. Grab a drink at Green Door Blues Bar & Grill, Harrison Road House, or Dublin Square.

Minnesota: Both the Lincoln and Omaha airports offer direct flights to Minneapolis; otherwise it's about a seven-hour drive from Lincoln. There are several different areas to grab food and drinks as downtown, the campus area, and the Mall of America all offer many different options. A few good spots to grab a bite are Matt's or the 5–8 Club (home of the Juicy Lucy hamburger), The Big Ten Restaurant and Bar, Burrito Loco, J.D. Hoyt's, Joe Senser's, and Mancini's Char House. The college bar district in Minneapolis is called Dinkytown. Also hit up Stub & Herb's, Sally's, Cuzzy's (a great dive bar), and Brit's Pub & Eating Establishment. Definitely note that Minnesota is the only Big Ten school that sells beer in its stadium. They also have a Buffalo Wild Wings literally feet from the stadium's entrance.

Northwestern: Evanston is a Chicago suburb, so there are plenty of ways to get there with direct flights through Omaha or Lincoln instead of driving for eight or nine hours. Within Evanston itself make sure you eat a classic Chicago-style hot dog at Mustard's Last Stand. Also check out Pete Miller's for a steak or grab a deep dish slice at Giordano's, which has a location in downtown Evanston. The bar district is not huge in Evanston, but Tommy Nevin's Pub, Bluestone, and Bar Louie are all spots to grab a drink. But if you go to a road game here, definitely visit Chicago, which is only a 30-minute L ride away. I could write a whole book on places to eat and drink there.

Ohio State: Columbus is the largest city in the state of Ohio, so there are plenty of single-connection flight options from both Omaha and Lincoln. It takes about 13 hours in a car. When in Columbus getting a hamburger at Thurman Cafe is a must but be prepared to wait. I waited about two hours at 2 PM on a Friday afternoon. Hyde Park, Due Amici, and Columbus Fish Market are also good places for meals. Columbus has a great bar district, but Varsity Club sits right across the stadium. R Bar is another great place to hit up.

Penn State: This is probably the hardest trip to make. Detroit is the only airport that allows you to get to State College from Omaha with just one connection. Harrisburg is the closest major airport. If you are driving, be prepared for a 17-hour trek across Interstate 80 with plenty of tolls through Indiana and Ohio. Grab a bite to eat at The Allen Street Grill for lunch or a drink there at night. Champs Sports Bar is also a great place to watch a game, get a drink, or grab a bite to eat. Otto's Pub and Brewery is basically State College's version of Lazlo's or Upstream and definitely worth a visit.

Purdue: West Lafayette is about an hour from Indianapolis or two and a half hours from Chicago's Midway Airport. If you are road tripping it, be prepared for an 11-hour drive from Lincoln. A few good places to eat are Lafayette Brewing Company, Triple XXX, Bruno's, or the South Street Smokehouse. Grab a drink at Nine Irish Brothers, Harry's Chocolate Shop (old school classic bar), Chumley's, or Scotty's Brewhouse.

Wisconsin: Madison is either a seven or eight-hour drive from Lincoln, or you can fly to Milwaukee or connect into Madison through Chicago and Minneapolis. The food options in Madison may be some of the best in the Big Ten. The Old Fashioned is a must stop and a great place to do lunch Friday before the game. Check out Dotty Dumpling's Dowry for a great burger or L'Etoile for fine dining. There are lots of great places to grab a drink, but do yourself a favor and have a beer inside Wisconsin's student union. (Yes, they have a bar on campus.) Then swing over to State Street Brats. Husker fans completely took over that bar in 2011. The Stadium is another great bar to hit up as well as Jordan's Big 10 Pub. Be prepared, though, to defend your turf as the Badgers have some of the more vulgar fans in the Big Ten.

72 Freshman Football

In today's star fishbowl world, football freshmen often arrive in college with hype and immediate expectations. However, it wasn't until 1972 that the NCAA allowed freshmen to play at the varsity level, so Nebraska used freshman and junior varsity games as a way to develop younger players.

From 1956 to 1990, Nebraska had a freshman-junior varsity record of 120–17–1. It played freshman and junior varsity games before 1956, but official records were not kept until that time. In most cases a freshman season consisted of five games, and NU would play other regional junior colleges and Big 8 freshman squads. Scott Downing coached Nebraska's freshman team in 1986 and he said typically a team was made up of 65 to 80 players—all true freshmen.

The freshmen had their own locker room in North Stadium and they held their own separate practices away from the varsity team. Usually the freshman team had about 10 separate coaches, who worked with them on a daily basis, but those coaches would also report up to the varsity program. Freshmen players did not travel with the team to bowl games back then or receive championship rings because as Downing said, "They were freshmen," and things were much different in those days. "The freshman program was a great way to develop guys whether they were scholarship or walk-ons," Downing said. "It also gave you a great read on who were the quality guys in your entire freshmen class—not only scholarship but walk-on guys. Let's face it. If you couldn't start or see significant time on the freshman team against freshmen, how were you going to be able to contribute later on against the varsity?"

In February of 1991, Nebraska announced they would discontinue the freshman-junior varsity program in anticipation of the NCAA's reduction in the allowance of football coaches—a cost-cutting measure that went into effect for the 1992 season. The Big 8 conference would soon follow suit and cut all freshman-junior varsity programs. In 1993, however, Nebraska would go on to play one more freshman game against Air Force. Head coach Tom Osborne scheduled the game as a favor to Air Force head coach Fisher DeBerry. It was a two-game series, but the second was never played that year in Colorado Springs due to inclement weather.

Graduate assistants Bill Busch (defense) and Gerry G[...] (offense) coached the team, and they only had one practice to g[...] things organized. Redshirt freshman quarterback Matt Turman out of Wahoo, Nebraska, led the Huskers to a 49–20 victory, completing 9-of-11 passes for 182 yards and three touchdowns.

The freshman games were an opportunity for players to get live reps, something younger players aren't given the opportunity to do today. "We're going to get two games when things are on the line and we have to show what we can do," the 5'10", 165-pound Turman told the *Lincoln Journal Star* after what was supposed to be the first of two freshman games with Air Force.

In a lot of ways, the freshman-junior varsity program was the key to building and developing depth in Osborne and Bob Devaney's programs. Incoming players would get solid game and practice experience with the freshman team their first year, play on the scout team their redshirt freshman season, and then get three years of playing time with the top units. It was a well-oiled machine. Several great players like running backs Roger Craig and Keith Jones or even defensive end Broderick Thomas got their start at NU by playing with the freshman team. "What was really cool was in the north end it was all freshmen," Downing said. "They bonded together and they created great bonds as a team and players. I still see some of those guys today, and they talk about what they did as freshmen. It was a great part of the history at the University of Nebraska. It was really cool."

The freshman-junior varsity program also allowed young coaches a chance to break into the profession as it provided several more jobs on coaching staffs at the Division I level. Frank Solich first earned his stripes coaching the freshman team where he went 19–1 over four seasons. When Dan Young was hired from Omaha Westside High, he started out as the freshman team head coach. Downing, who worked under Bill Callahan and now coaches at Tulsa, served as the freshman head coach at NU after Young. Shane

ial freshman coach before the program ended

more than 200 players and virtually unlimited bers, NU could get away with doing this and n any other school benefited by having a freshman program. On any given year, the Huskers would bring in 30 to 35 scholarship freshmen along with 50 to 60 walk-on freshmen. One could only imagine if Nebraska played freshman-junior varsity games today what type of attention the freshmen would have, mainly because of the fascination Husker fans have with incoming players and recruits.

73 1982 Nebraska at Penn State

When you talk about great Nebraska teams that didn't win a national championship, you immediately think of the 1983, 1993, or even the 1999 squads. Legendary head coach Tom Osborne, however, considers the 1982 Huskers the most complete team he ever coached not to win a national title.

The 1982 NU team had one setback to Penn State in State College, and it was arguably one of the more controversial finishes in school history. Ranked No. 2 in the country, Nebraska marched down the field late in the fourth quarter to take a 24–21 lead with 1:18 left on the clock after trailing 21–7 in the third quarter. Husker quarterback Turner Gill led NU down the field for a 13-play, 80-yard scoring drive that consumed nearly seven minutes of clock.

No. 8 Penn State would answer, though, as a personal foul penalty on the ensuing kickoff gave the Nittany Lions the ball at the 40-yard line. PSU quarterback Todd Blackledge (now an ABC/

Penn State's First Game Without Paterno

November 12, 2011 will be a day remembered in Penn State history. For the first time in 45 seasons, head coach Joe Paterno was not on the sidelines for the Nittany Lions. After a child sex abuse scandal involving former PSU defensive coordinator Jerry Sandusky, Paterno was forced to step down days before the Nebraska game.

PSU students were rioting through the streets of State College when the news became official that Paterno was out. Penn State was at the center of the national news, and some even thought the Nebraska vs. Penn State game may not happen that Saturday.

Nittany Lions fans were in mourning, and they were searching for healing after the news of the widespread child sex abuse charges became official. In a sign of solidarity between the two programs, Nebraska running backs coach Ron Brown led a prayer at midfield as the 107,903 people in attendance watched in silence. As Brown said the prayer, NU and PSU players and coaches joined hands. Tears were being shed throughout the stadium. It was one of the more emotional pregame scenes you'll ever see in college football. "It was two universities, two great football programs coming together, forgetting about football for one second and coming together as people and humans to reflect on what happened," junior defensive end Cameron Meredith said following the Huskers' 17–14 victory against PSU.

ESPN college football analyst) led Penn State down the field and connected with tight end Mike McCloskey on a third-down pass for a 7-yard gain to give PSU a fresh set of downs at the 2-yard line with nine seconds left. Replays show that McCloskey was two yards out of bounds when he made the catch, but there was no instant replay in college football in 1982. *The* (Harrisburg, Pennsylvania) *Patriot-News* in 2010 labeled the catch as one of the all-time worst officiating calls in college football history.

Blackledge would then connect with Kirk Bowman for the game-winning touchdown with four seconds left to give PSU a

27–24 victory. There was even some controversy on that game-winning catch because Bowman may have trapped the ball. The loss at Penn State ended up costing the 1982 Huskers a chance of playing for the national title, and PSU defeated Georgia in the Sugar Bowl to give Joe Paterno his first national championship.

"I know most everyone talks about losing to Miami [31–30] and missing the national championship the next season," Osborne told Huskers.com's Randy York. "But when you really look at that '82 team and that '83 team [the highest scoring team in college football history], our '82 team was really a lot more balanced than our '83 team. We were much better on defense in '82, and that '82 team was great on offense, too. We had Roger Craig and Mike Rozier and Turner Gill and Irving Fryar. I thought we were very deserving of a national championship."

Osborne told York the personal foul penalty on the kickoff after NU's go-ahead touchdown helped set up Penn State's game-winning drive. "I remember a couple of plays that our fans still remember and talk about," Osborne said. "I remember us scoring to go ahead 24–20. We kicked off; David Ridder ran down the field to cover. For some reason a Penn State guy kept trying to block him even after the play was over, and David threw him off him and was called for a personal foul. So instead of Penn State starting their winning drive on their own 25, they got to start on the 40."

After a bye week, Penn State would go on to lose to No. 4 Alabama, and Nebraska eventually jumped PSU in the polls. However, wins over No. 5 Pittsburgh and No. 13 Notre Dame, along with some lobbying from Paterno, allowed the Nittany Lions to vault the Huskers and play No. 1 Georgia for the national championship. Alabama ended the season as an unranked 8–4 team, and Notre Dame lost four of its final seven games, but PSU never was penalized for any of this in the final polls in November.

The Huskers beat No. 20 Auburn 41–7 and No. 11 Oklahoma 28–24 to close out the regular season 11–1, and they beat No. 13 LSU 21–20 in the Orange Bowl. It wasn't enough, however, as Penn State shutdown UGA and Heisman Trophy winner Herschel Walker 27–23 in the Sugar Bowl. "I still think about that 1982 Penn State loss today," Husker lineman and Outland Trophy winner Dave Rimington said. "It was the toughest loss of my career and kept us from playing for a national championship. I wasn't on that 1983 team, so 1982 was my only shot at a title."

74 The Legionnaire Club

From the late 1950s into the 1980s, there was really only one place to be seen in Lincoln—the legendary Legionnaire Club. It became known as the hangout spot for former head football coach Bob Devaney and his assistants. It also hosted the Friday night media dinner put on by sports information director Don Bryant for several years.

The Legionnaire Club was a throwback. It was Lincoln's original supper club that featured fine dining, plenty of cocktails, live musical acts, and dancing. And fans congregated on Saturday nights after Husker games to rub elbows and have drinks with Devaney and his coaching staff. Technically the Legionnaire Club was for veterans of World War II and the Korean War, but members were allowed to bring guests...and let's just say there were plenty of guests on a nightly basis who made appearances at the Legionnaire. The club was affiliated with American Legion Post No. 3, which at one time claimed the world's largest membership at more than 8,000. The club was owned by the late Bob Logsdon, one of Devaney's closest confidants and even a pallbearer at his funeral. Logsdon, a native of Tecumseh, Nebraska, took over the club in 1958 and moved it from where the Federal Building is now to 5730 O Street.

In Logsdon's obituary in the *Lincoln Journal Star*, Richard Piersol may have put it best by describing the Legionnaire as "lightning in a bottle when Devaney's magic moved into the lower level of the club."

"One of those football Saturdays, we fed like 1,800 or 1,900 people, and that was before we put on the second story," Logsdon told the *Journal Star* in the early 2000s after the club officially closed.

There were multiple years where the club did more than $2 million in business, and they were only open for dinner. The club had a mystique about it, and the fact that Devaney called it his hangout only added to its legend. When the Huskers once won the Big 8 title in the 1960s, the party was one for the ages. "The coaches used to have a party room in the basement," Logsdon told the *Journal Star*. "They came upstairs, and everybody in that place was on the tables cheering. It just about brought tears to your eyes. I remember people by the hundreds. Legionnaires from out of state came because they heard the coaches were out there after games."

From that point on, a legend was born. When Devaney died in 1997, former Iowa State head coach and Husker assistant Jim Walden even proclaimed the post-funeral gathering should move to the Legionnaire. "The party is moving to more of Devaney's type of element," Walden said at the time. "He wouldn't have wanted us not to have a good time today."

Logsdon received the Clarence Swanson Award in 1984 from the Nebraska Football Hall of Fame "for outstanding contributions to the University of Nebraska and the Husker athletic department through personal service, personal support of the athletic department programs, and dedication to the Husker football program and intercollegiate athletics."

Logsdon passed away at the age of 84 in June of 2012. "It's a great sorrow to thousands of people who knew and thought the world of him," Bryant said. "He was a tremendous personal friend. We for years had Friday night dinner for the media out there. He was just a tremendous leader, meeting people at the door, creative, just a wonderful guy. He did a great thing for Lincoln and the American Legion."

In today's social media world, places like the Legionnaire could never exist, but it was a major part of the social scene surrounding Nebraska football from 1958 all the way up until Devaney's death in 1997. "The Legion Club was special, as you say, because Bob [Devaney] and his assistants hung out there, and Bob became good friends with Bob Logsdon. There could be no Legion Club now in the same sense because college football has changed and with it coaches," Husker historian Mike Babcock said. "Devaney was well paid but not to the degree that Bo Pelini is now for example. Bob lived in the same house on C Street throughout his time at Nebraska and he was listed in the phone book.

"[The coaches] made good money, but again not to the degree that assistants do now. These days they're in an entirely different socioeconomic class from most of those who cover them. Plus there are so many more of us media types as well as the civilian media, folks who can tweet and take pictures with cell phones. Privacy is at a premium. The Legion Club was public, but it was private in the sense that people there weren't tweeting, talking on cell phones, snapping photos, or any of the instant media. Add that to the socioeconomic difference, and you can see why there wouldn't be a Legion Club equivalent now."

75 Remembering the Orange Bowl

For nearly 30 years, playing on New Year's Day in the Orange Bowl was always the goal for Nebraska. From 1968 to 1995, the Big 8 champion earned the right to play in the Orange Bowl against another championship-caliber opponent. In NU's program history, the Huskers represented either the Big 8 or the Big 12 conference 17 times in the Orange Bowl. It was a game that meant something to Nebraska fans. They would throw oranges onto the field after closing out the regular season with a conference title. It was an iconic moment to see Nebraska players walking off the field with oranges in their hands.

Like a lot of things over the years, however, the Big 8 conference's tie to the Orange Bowl ended with the formation of the Big 12 in 1996. The Big 12 chose to send its league champion to the Fiesta Bowl instead of the Orange Bowl. The Huskers still played in two more Orange Bowls as members of the Big 12, including the 1997 championship against Tennessee. But most college football historians will tell you the bowl has never been the same without the likes of Nebraska and Oklahoma making their way down to Miami on an annual basis. NU holds an all-time record of 8–9 in the Orange Bowl while OU is 12–6 in 18 Orange Bowl appearances.

Since the old Big 8 schools ended ties with the game, we've seen the Orange Bowl become a shell of itself, being forced to take lower level league champions from the Big East and the ACC. They even became a dumping ground for Northern Illinois in 2012 when the Orange Bowl was forced to take the MAC champions because of a BCS ranking technicality.

Cory Schlesinger, one of many in a long history of great Nebraska fullbacks, scores the game-winning touchdown in the 1995 Orange Bowl to give Tom Osborne his first national championship as head coach.

With 17 appearances there are a lot of great games to choose from, but here are Nebraska's top five moments in the legendary Miami bowl game. Four of Nebraska's five national championship victories came in the Orange Bowl.

1971—Nebraska 17 LSU 12

After both No. 1 Texas and No. 2 Ohio State lost earlier in the day, the Huskers captured their first national championship in school history with a 17–12 victory against LSU. Trailing 12–10 in the fourth quarter, Husker quarterback Jerry Tagge showed his moxie by driving Nebraska 67 yards and scoring a 1-yard touchdown with 8:50 left.

1972—Nebraska 38 Alabama 6

This was dubbed another Game of the Century as No. 1 Nebraska was 12–0 and No. 2 Alabama was 11–0. However, this would prove to be no contest as the Huskers jumped out to a 28–0 lead at halftime, and future Heisman Trophy winner Johnny Rodgers broke a 77-yard punt return for a touchdown, giving Nebraska head coach Bob Devaney his first win over Alabama's Bear Bryant in three tries.

1984—Miami 31 Nebraska 30

The 1983 Nebraska team will go down as one of the best ever to never win a national championship. Playing Miami in their home stadium, the top-ranked Huskers fell behind 17–0 in the first quarter, but Nebraska stormed back to make it 31–30 with 48 seconds left. Instead of kicking the extra point, Nebraska head coach Tom Osborne elected to go for two but came up empty. The 1984 Orange Bowl loss still ranks as one of the more crushing defeats in program history.

1995—Nebraska 24 Miami 17

Osborne finally got his long-awaited national championship, beating a loaded Miami Hurricanes squad on their home turf. Down 17–7 in the second half, the Huskers stormed back to win the game 24–17 after a pair of touchdowns from fullback Cory Schlesinger in the fourth quarter. The 1995 Orange Bowl win against Miami snapped a seven-year bowl game losing streak for the Big Red.

1998—Nebraska 42 Tennessee 17

In Osborne's final game at Nebraska, the Huskers dominated a Tennessee squad led by quarterback Peyton Manning 42–17. The future Super Bowl-winning quarterback passed for only 134 yards against the Blackshirts. Coming into the Orange Bowl, Manning was averaging 300 yards per game. The 1998 Orange Bowl victory gave Osborne that final signature moment to end his career at the top of the college football world.

76 Kicker/Punter U

When you think of NFL pipeline positions, most regard Nebraska as a great producer of linemen or even skill position players. Over the last 20 years, however, you could argue that kicker and punter have been the Husker positions that have produced the most successful NFL players. The one common theme with most Nebraska's NFL kickers and punters over the years is that almost all of them were outstanding all-around athletes and more than just guys who kicked a football.

The tradition all started in 1994 when head coach Tom Osborne gave baseball player Darin Erstad the opportunity to punt on NU's national championship team. Earlier that summer Erstad was the MVP of the prestigious Cape Cod Baseball League and in 1995 he would go on to become the No. 1 overall pick in the MLB draft by the then-titled California Angels. During the 1994 national championship season, Erstad played a vital role as the Huskers punter, averaging 42.6 yards per attempt—good for 14th overall in the country.

Erstad would start a trend at Nebraska that continues with the program today. In 1995 the Big Red signed Kris Brown out of Southlake Carroll High in Texas. Brown was a quarterback and kicker on consecutive 3A state championship teams in 1992 and 1993. As a four-year starter at NU, Brown would rewrite the kicking record books, scoring 388 points and making 57 field goals. He would go on to have a 12-year NFL career with the Pittsburgh Steelers, Houston Texans, San Diego Chargers, and Dallas Cowboys, connecting on 256-of-331 career field goal attempts in 179 NFL games.

Brown's successor at NU was the highly recruited Josh Brown out of Foyil, Oklahoma. While in high school, Brown was featured

Dale Klein's Big Day

Dale Klein may not have kicked in the NFL, but his 1985 performance against Missouri is certainly worthy of a mention in Nebraska's great history of kickers and punters. The Seward, Nebraska, native tied an NCAA record by kicking seven field goals in the Huskers' 28–20 victory against the Tigers in Columbia.

Klein connected on kicks from 32, 22, 43, 44, 29, 43, and 43 yards and he added an extra point for a Big 8-record 22 points. Klein's seven attempted field goals in a game also remains an NU school record. "Kicking is a lot like playing golf," Klein told Huskers.com in 2010 when thinking back to that 1985 day. "Making the first two kicks that day just made me all that much more confident, and I was able to get into a zone. It was weird because the field was pretty slippery. Mizzou had installed that new-fangled technology turf like we have now. I guess I had the right kind of cleats on, and our whole kicking team was putting everything together perfectly."

at running back, safety, and punter for an eight-man program. After redshirting in 1998 behind Kris Brown, Josh Brown would play in 46 games, scoring 315 points and connecting on 43-of-62 field goals. There was even a spring in 2002 when former head coach Frank Solich felt so comfortable in Brown's athletic ability that he let him play some wide receiver. Josh Brown would go on to become one of the better kickers in the NFL. He's had successful stints with the Seattle Seahawks, St. Louis Rams, Cincinnati Bengals, and he was signed in 2013 by the New York Giants. Over his first 10 years in the NFL, Brown connected on 231-of-284 field goal attempts.

Following Kris and Josh Brown, the Big Red would fail to produce another NFL kicker until 2011, but Sandro DeAngelis (2001 to 2004) would go on to be one of the more successful kickers in the Canadian Football League. The Niagara Falls native has an advantage playing in the CFL because he is a Canadian-born player. DeAngelis kicked for the Saskatchewan Roughriders in 2012. Before that he kicked for the Calgary Stampeders and the Hamilton Tiger-Cats.

The next real successful kicker from Nebraska to play in the NFL was Alex Henery (2007 to 2010). The Omaha Burke High product was also the state's best soccer player in high school. He received a scholarship offer from national power Creighton but turned it down to walk on at NU. Henery would go on to set nearly every school and several NCAA kicking records, making 68-of-76 career field goal attempts and scoring 397 points. Henery's 89.5 percent career accuracy mark is the best in NCAA history, and in 2011 he was drafted by the Philadelphia Eagles. "If you just look at his consistency and look at how consistent he's been through his whole career, that's really the mark of a great place-kicker," Kris Brown said of Henery in 2009. "He's done that since he got here Day One. Without a doubt he's light years ahead of where I was in my junior year for sure."

Henery was a first-team All-American in 2010 and a first-team All-Big 12 selection in both 2009 and 2010. He would also go on to punt in 2009 and 2010, averaging 42.2 yards per attempt and was named second-team All-Big 12 punter in 2010. Henery is now one of the top kickers in the NFL.

Following Henery, Kearney, Nebraska, native Brett Maher kicked and punted for NU in 2011 and 2012. Maher was the Big Ten's Kicker of the Year in 2011 and 2012 along with the Punter of the Year in 2011. Just like the great kickers before Maher, he was also a multi-sport athlete, winning state in both the long jump and pole vault. He was also Kearney High's top receiver with 775 yards and 10 touchdowns as a senior. He grew up learning how to kick from Kris Brown, who at one time was a student-teacher for Maher's father, Brian, in Waverly, Nebraska, in the late '90s.

Although the Husker kickers have certainly received most of the praise, the punters cannot be forgotten. Leading the way for the Huskers is Sam Koch, who has punted for Baltimore since 2006 and was part of the Ravens' Super Bowl championship team in 2013. Other punters in recent years to make the NFL from Nebraska are Kyle Larson (Cincinnati Bengals from 2004 to 2008) and Bill LaFleur (San Francisco 49ers from 2002 to 2003). Dan Hadenfeldt was part of several practice squads but never made an active roster.

Despite only kicking one field goal at NU and only doing kickoffs from 2007 to 2010, Adi Kunalic also was in the NFL for a handful of games with the Carolina Panthers in 2011 but never attempted a kick. Kunalic had 125 career touchbacks at Nebraska, which unofficially is an NCAA record because—during his four years at NU—kickoffs were from the 30-yard line. They were moved back from the 35 to create more kickoff returns.

77 "The Brown Brothers"

The first time Mike and Ralph Brown met one another was on an official visit to USC following the 1995 season. Something just felt right.

The two players were already familiar with one another since they were considered two of the top defensive back recruits in the country. Cornerback Ralph Brown played his high school football for Los Angeles-area power Bishop Amat Memorial High while safety Mike Brown was a standout at Scottsdale (Arizona) Saguaro High. "It's interesting because Mike and I had heard a lot about each other throughout high school—more our senior years because we were both highly touted defensive backs and running backs as well," Ralph Brown said. "We both took trips to USC on the same weekend because that was like their big weekend where they were bringing in the top talent, and they kind of wanted to sign the top guys that weekend. When I met Mike, and he met me as well, we both felt like we had already been boys for the last 10 years. When I saw him, I said, 'Yo, what's up?' And he said the same thing to me, and we had never spoken before. There was an immediate bond when we took our trip to USC."

Mike Brown went on to take his official visit to Nebraska without Ralph. The Huskers were fresh off their national championship beatdown of Florida in the Fiesta Bowl, so selling Husker football to high-profile recruits from the West Coast was never easier. Mike Brown committed that weekend, but Ralph wasn't scheduled to visit NU until the following weekend. "After [Mike Brown] left Nebraska, he called me and said, 'I'm going to Nebraska. You need to come.' I said, 'I haven't taken my trip yet.' So I took my trip out to Lincoln, and there was a blizzard and I didn't get a chance to see the campus," Ralph Brown said. "There was just a family and a brotherhood and just an aura about the players and the coaches that I hadn't felt when I took my trips to Colorado, USC, or UCLA. I didn't feel that focus or that winning mentality. After I left the campus, I felt this was the place I needed to come."

Even though Mike and Ralph Brown weren't brothers, the talented duo came to Nebraska with a bond you rarely see. "Mike and I were tight from the beginning," Ralph Brown said. "We just became inseparable once we both agreed to sign with Nebraska. He was ecstatic when I told him I was going to come be a Husker with him. It was a bond that a lot of people don't experience with others the first time they meet them. Still to this day, we are really close and best friends and we talk a lot."

Immediately the Browns were thrown into the fire on NU's defense in 1996 as Ralph earned a Blackshirt at the end of training camp while Mike played a valuable role on both the defense and special teams. Ralph Brown was the first true freshman player to start a season opener. He'd go onto finish his career with 52 total starts, the most ever by any offensive or defensive player in school history.

When Ralph Brown stepped on campus in the summer of 1996, he said NU's veteran players instilled a confidence in him from Day One that carried with him all four years of his career. "When I came to Nebraska to work out with the team in the summer time during 7-on-7s, the defense was already telling me, 'That's your spot. You're the right corner.' I had already been practicing and doing 7-on-7 work with the starting defense since the end of June and July," Ralph Brown said. "I had three months with the No. 1 defense before camp even started. I had so much experience and I felt so comfortable back there that those guys helped me become a Blackshirt. They cultivated me with the mentality of what it was to be a Blackshirt. By the time we got into training camp, I already knew certain routes the guys were running. I was a pretty good man-to-man guy. That mentality I took on being around those guys even before the season helped me mentally. When I got my Blackshirt, I was just so privileged. I remember the day when [Charlie] McBride handed out the Blackshirts and I was just overjoyed by that experience, being a freshman at age 17. I was just so amazed and overwhelmed by the situation."

Both Ralph and Mike Brown would go on to be first-team All-Americans in 1999. Ralph Brown was a three-time All-Big 12 first team selection and named the Big 12's Newcomer of the Year in 1996. Mike Brown was named a two-time first team All-Big 12 selection and he still holds the school record for most tackles in a season (102) and a career (287) by a defensive back. Perhaps most impressively Mike Brown was named a three-time Academic All-American from 1997 to 1999. Ralph and Mike Brown also are the only defensive backs in school history to be named first-team All-Americans in the same season.

Both enjoyed long NFL careers. A two-time All-Pro, Mike Brown played for the Chicago Bears from 2000 to 2008. Ralph Brown played for four teams, including the New York Giants, Minnesota Vikings, and Arizona Cardinals from 2000 to 2009.

Even though Ralph and Mike Brown aren't related, they played the game with a bond that seemed familial. "During the season players on the opposing team would even ask if we were brothers," Ralph Brown said. "We would kind of mess with them, and sometimes we would say, 'Yeah,' and sometimes we would say, 'No.' We just had a lot of fun with it. It felt good, though, that people would say the 'Brown brothers' because we were so close to each other that it was the perfect fit for us."

78 Athletic Director Steve Pederson

On October 13, 2007, Nebraska just suffered one of their worst losses in Memorial Stadium, losing to Oklahoma State 45–14. Earlier that same season, NU got shelled at home by USC 49–31 and it had just lost at Missouri the previous week 41–6. Program morale was at an all-time low, and the speculation was the next thing to go could be the precious sellout streak. Former players no longer felt welcome at NU, and there was a locked-door atmosphere within the Husker program that hadn't been there before.

Most of the blame pointed toward athletic director Steve Pederson. The former recruiting coordinator under Tom Osborne got his start working at NU as an undergraduate in the Husker ticket office. The North Platte, Nebraska, native was considered a slam dunk hire when chancellor Harvey Perlman brought him in to replace Bill Byrne in 2002.

At the time of Pederson's hiring, nobody could've predicted what was to come. Following a 31–22 victory at Colorado, which completed a 9–3 regular season, Pederson fired head coach Frank Solich the next day. Husker Nation was in shock. In the 2003 college football world, a nine-win football coach had never been fired before. Pederson's words at his press conference that Sunday afternoon were legendary. "I refuse to let the program gravitate into mediocrity," Pederson said with stern authority. "We won't surrender the Big 12 to Oklahoma and Texas."

At the time of Solich's firing, Nebraska had a 1–5 record against Texas since the formation of the Big 12 in 1996, and Bob Stoops' Oklahoma Sooners, who captured the 2000 national championship after beating the No. 1 Huskers in Norman, Oklahoma, were soaring. During that 2003 season, the Huskers lost to Texas 31–7, Kansas State 38–9, and Missouri 41–24. In 2002 and 2003, NU had a cumulative 8–8 record in Big 12 conference play. In comparison over the 1990s, Nebraska only lost eight league games in 10 years. In Pederson's eyes the program was slipping, and a change needed to be made. "The byproduct of excellence in every area of your program is winning," Pederson said, "and I don't apologize for having high expectations."

Following that 45–14 loss to Oklahoma State in Memorial Stadium, Husker Nation held Pederson to the same standards of excellence to which he held Solich. Even though that one game wasn't the sole reason Pederson was fired, it played a major part in the timing. Husker Nation needed strong leadership and most importantly they needed healing. Pederson was no longer the man for that job, and on October 15, 2007, Perlman turned toward former head coach Tom Osborne to step in as athletic director. "The selection of Steve Pederson in 2003 as athletic director was widely thought to be the only clear choice because of his experience, his roots, and his knowledge of our traditions," Perlman said.

"I know Steve made the decisions he thought were best for the interests of the program and the university. I am disappointed that I had to come to this decision."

Most will obviously remember Pederson for the bad decisions he made while at Nebraska, but he also was responsible for several good things, including the North Stadium renovation, brand new indoor football complex, and weight room facility. With these new additions, the Huskers had the nicest football facilities in the country.

Current Pittsburgh Panthers and Steelers play-by-play voice Bill Hillgrove worked with Pederson at Pitt before he came to NU in 2002 and he currently works with him again today. During a 2004 interview with Hillgrove, he may have summed up Pederson better than anyone. "Steve made some tough decisions here and he didn't flinch when he made them," Hillgrove said. "He's his own man and he makes his decisions based on what he thinks is best for the situation."

That type of leadership just wasn't meant to be at a place like Nebraska.

79 The Worst Loss in Program History

When you think about bad losses in Nebraska's history, it's hard to find one worse than the 1955 defeat at the hands of Hawaii. It was the season opener, and the year before the Huskers stomped the Rainbows 50–0 in Honolulu on the final game of the regular season before their Orange Bowl date with Duke. Despite losing to Oklahoma 55–7 in 1954, NU received the Orange Bowl bid over the Sooners because the Big 7 conference had a no-repeat rule, which kept OU from playing in the game a second consecutive year. Head coach Bill Glassford's Huskers lost to Duke in the Orange Bowl 34–7, losing three of their final four games in 1954 with the only win in that stretch coming against Hawaii.

NU opened the 1955 season in Lincoln against the Rainbows, and the game was expected to be another blowout. Don Bryant, who would eventually go on to become Nebraska's media relations director, was the sports editor of the *Lincoln Star* at the time. Bryant predicted the game against Hawaii to be another 50–0 win for the Big Red. Glassford's squad returned most of their key players, and the coach was quoted as saying they were the "best I've had at Nebraska since I've been here."

Hawaii featured a travel roster of only 28 players—none of whom were on scholarship. Henry Vasconcellos, who was Hawaii's athletic director, was also their head coach. All of Vasconcellos' assistants were volunteers, one of which was a lawyer who helped out in his spare time. None of the Rainbows players were highly recruited at all. They were almost like a club team. "These boys are not the top players produced in the islands," Vasconcellos said at the time. "The top stars are sent to the mainland by wealthy alumni. These are just kids—most of them from the outer islands—who are playing football for the fun of it."

Before their trip to Lincoln, Hawaii had a tune-up game against the Prep All-Stars and won 33–7. The following week the Rainbows would come into Lincoln with 28 players and their second-string quarterback and stun the Huskers 6–0. Before kicker Don Botelho missed the extra point, the game's only touchdown came in the fourth quarter on a one-foot run by Hawaii fullback Hartwell Freitas. "I stepped on top of our guard and dove over," Freitas recalled in a 2002 *Honolulu Star-Advertiser* story. "I landed on my head and I was in the touchdown zone."

Hawaii would finish 1955 with a 7–4 record, and its win against Nebraska was its only victory against a real college. The Rainbows played mostly service teams based in Hawaii.

According to the *Lincoln Sunday Journal and Star*, by halftime "the Hawaiians had gained about 23,000 supporters, and the Cornhuskers were getting horse laughs." The paper also wrote the Huskers "were completely humiliated…before some 23,000 hot and disbelieving football fans," as the sellout crowd watched the game in 93-degree sweltering heat.

Following the loss Nebraska hosted a luau for Hawaii at a farm near Elkhorn, Nebraska, which had been intended as a goodwill gesture for coming to Lincoln and taking a beating. Nobody could've ever predicted the 40-point underdog Rainbows would actually come to Lincoln and win.

There were a few other theories why Nebraska played so poorly following the loss. One was the Huskers were looking ahead to games with Big Ten champion Ohio State, Pittsburgh, and Bear Bryant's Texas A&M squad. For the record NU lost all three of those games that season as well. The other—more comical, though a bit salacious—theory was that NU played so bad because several players were suspended for disciplinary reasons for making a panty raid on a girls' dorm.

Whatever the reason Glassford did not survive after a 5–5 record in 1955. NU lost to Oklahoma again that season 41–0. But the loss to Hawaii is easily considered the worst loss in program history. "Nebraska football no longer is something which a great state can point to with pride but a muddle of ineptness that defies the imagination," Bryant wrote following the loss to Hawaii in the *Lincoln Star*.

80 Nebraska's Partnership With Adidas

From the late 1960s to 1994, Nebraska had a long-standing partnership with the apparel company Russell to make their jerseys. Former Husker equipment manager Glen Abbott was responsible for ordering all jerseys, pants, shoes, helmets, and patches. According to the website HuskerGameUsed.com, each Russell jersey had a patch sewn on it by a private seamstress in Lincoln. It was former head coach Bob Devaney who set up the relationship with Russell, which began in the mid 1960s.

It wasn't until the 1990s when Nebraska opened up the bidding for a new apparel partner. No longer were teams paying for jerseys anymore, but instead apparel companies were paying teams to wear their product. A little-known company by the name of APEX won the initial uniform contract for the 1995 season. The agreement paid Nebraska $1 million in apparel as long as the Huskers wore APEX game jerseys. There was some controversy, though, when Nebraska played for the national championship on January. 1, 1995 against Miami in the Orange Bowl.

Both Russell and APEX printed and made Orange Bowl game jerseys for the Huskers to wear against Miami. Russell was under the impression its deal ran through the bowl game, and APEX thought its deal started in 1995. Abbott gave the players both jerseys and let them decide which one they wanted to wear. Some players actually wore the Russell jersey for the first half and the APEX jersey in the second. It was a bizarre deal that never would've flown in today's world of huge endorsement contracts.

Heading into the 1995 season, APEX figured being partnered with the No. 1 team in college football would skyrocket its business. The only problem was the small start-up company overextended itself, and by Week 3 of the 1995 season, it sold to Adidas. Adidas did not want Nebraska wearing APEX or Russell gear, so it shipped another $ 1 million worth of gear for Nebraska's players and coaches to wear.

Since that time Nebraska and Adidas have been an inseparable force in college athletics. When Adidas made the decision to get into college football, Nebraska was the first team it signed to a contract. Now you'll find Adidas gear on several major teams, including Notre Dame, Michigan, Tennessee, Wisconsin, Indiana, Kansas, and UCLA.

Nebraska's deal with Adidas originally only covered football, and every other sport and coach was responsible for coming up with their own apparel contracts. During the mid to late '90s Nebraska's men's basketball team wore both Converse and Nike gear. It wasn't until 2005 when NU signed an eight-year, $22.7 million agreement with Adidas, which included a $1.5 million signing bonus. What made the deal even more valuable was that Adidas agreed to provide apparel for all 23 of Nebraska's varsity programs. "We do very few of these all-school deals," said Tim Haney, Adidas' director of licensed properties. "But a school like Nebraska—just because of the history and tradition—is one of those unique situations."

Nebraska's initial deal with Adidas ended in 2012, but the two sides agreed to a new partnership going forward through the 2017 season. Adidas agreed to a five-year extension that pays Nebraska $15.53 million—$8.03 million in cash and $7.5 million in athletic apparel and equipment products for NU's 24 varsity programs— for exclusive sponsorship.

During the 2012 season, Adidas flexed its muscles in the partnership by getting Nebraska to wear alternate uniforms in its game against Wisconsin, which featured black helmets with red "N"s on them. Wisconsin, also an Adidas school, wore alternate uniforms. On September 14 Nebraska is planning on wearing an alternate black TECHFIT jersey against UCLA.

81 The 2003 Alamo Bowl

Were you listening, Steve Pederson? Did you hear them? In the waning minutes of Nebraska's 17–3 win against Michigan State on Monday night, the Alamodome rocked to the chants of "We want Bo." The Huskers found interim head coach Bo Pelini and showered him with a tub of Gatorade. Interim schminterim.

—Omaha World-Herald (now ESPN.com)
sportswriter Elizabeth Merrill

Merrill used these words to describe Nebraska's dominating 17–3 victory against Michigan State in the Alamo Bowl on December 29, 2003 in the San Antonio Alamodome. After Husker fans watched defensive coordinator Bo Pelini turn around the Blackshirt defense, the 2003 Alamo Bowl was his audition to become Nebraska's head coach because Frank Solich was fired as NU's head coach by athletic director Steve Pederson on November 29.

Pelini was named the interim head coach on November 30 for the bowl game after the Huskers' 9–3 regular season. Pederson gave the 35-year-old Pelini the interim head coach title over longtime Nebraska assistant and former quarterback Turner Gill despite the fact Gill carried the assistant head coach title.

For Pelini this was his chance because Pederson was scrambling to find a head coach to replace Solich. Pederson's reported leading candidate to replace Solich was Miami Dolphins head coach Dave Wannstedt, but on the day before the Alamo Bowl, Wannstedt was retained by the Dolphins after a 23–21 win against the New York Jets. The Dolphins finished the season at 10–6 but failed to make the playoffs. It was speculated that Wannstedt was going to be fired, but owner Wayne Huizenga decided to keep him another season.

With no top candidates knowingly interested in the job, Pelini's name quickly began to gain popularity both with the fans and the players after he turned around Nebraska's defense. The assistant coaches, who knew their jobs were most likely gone after the bowl, had little to lose. When Nebraska got to San Antonio on December 23, it was almost like a load came off its back after the stressful month everyone endured when Pederson fired Solich.

Some of the more memorable moments on that trip were following a 2 AM curfew on Day One. Nebraska's players had a little too much fun on the River Walk, and it showed during their first morning practice at Trinity University. "We were a little bit

Bo Pelini, then the interim head coach, argues with a referee during Nebraska's 17–3 win against Michigan State in the 2003 Alamo Bowl.

sluggish today," Gill said. "Unfortunately I think our guys were a little tired from going out last night. They were not in tune from where we want them to be with our standards. So tomorrow we're hoping they'll come out here and get some things done at a better pace and be a little bit more efficient."

Then there was the notorious near brawl at a team fiesta put on by the Alamo Bowl. A group of Michigan State players surrounded Husker quarterback Jammal Lord only to be greeted by some pushing and shoving and a tossed chair by fiery offensive lineman Richie Incognito. "I just heard talk, talk, talk," Nebraska offensive lineman Dan Vili Waldrop said. "Then everybody stood up. And I was like, *huh…that's interesting*. But I kept eating because it was pretty good food."

Michigan State quarterback Jeff Smoker had his own view of the near team brawl at the La Villita Assembly Hall. Witnesses from Nebraska who saw the confrontation said it happened within seconds of MSU's arrival into the building. "We weren't going to be intimidated by them," Smoker said, "and we were going to show that."

Other classic moments on that trip were Husker coaches getting up to sing at the piano bar Howl at the Moon. Then days before kickoff, defensive tackle Le Kevin Smith predicted a Husker "blowout" and that Smoker might be in for a long night.

Through it all nobody really knew how Nebraska would respond after an emotional trip led by a coaching staff that was going to be jobless in a few days, but Pelini impressed in his debut as Nebraska crushed the Spartans 17–3. Not only were the Huskers ready, they also played a near perfect game on defense, holding Michigan State to 174 total yards, including just 18 yards rushing on 23 carries.

A proud Pelini addressed the media one final time in San Antonio the morning after the game, knowing he had accomplished the job he was brought in to do. "We've come a long way," Pelini said. "I can look back and I can see there are a lot of football players especially with what I was dealing with on the defensive side of the ball that improved a great deal. And as a coach that gives you a tremendous level of satisfaction that you brought guys a long way. And I think myself and our staff did that, and we got better. We got a lot out of these guys, and it was a lot of fun doing it."

Before the season Pelini entered the college ranks as a fairly anonymous coach, but after the job he did with the Blackshirt defense, Pelini become a household name and left Husker fans craving more. "I was an unknown quantity in the college game, but people in the pros knew what I could do," Pelini said. "So obviously it helps me to show that I can have success at both levels."

82 Clarence Thomas: The Highest Husker Fan in the Land

When you walk into the office of U.S. Supreme Court Justice Clarence Thomas, it doesn't take very long to figure out he's a Husker fan. Thomas has countless Nebraska items displayed both at his office and in his home. He wears a Husker watch to work each day. Both his cell phone and iPad sit inside customized Husker carrying cases.

Thomas' homepage on his computer is HuskerOnline.com. When Thomas works out at home, he often watches old Nebraska football games he's collected over the years. His favorite games to watch were during the national championship years in the 1990s. Each year Thomas gets a new group of clerks to work under him at the Supreme Court, and they are immediately immersed in his love for the Huskers.

The question posed by many is how did Thomas become such a big Nebraska fan? He was born in Georgia, went to Holy Cross for his undergraduate degree, and Yale for law school. Thomas explains a number of things led him to become a Husker fan, starting with his wife, Virginia Lamp, who is an Omaha native. Lamp attended Omaha Westside High School, graduated from Creighton University, and married Thomas in 1987. Most of Lamp's relatives attended the University of Nebraska, and their love and passion for the Huskers really caught his attention. "I started trying to get involved and following things, and my in-laws were very much involved with Nebraska, and that was the hook," Thomas said. "That's when I started having real contact with Nebraska. Her family was really into it. Both of her parents went to [NU], and her sister went there. She went there for a year, and her brother went there. The family is very much invested into it. I really, really admired my in-laws and had great affection for them, so [being a Nebraska fan] was a natural. I became a guy that just sort of inherited the passion. It just became a way of life. This is what I do, and it's permanent. As long as Nebraska continues to do things the right way, I'm a Nebraska fan."

Thomas also recalls in 1995 when former head coach Tom Osborne invited him to speak to the team for the very first time. His knowledge of the Huskers in 1995 was somewhat limited. What he remembers about that day was Osborne explaining to him why he was going to keep running back Lawrence Phillips on the football team after his legal problems. It was a decision heavily scrutinized by many national media members. "[Osborne] was saying that, 'They want me to do bad things to [Phillips].' He said, 'If you take away football from him, we have no leverage to at least try to get him to do well.' This kid has nothing else—no family, nothing. Football is everything," Thomas said. "He said, 'I think I owe it to him to try and help him and I know I'm going to catch grief for it.' That's when I went over there and I said, 'Wow.'"

The way Osborne handled that situation was always something that stuck out to Thomas. Letting Phillips continue to play football

Other Celebrity Huskers Fans

Although Supreme Court Justice Clarence Thomas may be the highest profile Nebraska football fan, here is a list of some other notable celebrity Huskers fans.

Larry the Cable Guy—The comedian, whose real name is Dan Whitney, is a Nebraska native and has a skybox in North Stadium.

Gabrielle Union—The Omaha native and actress originally attended the University of Nebraska and is a die-hard Husker fan. A picture of her posing in a No. 3 Taylor Martinez jersey ran in *ESPN The Magazine*.

Andy Roddick—Born in Omaha, the retired professional tennis star has attended several Husker games and will even tweet about his love for Nebraska from time to time.

Chuck Liddell—The famous MMA fighter was part owner of the NZone and Dillinger's bars in Lincoln. He's been seen at Nebraska games wearing Husker gear.

Johnny Carson—The former king of late night television, Carson was from Norfolk, Nebraska, and attended the University of Nebraska. All the way up to his death in 2005, Carson donated generously to the university.

Warren Buffett—The billionaire investor is one of the most powerful people in the world and graduated from the University of Nebraska in 1950. Buffett is a regular at Husker home games.

was not the most popular decision, but Osborne didn't care because he only wanted what was best for Phillips' future.

However, the moment where Thomas really became a passionate Husker fan was in 2003 after Steve Pederson fired head coach Frank Solich. Thomas said he had started to become close to Solich's staff at that time and began making regular check-in phone calls to assistant coach Scott Downing. "I liked [Solich], and he got fired and I never understood why he got fired," Thomas said. "I really never understood it. That team won 10 games, and he got fired. I liked the athletic director, Pederson. He was a nice guy to me, but I still never understood why [Solich] was fired. I don't understand how you win 10 games and get fired. There was nothing I could do about that, but that perplexed me. I liked Pederson and got to meet him and know him and his family, and he was fine, but I still didn't understand that, but there's a lot in life I don't understand."

Coincidently, Downing was one of only two coaches retained by new head coach Bill Callahan in 2004, so Thomas continued to check in with him for regular updates. "[Downing] was a really nice guy. He would always take my calls, and I would call him," Thomas said. "When the new people came, he was still there for two more years. So he was my contact. Then he would invite me over to the team, so that's when I really started following them hard when people where hating on Callahan because he was an outsider. That's when I started saying, 'Either you are a fan or you are not a fan.' When you get married, it's for better or worse. When you really are a fan, it's during the dark days, and these are the dark days. The kids are still playing. You may not agree with the coaches or you may not agree with that, but the kids are still playing, and it's still the Huskers. That's when I became a die-hard fan when other people were questioning their loyalties."

It's not just Husker football that Thomas follows. He watches every Nebraska volleyball, men's and women's basketball, wrestling, and baseball game when they are on the Big Ten Network. Thomas even finds himself supporting and rooting for coaches who have left Nebraska. He cheers for Solich at Ohio, Shawn Watson at Louisville, Scott Downing, and Craig Bohl at North Dakota State.

Some of Thomas' favorite players he's been able to strike up relationships with during his visits to Lincoln were running back Rex Burkhead, cornerback Prince Amukamara, brothers Courtney and Steven Osborne, running back Marlon Lucky, defensive end Barry Turner, and safety Austin Cassidy. Thomas also has an extreme amount of respect for current head coach Bo Pelini and loves the discipline with which he runs his football program. "I like black and white," Thomas said. "I like clarity. I like passion. People pick on [Pelini] because he gets upset. I watched the Super Bowl and I watched [Jim and John Harbaugh] get upset. I also like honesty. I like the way he tries to get these kids involved with the whole program—to take care of your stuff off the field and to take care of your business in the classroom. These younger people make fun of the process. Well, that's been my whole life. If you go into court, you have a system. You better have a system. You have to have a predictable approach to everything, a level of preparation to everything, and it has to be steady day in and day out."

If anything when Thomas looks at his passion toward Nebraska athletics, he looks at it as his hobby. Thomas doesn't golf. He doesn't hunt or fish. The Huskers are his No. 1 hobby. Being a Nebraska fan has given him more balance in his life, and that's something he's always believed in ever since being appointed to the Supreme Court in 1991. "You can be serious about everything, but it makes you really dull," Thomas said.

Thomas jokes that if he could retire someday he'd move to Waverly, Nebraska, because of its close proximity between Lincoln and Omaha. In his perfect world, he'd be able to drive his own RV to all the Husker football games and tailgate like a regular fan. When Thomas travels to a Nebraska game now, a security detail as large as 20 people may come with him, and he has to sit in the sky-boxes up above. If Thomas had it his way, he'd be sitting in row 45 in East Stadium with the regular fans. "After you have seen as much life as I have and you've seen Washington, you really see something very special coming out to Nebraska," Thomas said. "I really don't think people understand what they have. I really don't. I don't get to retire, but my wife asks me, 'Where would you retire?' And I say, 'Waverly' and I mean it. Waverly seems to be a nice community. I don't want to live in a college town, and I don't want to live 45 minutes away from the Huskers. I want to go to the practices and I want to see all my games, and Waverly is right there. That's my kind of community. I don't want to be in a college town. I want to be near regular folks, working class people."

83 *Sports Illustrated* Cover Boys

If you grew up a Husker fan in the state of Nebraska, odds are you own at least one old *Sports Illustrated* issue in your house that features the Big Red on the cover. When you count regular weekly issues and special commemorative issues over the years, Nebraska has appeared on 35 different *SI* covers. Here's a complete rundown of Nebraska's *Sports Illustrated* cover history.

September 20, 1965—The first *Sports Illustrated* cover that featured Nebraska had a cover headline that read, "Nebraska goes for No. 1" and it had fullback Frank Solich breaking a run against Oklahoma from the 1964 season. The Huskers finished 10–0 in the 1965 regular season but lost to Alabama 39–28 in the Orange Bowl.

January 3, 1966—Nebraska and several other teams were featured on *SI*'s bowl preview issue as the Huskers were getting ready to play Alabama in the Orange Bowl.

January 2, 1967—Husker cheerleader Kitty McManus was featured on the bowl preview issue as Nebraska got ready to play Alabama in the Sugar Bowl.

September 13, 1971—Nebraska and several different teams were featured on the cover. It had a profile story on head coach Bob Devaney on page 53.

November 22, 1971—The 1971 "Game of the Century" preview was featured on the cover.

December 6, 1971—This was an Orange Bowl preview for Nebraska's national championship game against Alabama.

January 10, 1972—Nebraska beats Alabama 38–6 to win a second straight national title as the cover read, "Awesome Nebraska."

September 11, 1972—A cover featuring Bob Devaney titled "Nebraska goes for three straight."

November 20, 1978—The cover read "Nebraska bursts Oklahoma's bubble" as NU beat OU to win the Big 8. That cover featured running back Rick Berns running through the OU defense.

November 12, 1979—The cover was headlined with "Who's really No. 1?" It featured five different players from five different schools, including Nebraska running back Jarvis Redwine holding up his finger, proclaiming Nebraska should be No. 1.

October 4, 1982—Nebraska lost a controversial game at Penn State where an out of bounds PSU pass was called a touchdown. The cover showed Nittany Lions quarterback Todd Blackledge being chased by Nebraska defensive lineman Jeff Merrell and read "Prodigious Penn State."

September 5, 1983—Nebraska got its revenge against Penn State, routing the Nittany Lions 44–6 in the Kickoff Classic. The cover featured running back Mike Rozier and read, "Oh, those Huskers."

January 9, 1984—The Huskers lost the national championship to Miami in the Orange Bowl, and the cover featured Hurricanes running back Keith Griffin running away from Nebraska. The issue was titled, "Miracle in Miami."

October 1, 1984—The cover read, "The Big Red Machine" as Nebraska running back Jeff Smith was featured when the No. 1 Huskers beat No. 8 UCLA 42–3.

November 30, 1987—Dubbed as the "Game of the Century II," Nebraska and Oklahoma were featured on the cover. The Sooners beat the Huskers 17–7, and the cover had NU quarterback Steve Taylor getting wrapped up as the headline read "Oklahoma O.K."

January 9, 1995—Nebraska head coach Tom Osborne was featured on the cover when Nebraska beat Miami for the national championship in the Orange Bowl. The headline read, "How sweet it is."

January 1995 (special issue)—*SI* put out a special national championship issue that featured offensive lineman Aaron Graham and tight end Matt Shaw on the cover. The issue was titled, "The Championship Season: 1994 Nebraska."

Spring 1995 (special issue)—A special leather-bound issue put out by *Sports Illustrated* was offered to new subscribers after Nebraska's 1994 national championship season. The commemorative cover featured the same picture as the January 9, 1995 issue.

August 1995 (college football preview)—Nebraska running back Lawrence Phillips was featured on a cover that read, "Heart of the Huskers." The issue previewed the 1995 college football season and was not a regular *SI* issue.

December 25, 1995—Quarterback Tommie Frazier was featured on a cover that was titled, "Husker Hero." The issue previewed the upcoming Fiesta Bowl game against Florida.

January 8, 1996—Frazier was featured on the cover again as the Huskers routed Florida to win their second straight national championship. The cover read, "Nebraska No. 1 (again)."

January 1996 (special issue)—Similar to the 1994 national championship season, *Sports Illustrated* put out a special issue commemorating the 1995 season. The cover featured Frazier and read "Champions Again."

Spring 1996 (special issue)—Frazier was featured on a special leather-bound, hardcover issue for new *Sports Illustrated* subscribers in the spring of 1996.

August 1996 (college football preview)—Running back Ahman Green was on the college football preview issue, and the cover read, "One more time?"

September 16, 1996—The cover featured Green and was titled, "Red Alert: Ahman Green and Nebraska set their sights on a third straight national title."

October 1996 (special merchandise issue)—A special *Sports Illustrated* merchandise issue featured Osborne on the cover after Nebraska's 55–14 win against Michigan State. The cover read, "Gear up for '96 with No. 1 Nebraska."

January 21, 1998 (Tom Osborne commemorative issue)—A special tribute issue to Tom Osborne following his 25-year coaching career at Nebraska.

Spring 1998 (special issue)—Osborne was featured on a special leather-bound, hardcover issue for new *Sports Illustrated* subscribers in the spring of 1998.

November 6, 2000—The cover read, "Back on top" as Oklahoma beat Nebraska to take over the No. 1 ranking. The cover showed OU running back Quentin Griffin running away from Nebraska defensive tackle Jon Clanton.

November 26, 2001—Quarterback Eric Crouch was on a cover that read, "Who is Eric Crouch?" The issue talked about Crouch's unlikely path to his Heisman Trophy candidacy. Nebraska ended up losing that week to Colorado 62–36, but Crouch still won the Heisman.

January 7, 2002—Miami romped Nebraska to win the national championship. Hurricanes running back Clinton Portis was shown running through the Husker defense.

September 24, 2007—USC was featured on the cover blowing out Nebraska 49–31 in Memorial Stadium.

August 23, 2011—Nebraska defensive tackle Jared Crick was on the college football preview issue as the cover read, "Nebraska: The Big Ten's new Bully." Crick was featured on the cover with Oklahoma quarterback Landry Jones and Stanford quarterback Andrew Luck.

August 2010 (Big 12 preview)—Nebraska wide receiver Niles Paul was featured on a special Big 12 preview issue.

August 2011 (Big Ten preview)—Nebraska quarterback Taylor Martinez was featured on a special Big Ten preview issue.

84 Huskers Football, Tokyo Style

With a Big 8 championship on the line, Nebraska played their final game of the 1992 season against Kansas State in Tokyo, Japan, in what was dubbed the "Coca-Cola Classic." From 1977 to 1993, Tokyo played host to one college football game per year on the final week of the regular season.

In 1992 Kansas State and head coach Bill Snyder's team agreed to give up a home game for a guaranteed $200,000 to play the Huskers in front of 50,000 people in the Tokyo Dome on December 5. What was even more unusual about this game was there was no local television broadcast, and it actually kicked off Sunday afternoon in Tokyo, which was 15 hours ahead of Nebraska time. That meant the only over-the-air broadcast was on the radio in the wee hours of the morning.

Nebraska ended up winning the game 38–24 to clinch the Big 8 title, but what will be remembered most about that trip are some of things that happened off the field. The Coca-Cola Classic featured a rock band that played while the game was going on. And before the two teams arrived for that game, they flew on the same plane from Kansas City to Vancouver, British Columbia, to Tokyo. It was a 13-hour flight, and a number of boosters and entourages from each school joined the two teams on the flight. At this time Snyder wasn't a relatively well-known coach in college football, but over the years he would develop a reputation as the most detail-oriented coach in the country. Nebraska got to see it firsthand on the flight to Tokyo when Snyder arranged for his players to all sit on the side of the plane with more shade, allowing them to get more rest on the 13-hour flight than the Husker players.

Snyder's meticulousness would eventually help Kansas State make the greatest turnaround in college football history. He also hired some unbelievable coaches. On that trip to Japan some of his assistant coaches were Bob Stoops (co-defensive coordinator), Jim Leavitt (co-defensive coordinator), Mike Stoops (defensive line coach), and Tim Beck (graduate assistant). Brent Venables and Mike Ekeler, who would become noted defensive coordinators, were also on that 1992 KSU team.

Former Nebraska media relations director Don "Fox" Bryant had an interesting blurb about the trip to Japan in his *Tales from the Nebraska Sideline*. Bryant wrote that each Japanese city "adopted" a team, and their citizens comprised cheering sections. Because of Nebraska's superior reputation nationally, the Cornhuskers had a much bigger draw than the Wildcats. "The hosts were somewhat more attentive to coach Tom Osborne than the Wildcats and coach Bill Snyder," Bryant wrote. "Bill is one of the top football coaches in the profession and he has done a tremendous job with the Kansas State program for a long time. But I know he did not enjoy that trip to Tokyo."

Former Husker play-by-play man Kent Pavelka remembers calling the game from behind home plate in a press box designed for baseball. "The nearest sideline was a long, long ways away," Pavelka said. "The far sideline? Forget about it."

Ticket prices for the game averaged $230, which even by today's standards is extremely high. Only about 500 Nebraska fans attended while about 100 from K-State made the trip. The rest of the 50,000 were locals. Osborne still couldn't believe people in Japan paid that kind of money to watch something they really didn't follow. "Can you imagine that…$230 and then not even understand what you're seeing out there?" Osborne told the *Lincoln Journal Star*. "It'll be a little bizarre."

The Coca-Cola Classic came to an end following the 1993 season as conference title games took over the first weekend of December in its place.

85 Skyboxes, Skyboxes, and More Skyboxes

When former athletic director Bill Byrne came to Nebraska from Oregon in 1992, Memorial Stadium had zero skyboxes or club seating of any kind. The athletic department was making revenue but nowhere near the $90 million operating budget they have today.

One of the biggest things Byrne did while at Nebraska from 1992 to 2003 was build NU's development office from scratch, and that became what is now referred to as the Husker Athletic Fund. Before the creation of the Husker Athletic Fund, most of the fund-raising at Nebraska was done from what associate athletic director Paul Meyers called a "grassroots effort" through organizations like the Touchdown Club and the Cattle Club.

Former NU coaches would go around the state to encourage and build membership to these types of booster club organizations. This created revenue, but Nebraska was leaving millions of corporate dollars on the table each year by not having any sort of skybox or club seating in Memorial Stadium.

After starting the development office in 1994, Memorial Stadium opened its first skyboxes in 1999. The initial project included 30 skyboxes that were leased for $75,000 per year on a 10-year contract, and another 10 skyboxes were leased for 25 years for a one-time gift of $2 million at a more prime location. "It wasn't an easy sell," Meyers said of the initial West Stadium skyboxes. "It took a while to sell those because we were selling something people hadn't experienced before. It took a while, and in some cases, the project came close to failing simply because it was predicated on 10 people, saying they were willing to invest in the program at the level they did, which was the $2 million mark…It was not an easy project, but it was one that really catapulted us to all these other projects."

The suites were more than 700 square feet with a maximum seating capacity of 28. Each skybox was equipped with three televisions, a radio, a fax machine, Internet hook-up, a refrigerator, microwave, mini-kitchen, and restroom. The initial wing of west skyboxes was located on the fourth and fifth levels of Memorial Stadium while the entire third level was club seating. The new addition brought the stadium capacity from around 75,000 to 77,000 on gamedays.

In 2006 Nebraska introduced more skyboxes in North Stadium along with expanded end-zone seating to bring the stadium capacity to approximately 86,000. In 2013 NU opened up their East Stadium skyboxes to bring the gameday capacity up to around 91,000.

In all Memorial Stadium will have 101 skyboxes—the most of any school in the Big Ten. Michigan has 82, and Ohio State has

81 skyboxes. Nationally, Alabama has 159 sky boxes and Arkansas 132, according to their schools' websites. Oklahoma State has 99, but many of its boxes have not been leased in Boone Pickens Stadium.

Nebraska's new East Stadium skybox addition was a $63 million project, but it will be paid off in its entirety within seven years. In all Meyers said five donors paid $2.5 million to get prime East Stadium skyboxes for 25 years, which gives NU a total of 15 suite owners who paid either $2 million in 1999 or $2.5 million in 2013 to lock up a skybox for 25 years in a prime stadium location.

Heading into the 2013 season, Meyers said all of the 101 suites are sold out. The skyboxes lease for 10 years at $85,000 to $90,000 per year for a larger suite and $45,000 to $55,000 per year for a smaller suite. In comparison Ohio State's 81 suites lease for five to seven-year terms for $24,000 to $80,000 per year. The 101 skybox suites will bring Nebraska an annual revenue stream of $6.3 million per year. A total of 2,550 people occupy the skybox suites on gameday, according to figures released by Meyers.

Memorial Stadium also has 5,400 club seats to go with their 101 skyboxes, and those are priced in annual donation tiers of $1,500 to $2,500 per seat on top of the ticket's regular price, which is $448 in 2013. So a pair of 50-yard line club seats would run just under $6,000 for the 2013 season while a pair of seats closer to the end zone would run just under $4,000. "Really, Bill Byrne lit the match to dynamite," Meyers said. "When you look at this East Stadium structure, it not only creates a lot of valuable seating for people who wanted club suites and all those things, but the revenue off of that facility is going to be about $9 million annually. When you look at that structure from a business perspective, just by building that structure we'll be able to pay it back in about seven years. That turnaround is pretty spectacular in business terms."

Meyers said only around 40 percent of Memorial Stadium's seats paid a seat donation fee in 1994, but in 2013 that number is around 60 percent. If you had your season tickets before seat donations were enforced, you are not required to pay any extra money for season tickets. If you don't renew your seats, a new season-ticket holder can purchase them with an annual seat donation tied to them. A season-ticket holder can also choose to transfer them to a family member, but a seat donation fee of half of what the general public pays would still be tied to them. The lowest donation level recommended by NU is $150 per seat, but $500 to $750 per seat will increase your chances to get Husker season tickets.

When new athletic director Shawn Eichorst took over in January of 2013, Meyers said he was "blown away" with the overall financial stability of the Nebraska athletic department. "We are extremely blessed," Meyers said. "It really comes down to the responsibility of your leadership for the dollars that come in here for any reason—whether it's for tickets, a donation, or a hot dog purchase. Our responsibility is to treat it like it were our own, and you don't spend it frivolously and you don't buy things that you can't afford. You plan and you plan ahead. You try and invest in the areas where you think you are going to make the greatest impact.

"We could put stone all over the outside of the stadium and gold railings in if we wanted to, but we choose not to because it's not the Nebraska way. I think we treat, and all of our leaders treat the budget, the revenues, and the daily activities in a way that Nebraskans would expect us to."

86 Rex Burkhead

From 2010 to 2012, it was hard to go to any apparel store in Nebraska and not see the shelves stocked with No. 22 Rex Burkhead jerseys. For many young boys across the state, the 5'11", 210-pound Burkhead served as an inspiration. He was a poster child of hard work on the field, but it was the manner and class with which the Plano, Texas, native conducted himself off the field that brought him so much attention.

Statistically, Burkhead finished his career with 3,329 yards rushing despite the fact he missed nearly half the 2009 and most of the 2012 season with injuries. Burkhead was a first team All-Big Ten running back in 2011, but perhaps his biggest career honor was being named the honorary captain of the Allstate AFCA Good Works Team, which recognizes football student-athletes for exemplary community service.

Burkhead led the charge to raise awareness for pediatric brain cancer after meeting then-six-year-old Jack Hoffman of Atkinson, Nebraska, in 2011. Hoffman has undergone several surgeries and treatments to fight his brain tumors, and Burkhead not only has been with him almost every step of the away, but he also helped bring national attention to pediatric brain cancer. Burkhead helped promote "Team Jack," and the organization served as inspiration to the entire Husker football team. By the end of the 2011 season, Burkhead and several other Husker players wore Team Jack red bracelets to show their support for Hoffman.

A Team Jack T-shirt campaign was also launched to raise money for pediatric brain cancer research. Led by Burkhead's efforts, more than 14,000 Team Jack T-shirts were sold initially, and a check of $275,000 was presented to pediatric brain cancer

Known for his good deeds off the field, running back Rex Burkhead poses with Jack Hoffman, a child fighting brain cancer, in front of the White House.

researchers at the Dana-Farber Cancer Institute in Boston. Led by Burkhead the Nebraska Uplifting Athletes Chapter donated $100,000 toward the total contribution presented by Team Jack. "Nebraska should be very proud of what it accomplished today in the fight against pediatric brain cancer," Andy Hoffman, the father of Jack Hoffman, told KOLN-TV of Lincoln. "Cornhusker fans showed this past fall that when they get behind a team, they get behind a team. Their unending loyalty to the cause [and] campaign of pediatric brain cancer has put the disease in a position to be further researched by one of the most accomplished cancer research centers in the world. We have never been more proud than today to be from Nebraska."

During the 2012 Wisconsin game, Hoffman and six-year-old Isaiah Casillas of McCook, Nebraska, led the Huskers through the Tunnel Walk. It was a special moment that brought tears to the eyes of many as Burkhead and wide receiver Kenny Bell lifted up the two young boys to touch the horseshoe on their way out of the tunnel for arguably the biggest home game of the season. Casillas, who also had pediatric brain cancer, passed away just two months later.

At Nebraska's 2013 Red-White spring game, NU came up with the idea to insert Hoffman into the game for one play. Wearing a red No. 22 jersey and Husker helmet, Hoffman raced for a 69-yard touchdown as quarterback Taylor Martinez handed him the football, and 60,000 people in Memorial Stadium went crazy. The story and video of it went viral. A YouTube clip drew more than 8 million hits and was featured on several national news shows, including ABC's *Good Morning America*. The touchdown run won the 2013 ESPY award for best moments in sports, and President Obama even welcomed Hoffman to the White House during late April. The president gave him a football with a personal note during a 15-minute meeting where Obama discussed Jack's run and cancer research efforts.

It's something Burkhead helped spearhead, and moments like this are why the player, drafted in the sixth round of the 2013 NFL Draft by the Cincinnati Bengals, will be forever remembered by Husker fans. The unfortunate thing for Burkhead is that he never got to play a full senior season and help Nebraska capture a conference championship.

Even though Burkhead left his senior season empty-handed, his accomplishments outside of football are far greater than anything he could've accomplished solely as a player. "It's been an unbeliev-able experience," Burkhead said of his career, following Nebraska's loss in the 2013 Capital One Bowl. "I'm going to miss the senior class especially and the coaches and everyone associated with the football program. All the opportunities I've had on and off the field at the university have been unbelievable. If I had gone to another place, I probably wouldn't have experienced it. Just from the players to the staff, everything was top notch. I'm really going to miss them and I love them all."

87 Enjoy the Big Red Breakfast

Since the early 1970s, Nebraska fans have gathered on Friday mornings in Omaha for the Big Red Breakfast. It's a tradition you won't find at any other school. Still to this day, 200 to 400 Husker fans gather at 7 AM to listen to either the head coach or an assistant coach preview the next day's game with a film breakdown and an in-depth Q&A session. Individual tickets for the event are $30, and it is something that all the major media outlets in the state cover each week.

The event itself started at Johnny's Café in South Omaha on 27th and L Street with former head coach Bob Devaney. The Big Red Breakfast eventually moved to the Holiday Inn on 72nd and Grover in 1985. The event is still at the same location, but the Holiday Inn is now the Ramada Plaza Hotel and Convention Center. From 1985 to 2010, Omaha attorney and longtime program booster Dean Kratz ran and organized the Big Red Breakfast.

The Big Red Breakfast was started by Omaha businessman Lee Roberts, who held the event at Johnny's Café with Devaney and

Tom Osborne. Johnny's hosted the breakfast all the way through the 1984 season. But after Osborne had double bypass heart surgery in 1985, he told Roberts he could no longer do the breakfast. At that time Kratz said they filled a room at Johnny's with around 70 to 80 people each week. "Osborne came every Friday, and it was a good show," Kratz recalls of the early Big Red Breakfasts.

It was Kratz who approached Osborne in 1985 with a solution to continue the Big Red Breakfast. "When Osborne had his heart surgery, he told Roberts he couldn't do it anymore," Kratz said. "Well, Roberts and his committee said, 'Then we aren't going to do it, and there would no longer be a Big Red Breakfast.' Me and another guy got in the car one day, and we met with Osborne and told him we'd be glad to sponsor and carry on the Big Red Breakfast if he'd come once in a while. His deal was he'd come three times a year, and the other times, the assistant would come. We set it up, and that's the way it worked. Osborne came to the first one and the last one and one in between. The other times we had assistants."

Kratz said for the 25 years he ran the Big Red Breakfast either Osborne or the assistant coach speaking received a check for $1,000. In those days a $1,000 check to speak on a Friday morning for an hour was very good money. "That money helped pay the bills," longtime defensive coordinator Charlie McBride said. "You have to remember. Even in my final few seasons, my base pay wasn't even six figures yet, so back then events like that really helped the coaches out."

In the peak years of the Big Red Breakfast, Kratz said the event drew a solid 600 to 700 people each week during the national championship run in the 1990s. "You kind of got confidential information at that time," Kratz said. "You didn't have to worry about social media or anything back then."

The Bugeaters Booster Club that meets at the Champions Run Golf Club in West Omaha would also take advantage of the opportunity to get an assistant coach each week. The Bugeaters brought the Big Red Breakfast coach in on Thursday night to talk with smaller VIP group of people, and then the coach typically stayed at the hotel on 72nd and Grover to speak at the breakfast on Friday morning. "The coach would come over and stay, make the speech at the breakfast, and go home. We would pay them $1,000, and the Bugeaters would pay them $1,300," Kratz said. "It was a good deal for them. We always paid them $1,000. We gave them a check when they came in and my nephew, Paul Kratz, would wait for them, and when they'd come in, he'd hand them a check for $1,000. In those days that was a big deal. It was a lot of money, but we could afford it. It was really a break-even deal for us, but that's what we wanted to do."

In 2011 the Bo Pelini Foundation took over the Big Red Breakfast when Kratz and his board gave it up. They held the event at the Embassy Suites in La Vista, along with the original 72nd and Grover location. The Pelini Foundation only ran the event for one year, but 1110 KFAB radio stepped in to make sure the Big Red Breakfast would continue its almost 45-year history of hosting an NU coach each Friday morning before the game.

Former Husker radio color analyst Gary Sadlemyer was instrumental in making sure the event stayed alive. The Big Red Breakfast now pays the coach $1,200 each Friday morning, and the head coach only appears at the breakfast at the start of the season. The other nine assistant coaches and graduate assistants rotate to speak at the other 12 breakfasts. "One of the things we love most about college football is its embrace of tradition, and one of the best of those in Nebraska is the Big Red Breakfast," Sadlemyer said. "We were so glad to be able to keep this iconic Omaha event alive."

If you are coming into town for a game, the Big Red Breakfast on Friday mornings is the perfect way to kick off your Husker weekend. KFAB sells individual tickets on both its website and at its station headquarters on 50th and Underwood.

88 The Kick

Alex Henery stood at the press conference podium in his black Omaha Burke High School T-shirt, looking more like a kid you'd see hanging out at the mall than the day's Nebraska football hero. But there he was—the sophomore kicker who rewrote the school record books with a 57-yard game-winning field goal that eventually led the Huskers to a 40–31 win against Colorado on Black Friday of 2008 in Memorial Stadium.

With 1:43 left in the game and Nebraska facing a fourth-and-25 from CU's 40-yard line, head coach Bo Pelini decided to entrust Henery with the outcome of the game instead of opting for a Hail Mary pass to get a first down or touchdown. On second down, quarterback Joe Ganz took a costly sack that forced the Huskers into the difficult situation they faced.

Under more pressure than he's ever been in his entire career, Henery drilled the kick perfectly, sending it through the uprights with room to spare to put the Huskers up 33–31. An interception return by defensive tackle Ndamukong Suh then put the game out of reach at 40–31 and gave NU a much-needed victory.

The kick not only was the longest ever by an NU kicker, it also gave the Huskers their eighth win of the regular season and paved the way for a Gator Bowl invite on New Year's Day to play Clemson. Henery's kick was the signature moment of Pelini's first season at Nebraska. "I hadn't been hitting it that far in pregame," Henery said. "We have our distances set, and I didn't hit one [from that far] in pregame, so it was weighing the yardage and whatnot… It took forever—first off because of the TV timeout. It seemed like a year. Going up there all I remember is hitting the ball. I don't remember much after that. [T.J. O'Leary] had a great snap, [Jake

Wesch] had a great hold. They get a lot of the credit, too. I don't remember watching it go through at all. I was pretty sure I made it. I hit the ball really well."

Pelini said he wanted to gauge Henery's confidence in making the kick before sending him out to try it, but Henery was generally one of the more reserved personalities on the team. Pelini sent him out anyway. Judging from the result, it was obviously the right decision. "I just wanted him to look me in the face and tell me he felt he had it in him," Pelini said. "He kind of looked at it. Normally his range is around 52 [yards]. He looked at me and said, 'I made it in warm-ups. I've been hitting it good.' And I said, 'Alright, let's go.' He cleared it pretty good. Obviously he hit it well. It doesn't surprise me. The guy's a stud. He's been doing it since he got here. He's just made kick after kick, and I'm glad he's on our team.'"

Henery's kick also assured Nebraska's 21 seniors a happy ending on Senior Day as the Colorado game marked their final moment in Memorial Stadium as Huskers. "I've been saying it all year, man. Alex Henery is my favorite person on this football team," senior wide receiver Todd Peterson said. "It was so funny. Coach Pelini, we were there at like fourth-and-25, and he was like, 'Can you hit it? Can you hit it?' And Alex is like, 'Well, I've been hitting it pretty good today, Coach.' Coach Pelini got a kick out of that after the game. But that's big time for him to hit that in crunch time on Senior Day for all of us."

Peterson said the way the Huskers pulled out the victory in their final regular-season contest was only fitting considering the way the season has gone this year. After taking some hits early and falling behind 14–0 in the first quarter, Nebraska was able to fight its way back and end on a high note.

Oddly enough, the same can be said about the way the whole season went. The 2008 Huskers would go on to finish the year with a 9–4 record after starting off the year at 3–3 with three straight losses to Virginia Tech, Missouri, and Texas Tech. The Huskers would go on to win six out of their final seven games in 2008 with their only loss coming to Oklahoma, who played for the national championship that season against Florida. "It's very memorable," Peterson said. "It's a lot more memorable than it needed to be, but it's great. It's kind of a metaphor for our whole year. We've been punched in the mouth a couple times and we had to come back kicking and fighting. Things haven't always gone our way, but we found a way to get it done."

89 Visit Misty's on Friday Nights, the Sidetrack Band, and Barry's

If you are in Lincoln on a Husker gameday weekend, there are three things you must do to get the full experience.

No. 1: Eat a prime rib dinner at Misty's in Havelock on Friday with the pep band and cheerleaders.
Each Friday night in the fall, the Nebraska pep band and cheerleaders make their way to the three Misty's restaurants in Lincoln, but the original Havelock location serves as a Husker museum with loads of memorabilia and history throughout the restaurant.

Misty's in Havelock was opened by Bob and Grace Milton in 1963 and earned an early reputation by being strong supporters of the football program. The Miltons provided employment to several Husker football players over the years. The players greeted and served guests at the restaurant, helping brand Misty's into what it is today.

Former head coach Bob Devaney was also a frequent visitor to Misty's and even has his own steak on the menu named the

Former coach Bob Devaney, pictured with halfback Mick Ziegler during 1968, has a steak dish named after him at Misty's restaurant.

"S.O.B. Sirloin," which doesn't mean what you think. The initials stand for "Sweet Old Bob's" Sirloin.

On Friday night's before football games, Devaney would often eat at Misty's and visit with media members in town covering the game. Former Oklahoma head coach Barry Switzer was also known to be a regular guest at Misty's on the night before games in Lincoln.

No. 2: Head down to the Single Barrel Bar and listen to Joyce and the world-famous Sidetrack Band.

I can promise you the Sidetrack Band is something you only will find in Nebraska. Each Friday and Saturday, they play at the Single Barrel on 10th Street. They used to play at the Sidetrack Bar on O

Street, but they were forced to switch locations after a fire burned down their building. Led by lead singer Joyce Durand and sidekick Paul Newton, the Sidetrack Band has been around for nearly 40 years.

The band began playing in the Haymarket in 1977 and is known for its raunchy, Husker-related parodies and cover songs. Each week Durand and Newton come up with new lyrics that feature Nebraska's upcoming opponent or different lyrics about current Husker players and coaches. They will even take their show on the road and play at away sites and conference championship games.

No. 3: Stop at Barry's—the original Husker bar—and have a beer to end your night.

Barry's dates back to 1959 and is located on 235 North 9th Street in the heart of downtown. It is the biggest Husker bar in Lincoln, featuring multiple rooms and a rooftop bar that was just opened in 2012.

New owners purchased Barry's from a group that owned the bar since 1988. The slogan on Barry's website says it all: "Our mission is to provide a friendly environment where our customers can go to relax, watch games on our state-of-the-art AV system, have a great meal, a cold beer, and debate whether Johnny Rodgers or Mike Rozier was the greatest Husker of all time."

90 Star Gazing for Recruits

Some might call Nebraska fans' obsession with recruiting and five-star rankings an unhealthy obsession. You won't find very many schools that follow recruiting like Husker fans. The obsession with recruiting seemed to really take off after the hiring of head coach Bill Callahan in January of 2004.

Callahan made it an emphasis to recruit high-profile players and he made it known during his hiring that the Huskers would only go after the best. Callahan wanted Nebraska fans to follow the recruiting and know who the big-time players were. Having served as Tom Osborne's recruiting coordinator in the 1990s, athletic director Steve Pederson also made it a major point of emphasis.

Recruiting websites like HuskerOnline.com, which is part of the Rivals.com network, began to explode. For a short while in 2006, HuskerOnline.com was actually the biggest website in the Rivals.com network—in large part due to Callahan's ability to keep Nebraska fans intrigued with his year-round recruiting efforts.

The Cornhusker Breakfast Club was responsible for lining up the annual recruiting dinner each year. Event organizer Dean Kratz said before Callahan there just wasn't the interest in the recruiting dinner like there is now. Kratz joked that he and fellow Omaha attorney Bob Knowles may have been the only Husker fans who followed recruiting before online websites like HuskerOnline. com took off. "It started out as 50 or 60 people, and we couldn't get the head coach," Kratz said of the early recruiting dinners. "I remember one year we got [assistant coach] Ron Brown and I can even remember one year we brought in [recruiting analyst] Max Emfinger. We always had it at the Holiday Inn on 72nd and Grover, and it started out as 50 or 60 people. In those days there wasn't that much interest in recruiting.

"It's so much different than it is now. Back then people didn't care. They didn't know or understand, and you didn't have all these ratings. I remember I used to scramble around to figure out who each recruit was, and you'd measure him by who else was recruiting him. Nebraska used to put out a sheet of paper with who was recruiting that guy, but it wasn't really reliable."

When Callahan took over in 2004, the Husker recruiting dinner exploded. Celebrity Husker fan Supreme Court Justice Clarence Thomas even made it a point to attend one of Callahan's recruiting dinners. "The first year Callahan was here, it was a snowstorm. I mean it was a blizzard," Kratz said. "Callahan was in Lincoln and said, 'Well, they won't have this,' and somebody said, 'Yeah, they will.' I remember that night so well. There had to be 600 or 700 people in there, and they were hanging from the rafters, and it was a blizzard outside. I remember so well Callahan sitting there and I just watched him, and he just kept shaking his head. Then in 2005 we had 1,200 people, and [Callahan] was so absolutely amazed with the Nebraska fans that he decided that he had to do something about this and he decided to give me a plaque. I've got a plaque, and it's in appreciation from Bill Callahan and the staff for service to the football program. There were 1,200 people there at that event. It was just jammed."

Kratz said the Omaha Recruiting Dinner drew crowds of more than 1,000 people in 2005, 2006, and 2007. Tickets for the dinner were $55 during those years, and all the proceeds would go directly to the coaches after expenses were paid.

During the dinner the head coach typically addresses the crowd about the recruiting class before the assistant coaches do a film breakdown of each position. Now the event is put on by the Husker Athletic Fund and still draws around 500 people, but that's nowhere near the crowds it drew in the peak years from 2004 to 2007. On the night after signing day, there is also a Lincoln Recruiting Dinner at the downtown Embassy Suites. Other schools around the country hold booster club events like Nebraska does for recruiting, but nothing comes close to what you'll find in Omaha.

91 The Big Red Invades Notre Dame

From 1949 to 2000, Nebraska and Notre Dame only played one time. Before that NU and ND met on an annual basis for 11 straight years from 1915 to 1925 and also played in 1947 and 1948 along with the 1973 Orange Bowl. When the two historic programs agreed to play a home-and-home series in 2000 and 2001, NU's trip to South Bend in 2000 was arguably the most anticipated road game in school history.

Husker fans from Nebraska and all over the country wanted to be in South Bend, Indiana, that Saturday afternoon to watch their team run out of the historic Notre Dame tunnel. The university received 28,000 requests through the ticket office for the school's 4,000-seat ticket allotment. In comparison NU received around 20,000 ticket requests for the Huskers' first Big Ten game at Wisconsin in 2011 for its allotted 3,000 seats.

Notre Dame head coach Bob Davie was worried going into the game of the possible Big Red takeover in South Bend and even warned fans not to sell their tickets. Apparently they didn't listen as the *Omaha World-Herald* estimated 25,000 Nebraska fans made up the crowd of 80,232 that day in Notre Dame Stadium.

Like troops marching into a foreign country, Husker fans took over South Bend that weekend and made it their own. To this day you can still find countless stadium pictures of the Sea of Red in Notre Dame Stadium on September 9, 2000. The late Leon Hart, who won the 1949 Heisman Trophy at Notre Dame, sat next to me in the press box that afternoon. Hart said in all his years associated with Notre Dame football he had never seen anybody come into Notre Dame Stadium and take over like that. Veteran

Huskers Fans Cause the Other NU to Use a "Silent Count"

Nebraska's 2012 visit to Northwestern in Evanston, Illinois, had a similar feel to the 2000 Notre Dame game in South Bend. An estimated 25,000 Husker fans made their way into Ryan Field, making up over half of the 47,330 in attendance.

The large Husker following made their way to Chicago that weekend despite bad losses earlier in the season at UCLA and Ohio State. For over three quarters, it appeared Nebraska was about to suffer another disappointing loss, but the 25,000 fans in attendance kept Nebraska on life support, willing the Huskers to a 29–28 victory.

The 25,000 fans in attendance were so impactful that they forced Northwestern to move to a silent snap count on offense in the fourth quarter, which is unheard of when playing at home. Wildcats head coach Pat Fitzgerald said his team didn't even practice its silent snap count that week leading up to the game.

sportswriter Dick Weiss of the *New York Daily News* wrote that scalpers were getting "upwards of $500 a ticket."

Several national writers were in town to watch the No. 1 Huskers take on the No. 23 Fighting Irish. They were as blown away as Weiss and Hart. "The last time there were more outsiders at Notre Dame was the first day of freshman orientation," wrote CBS SportsLine.com's Dennis Dodd. "There were estimates that 20,000–30,000 Nebraska fans had wedged their way into the 80,000-seat stadium despite the school getting only 4,000 tickets from Notre Dame."

NU quarterback Eric Crouch, who scored the game's winning touchdown in overtime, had his own take. Crouch finished that game with 183 yards of total offense as the Huskers won ugly 27–24. "It looked like they stole tickets or beat people up outside to get in," Crouch told reporters after the game. "There was way more people than I anticipated being here."

The timing of the trip was perfect as NU was in its glory years, winning three national championships in a four-year period and picked to win another that season before losing to eventual national champion Oklahoma in Norman, Oklahoma. Nebraska fans have proven they will travel anywhere, and no matter what, they'll figure out a way to get in—even if that means paying top dollar. "This will be remembered as the Saturday when the only green that mattered to many Notre Dame ticket holders was the color of money," wrote Skip Bayless in the *Chicago Tribune*. "On Sept. 9, 2000, a priceless tradition finally had a price—up to 500 bucks a ticket."

92 Harvey Perlman and the Move to the Big Ten

When Harvey Perlman was named Nebraska's chancellor on April 1, 2001, little did the York, Nebraska, native know the impact he'd have on NU athletics. Under Perlman's watch at Nebraska, he's been involved with the hiring of three different athletic directors—Steve Pederson (2003 to 2007), Tom Osborne (2007 to 2012), and Shawn Eichorst (2013 to present). Perlman has also been involved in the firings of Pederson (2007) and football coaches Frank Solich (2003) and Bill Callahan (2007) along with the hiring of Callahan (2004) and Bo Pelini (2007).

In most cases it would be hard for any Chancellor to top this, but what Perlman did in 2010 arguably changed the landscape of college athletics as we know it. During a January meeting in 2010 at the NCAA's annual convention in Atlanta, Perlman was tipped off that the conference realignment carousel was about to turn and he figured Nebraska better get its ducks in a row otherwise it might be left in the cold. Perlman told the *Omaha World-Herald* he remembers firing off an email to Big Ten commissioner Jim

Delany that day just to put a feeler out there. Delany was also in Atlanta, and the two talked briefly during the convention. "I don't know what you guys are thinking," Perlman said. "But if you think about looking west, Nebraska would be interested in at least having a conversation with you."

Delany plays an excellent poker face and didn't really give Perlman an indication either way what he was thinking in regards to the future of the Big Ten, but after that e-mail, he at least knew there was some interest from Nebraska. Fast forward five months later to May, and Perlman and Osborne conducted a secret meeting with Delany at a location that still hasn't been revealed to this day. Conference realignment talk was everywhere by this time, and Nebraska, Missouri, Notre Dame, and Rutgers were all rumored to possibly be joining the Big Ten.

The meeting with Delany was Osborne and Perlman's chance to show him that Nebraska was a perfect fit for the Big Ten. This was their one and only shot, and like an experienced football coach in the living room of a recruit, the pair delivered. Instead of coming into the meeting with a bunch of bells and whistles, Perlman and Osborne came at Delany with facts. They demonstrated why Nebraska would be a great fit for the Big Ten, and Perlman told the *World-Herald* they showed Delany, "We try to do things the right way." They talked about the Academic All-American tradition and other great things outside of sports that make NU a good fit for the Big Ten.

Delany was sold, but he didn't give Osborne and Perlman any idea where they stood that day. The following week things got awkward in Kansas City at the Big 12's spring meetings. Rumors of Nebraska and Missouri going to the Big Ten were widespread. Missouri's governor was openly campaigning to join the Big Ten. Perlman and Osborne took a different approach, denying all reports. There was also talk of Texas, Texas A&M, Oklahoma, Oklahoma State, Texas Tech, and Colorado leaving the Big 12 and forming a Pac-16—merging six Big 12 and 10 Pac-10 schools into one mega-conference.

The normally boring spring meetings in Kansas City turned into a media circus. There was smoke all over the room, and it was only a matter of time before there was fire. Big 12 commissioner Dan Beebe wanted answers particularly from Nebraska and Missouri. Beebe wanted a commitment from the Big Red to the Big 12 and he basically gave NU one week to let him know its future.

With the future of the Big 12 in major doubt, Perlman had to move and he had to move fast. While driving back from Kansas City on I-29 on Friday night, Perlman placed a phone call to Delany. "This is not an ultimatum to you, but in fairness, this is what the situation is," Perlman told the *World-Herald* in August of 2010 when recalling that phone conversation. "If I don't have something definitive from the Big Ten, I'll have to commit to the Big 12."

It was a tough call for Perlman to make to one of the most powerful men in college athletics, but it was a call that had to be made. The Big 12 put the screws on Perlman, and he had no choice but to contact Delany. Later on Delany would say he completely understood why Perlman made that phone call and had no problem with how he did it—mainly because of the position Beebe had put Nebraska in.

In a perfect world, this process would've taken months to complete, but Delany and the Big Ten had to make a decision in a week. Along the way Nebraska received assists from then-Penn State and former Nebraska president Graham Spanier and Wisconsin athletic director and former Husker football player Barry Alvarez. The two were instrumental in helping NU forge a relationship with Delany and the Big Ten behind the scenes.

Just seven days after the phone call Perlman placed to Delany around Mound City, Missouri, Nebraska was officially part of the Big Ten. Delany flew to Lincoln and announced the news at a press conference that Friday afternoon. "The most important reason, in our reasoning, is this will bring Nebraska stability the Big 12 will not offer," Perlman said of NU's decision to join the Big Ten. "Our obligation was to protect Nebraska from the vulnerability of not being in a conference altogether."

Many detractors of the move were pointing the finger at Nebraska for possibly breaking apart the Big 12. However, Perlman pointed out that talks of other Big 12 schools leaving the conference forced Nebraska to look out for its own best interests. "One school leaving a conference does not destroy a conference," Perlman said. "Nebraska did not start this discussion. After the Big Ten announced it planned to consider expansion, we saw reports that Missouri would want to go to the Big Ten, including a statement by their governor, a member of board of curators, and chancellor—comments that weren't clearly supportive of the Big 12."

Just days before NU left for the Big Ten, Colorado announced plans to join the Pac-10, which became the Pac-12. The following year both Missouri and Texas A&M would leave the Big 12 to join the SEC. The Big 12 replaced its four lost members with West Virginia and TCU.

As the Big 12 looked like a shell of its former self in 2012, Perlman's foresight to reach out to Delany will go down as one of the biggest decisions in Nebraska's history. Perlman will forever be known as the man who led the charge to get Nebraska in the Big Ten.

93 One Last Time: Nebraska vs. Oklahoma

The 2010 Big 12 Championship Game in Arlington, Texas, was emotional on multiple levels. No. 1, it was Nebraska's final game in the Big 12 as the Big Red would officially join the Big Ten in 2011. No. 2, it was the final time Nebraska and Oklahoma would ever meet as conference foes. Going into that 2010 title game, the two schools had met 85 times with OU holding a 44–38–3 advantage against the Huskers.

What also made this game special was instead of Switzer vs. Osborne, you had another great coaching story line between the two programs. Nebraska head coach Bo Pelini and Oklahoma head Bob Stoops grew up together in Youngstown, Ohio, and both attended Cardinal Mooney High. Pelini is younger than Stoops, but growing up he played on the same high school football and basketball teams with Stoops' younger brother Mark (now the head coach of Kentucky). Stoops' father, Ron, was also one of Pelini's high school football coaches. Another connection between the two staffs was that both Nebraska assistant coaches, Carl Pelini and Tim Beck, also attended Cardinal Mooney.

For many people close to the Stoops and Pelini families, it was hard to pick a side to cheer for in the 2010 Big 12 Championship Game. "[The people in Youngstown] are probably hoping it's a tie, but I don't think that's going to happen," Pelini said in his pregame press conference. "You know, we obviously share a lot of mutual friends. I don't know. I'm glad I'm not there to watch it because I don't think there is going to be anybody fighting over the whole thing. I can tell you that much. It's interesting you asked that because I think Bob said it earlier in the week—the best thing about when we played against each other [is] you know that one of us is going to walk away with the Big 12 championship. That's a good thing."

The previous season Pelini took the bragging rights back to Youngstown with a 10–3 win against Oklahoma and a 33–0 win against Arizona in the 2009 Holiday Bowl. (The Wildcats were then coached by Bob's younger brother, Mike Stoops.)

Bob Stoops is not typically one to acknowledge the historical significance of a particular matchup, but even he knew the 2010

Big 12 title game was special. "It's kind of ironic to be involved in the OU-Nebraska game, one of the last times that we're playing here for a championship. As I said to him—as my brother Ron [Stoops] and another great friend, Jerry that are here are also close with Bo—I said it's not bad for a couple of poor kids from the south side," Bob Stoops said. "Here we are playing for the Big 12 championship with Oklahoma and Nebraska. So anyway, it's really pretty neat. The good part of it when you're in a game like this is one of you has to win. So one of you is going to have a championship."

Nebraska would race out to a 17–0 lead in the first half, but the Sooners amassed 17 consecutive points of their own to tie things up at 17–17 before Alex Henery hit a 42-yard field goal to put Nebraska up 20–17 at halftime. The Sooners defense would finally settle in during the second half, holding the Huskers scoreless for the final two quarters. OU outscored Nebraska 23–3 over the game's final 42 minutes, giving Bob Stoops his seventh Big 12 championship since 2000.

94 The Crazy Comebacks of 2012

There was a point during the 2012 season where you stopped trying to figure out Nebraska and its crazy comebacks. During the 2012 season, the Huskers found ways to come back four times from double-digit second-half deficits to finish Big Ten conference play with a 7–1 record. It was the first time the Huskers had won seven conference games since the 2001 season.

The string of comebacks all started in NU's Big Ten conference opener against Wisconsin when the Badgers jumped out to a

27–10 third-quarter lead, but Nebraska would answer by scoring the next 20 points to win 30–27. The following week the Huskers raced out to a 17–7 lead in the second quarter at Ohio State, but things would fall apart, and the Buckeyes would win 63–38 and rush for 371 yards in a game fueled by the play of quarterback Braxton Miller. It was after this loss that head coach Bo Pelini said during his postgame press conference that his team would have to "win out" its final six games if it wanted to make it to Indianapolis for the Big Ten championship game.

When a coach makes a statement like this, you never know how it's going to be received, and following a bye week, the Huskers traveled to Northwestern where for three quarters they played some of their sloppiest football of the season. Down 28–16 with 8:16 in the fourth quarter, junior Nebraska quarterback Taylor Martinez would engineer two perfect drives in the hurry-up offense to pull out a 29–28 come-from-behind victory, tying the largest fourth-quarter comeback in school history.

Two weeks later at Michigan State, the Huskers found themselves down 24–14 with 14:20 left in the fourth quarter. Once again Martinez would engineer another fourth-quarter comeback capped off by a touchdown pass to Jamal Turner with six seconds left to give the Huskers a 28–24 victory. "In the last couple of weeks, I feel like I've aged about 20 years," Pelini said.

With just three games down and three to go, the Huskers were halfway home to winning out. Every championship season has its fair share of breaks or moments like this, but 2012 was different. "The teams that I have been on that have been able to make that run, you have to find a way to win a couple of these games," defensive coordinator John Papuchis said. "This is two games where we've gone on the road, which in the Big Ten we're finding out is not an easy thing to do. They're all fistfights. We find a way to win the game. Statistics and all that stuff—you can throw out the window. Find a way to have more points than the other team and at the end of the day stay on track to what you want to get done. I think today is another great example of that."

The next week Penn State came to Lincoln, and the Huskers found themselves in a familiar position—down 20–6 at halftime, but it very easily could've been 28–6. The Huskers would once again find another way to come back from a double-digit deficit to win the game 32–23. It was NU's fourth double-digit, second-half comeback in six games and the Huskers' third of 12 points or more. Prior to the 2012 season, the Big Red had only made six second-half comebacks of 12 points or more in school history. "I'm going to call the Big Ten conference, and we are going to spot them 14 and we are good to go," Pelini joked after the Penn State game. "I love the kids on this team and the approach and the want-to and just how they respond. There's never a sense of panic with these guys. They believe in each other and they believe in what we are doing, and that at least gives you a chance."

The 2012 Huskers never got that conference championship, though, for Pelini, coming up short against Wisconsin in the Big Ten title game. However, they did become the first team to go undefeated at home since 2001, which was also the last time NU finished conference play with 7–1 record. The 2012 Huskers also were the first NU team to finish the regular season on a six-game winning streak since 1999, the last time the Huskers won a conference title.

The Fish Bowl: 24–7 Media Coverage

If an outsider who knew nothing about Nebraska football were to visit a normal Monday or Tuesday after practice in the fall, he or she might think a major news story was breaking. On any normal day during the season, around 25 to 30 media members show up to cover Nebraska football's post-practice session. A herd of 10 or more television cameras often surround the front of head coach Bo Pelini while another 10 or 15 reporters flank around the sides to listen in on his remarks.

This is the norm for Nebraska media relations director Keith Mann and his staff. Over the last five to 10 years, he's seen the amount of media that covers Husker football on a daily basis double with the addition of more websites and online videographers who now cover the day-to-day beat.

A typical practice at Nebraska is covered by five writers and a videographer from the *Omaha World-Herald*, three writers and a videographer from the *Lincoln Journal Star*, three writers and a videographer from HuskerOnline.com, three writers from Husker Illustrated, two writers from Big Red Report, and seven different television station cameras to go along with a handful of radio reporters and other website publications. Ten years ago you might get 10 media members covering practice on that same day. The demand for 24–7 Husker news has made Nebraska football one of the most heavily covered college football teams in the country.

Mann said it really shows in the amount of journalists who travel to cover the Huskers on the road. The *World-Herald, Journal Star*, and *Grand Island Independent* all send multiple people on the road as do the three major online publications. On top of that, the Nebraska media contingent will send at least six TV stations to road games, which nobody in the Big Ten or Big 12 even comes close to. "Our TVs travel more than anyone, and the *World-Herald* travels more than anyone we've ever had come in here," Mann said. "Maybe the *Columbus* [Ohio] *Dispatch* or somebody like that would travel that many, but the *World-Herald* travels more for road games than anybody."

ESPN *College GameDay* Appearances in Lincoln

ESPN's *College GameDay* is widely regarded as the pinnacle of college football media coverage. *GameDay* began traveling to college campuses in 1993, and the show has been involved with Nebraska games 16 times, including six stops to Memorial Stadium.

Overall the Huskers are 5–1 at Memorial Stadium and 9–7 in games when the *College GameDay* set has been present. Here's a quick rundown of Nebraska's history with *College GameDay* in Lincoln.

1994—No. 13 UCLA at No. 2 Nebraska **(49–21 Nebraska win)**
1994—No. 2 Colorado at No. 3 Nebraska **(24–7 Nebraska win)**
1998—No. 9 Washington at No. 2 Nebraska **(55–7 Nebraska win)**
2001—No. 17 Notre Dame at No. 5 Nebraska **(27–10 Nebraska win)**
2001—No. 2 Oklahoma at No. 3 Nebraska **(20–10 Nebraska win)**
2007—No. 1 USC at No. 14 Nebraska **(49–31 USC win)**

When the Huskers joined the Big Ten, Mann said he immediately heard about Nebraska's large traveling media entourage. In 2011 and 2012, Big Ten Media Days in Chicago saw record numbers of attendees in large part due to the added Nebraska media contingent. "I know when we joined the Big Ten a lot of the guys in other media relation departments were pretty surprised about the number of media that travels for us," Mann said. "In the Big Ten, the only one that would have similar numbers to us would be Ohio State. In the Big 12, there really wasn't anyone that traveled as much. Texas would probably be the closest and then Oklahoma. Not as many as we do. I know the Big Ten conference's Media Day numbers jumped quite a bit the first two years we've been there."

As for the most heavily requested player for interviews, Mann said in his time at Nebraska nobody has really come close to defensive tackle Ndamukong Suh (2005 to 2009). During the 2009 season, Mann said Suh received interview requests from just about every national media outlet imaginable. "One day I asked [Suh] to do an interview with the *Wall Street Journal,* and he remarked, 'I didn't even know they had a sports section, but that's cool,'" Mann said. "[Suh's] interview requests were by far the most we've ever had in the last decade."

96 The Gotham Bowl

In today's college football world where bowl game invites are handed out like YMCA participation ribbons, playing a postseason game in Yankee Stadium is not out of the spectrum of possibility. In fact Yankee Stadium currently plays host to the Pinstripe Bowl, and the Big Ten has agreed to send one of its teams to that bowl from 2014 to 2021. In 1962, however, playing a bowl game in Yankee Stadium was a very unique situation. After finishing the regular season with an 8–2 record, first-year Nebraska head coach Bob Devaney and his team accepted an invite to play in the Gotham Bowl against Miami (Florida).

The Gotham Bowl only lasted for two seasons with the Huskers playing the Hurricanes in 1962, and Baylor playing Utah State at the New York Polo Grounds in 1961. Event organizers tried to play a 1960 Gotham Bowl, but they failed to find an opponent for Oregon State. Jim Turner, who kicked in the 1961 Gotham Bowl for Utah State, told the Associated Press in 2003 that what he remembers most about the game were some of the strange promotional ideas they had for the two teams. Turner said one featured Utah State players marching through Times Square in their uniforms for an appearance on NBC's *Today* show with host Dave Garroway.

That 1961 game was played in frigid conditions with an announced attendance of 15,123, but as sportswriter Warren

Pack said, "Many of them came disguised as empty seats." The game itself lost $100,000, which led to speculation that the 1962 Gotham Bowl would not happen. The promoters still went on with the game and invited Nebraska and Miami. The Gotham Bowl was also moved to Yankee Stadium, which was reportedly much more luxurious than the Polo Grounds.

Both Nebraska and Miami were given allotments of just 300 tickets, which is far less than the 10,000-plus tickets teams have to sell in today's bowl games. Even with such a low ticket allotment, the Huskers sold only 30 tickets for the Gotham Bowl. NU actually sold 46 tickets to the Orange Bowl that same year, which featured rival Oklahoma taking on Alabama.

The Nebraska team plane for the Gotham Bowl sat on the runaway in Lincoln until officials got confirmation that the $35,000 check to cover the team's expenses had been deposited in their account. Miami also refused to travel to New York until its check cleared. Besides the money there were other problems that set the game back. ABC canceled their television broadcast after problems from the 1961 game. There was also a newspaper strike in New York during the time of the game, which prevented the kind of publicity the Gotham Bowl could've gotten from the local print media.

And, oh yeah, there was the weather. New York City on December 15 is not Miami on January 1. Freezing rain fell on gameday as just 6,166 fans took in the Gotham Bowl. "I really feel bad about getting you guys into this mess today," Devaney told his team before kickoff. "I know it's a terrible day, and this won't be much fun, but it kind of reminds me of the old back-alley fights we used to have when I was a kid in Michigan. There's nobody here to watch, but the toughest son of a bitch is going to win!"

Even with terrible 14-degree conditions, the fans were treated to a great game as the Huskers edged the Hurricanes 36–34. All-American Miami quarterback George Mira still managed to throw for 321 yards, but it wasn't enough to prevent Nebraska from winning its first bowl game in school history.

The 1962 Gotham Bowl is the last time NU has played a game in New York City, but the Huskers did make three appearances in the Kickoff Classic, which was played in East Rutherford, New Jersey, from 1983 to 2002.

97 20 Straight Years in the Super Bowl

Nebraska football has been known for several different significant streaks over the years. NU still holds the NCAA record for consecutive nine-win seasons at 33. The Huskers appeared in an NCAA record 35 straight bowl games from 1969 to 2003. They also still hold an NCAA record for playing in 17 straight January bowl games from 1981 to 1997. Nebraska had a streak of 348 straight weeks of being ranked inside the top 25, another NCAA record. From 1969 to 1989, NU finished inside the top 15 of the final polls, also an NCAA record.

In 2013 a new Nebraska streak was discovered. For 20 straight years, the Huskers have had at least one player on a Super Bowl roster. Both Notre Dame and Purdue are tied for second with a streak of 14 straight years. Below is a list compiled by Yahoo! Sports' online magazine, ThePostGame, of each of the last 20 Super Bowls and the Nebraska players on the roster for each game.

1994—**Dallas Cowboys vs. Buffalo Bills**—Nate Turner, Bills
1995—**San Diego Chargers vs. San Francisco 49ers**—John
   Parrella, Chargers

Known for his high motor, Grant Wistrom, who would play in three Super Bowls in the NFL, celebrates a 1996 interception return for a touchdown. (Getty Images)

1996—**Cowboys vs. Pittsburgh Steelers**—Brenden Stai and Donta Jones, Steelers

1997—**Green Bay Packers vs. New England Patriots**—Tyrone Williams and Calvin Jones, Packers

1998—**Denver Broncos vs. Packers**—Tony Veland and Neil Smith, Broncos; Williams, Packers

1999—**Broncos vs. Atlanta Falcons**—Smith, Broncos; Michael Booker, Falcons

2000—**St. Louis Rams vs. Tennessee Titans**—Grant Wistrom, Rams; Doug Colman, Titans

2001—**Baltimore Ravens vs. New York Giants**—Christian Peter, Giants

2002—**Patriots vs. Rams**—Wistrom, Rams

2003—**Tampa Bay Buccaneers vs. Oakland Raiders**—Adam Treu, Eric Johnson, and John Parrella, Raiders

2004—**Patriots vs. Carolina Panthers**—Russ Hochstein, Patriots; Mike Minter and Mike Rucker, Patriots

2005—**Patriots vs. Philadelphia Eagles**—Hochstein, Patriots

2006—**Steelers vs. Seattle Seahawks**—Josh Brown and Grant Wistrom, Seahawks

2007—**Indianapolis Colts vs. Chicago Bears**—Mike Brown, Bears

2008—**Giants vs. Patriots**—Hochstein and Le Kevin Smith, Patriots

2009—**Steelers vs. Cardinals**—Ralph Brown, Cardinals

2010—**New Orleans Saints vs. Colts**—Cody Glenn, Colts; Carl Nicks and Scott Shanle, Saints

2011—**Packers vs. Steelers**—Brandon Jackson, Packers

2012—**Giants vs. Patriots**—Prince Amukamara, Giants

2013—**Ravens vs. 49ers**—Sam Koch, Ravens

98 Roy Helu Breaks Single-Game Rushing Mark

When Nebraska left its option-based offense following the 2003 season, Calvin Jones' single-game rushing record of 294 yards seemed untouchable. To put that in perspective, from 2004 to 2012, only one other running back—Marlon Lucky in 2007 vs. Nevada—has ever rushed for more than 200 yards for NU.

When you look at Roy Helu's record-breaking day in 2010 against Missouri, it's hard to even imagine a modern-day Husker back putting up such numbers. Helu went off that day for a school-record 307 yards on 28 carries, lifting Nebraska to a

31–17 victory against the No. 7 Tigers. What made the feat even more impressive was that the week before, Missouri beat No. 3 Oklahoma 36–27 and held the Sooners to just 99 total rushing yards.

It was a record Helu had no idea he was closing in on, but with quarterback Taylor Martinez out for most of the game due to a foot injury, offensive coordinator Shawn Watson rode No. 10 to the finish line. "He did a great job. He was unbelievable," Watson said. "He put the team on his back today…He's stellar, man. I've never had a back—and I've been around some great backs—but I've never had a back do what he did today."

Teammates and fans at Memorial Stadium acknowledged Helu's record-breaking performance. "When the [public address announcer] said, 'Congratulations to Roy Helu Jr.,' that was pretty cool," Helu said. "It was weird. [My teammates] were acting like we won the Super Bowl or something…I didn't hear [the fans] chant my name. I wish I would've heard it. That would've been cool."

Helu's 307-yard performance also passes such greats as Mike Rozier, Ken Clark, Lawrence Phillips, and Ahman Green. Even head coach Bo Pelini, who doesn't get caught up in records or numbers, realized the significance of Helu's performance. "I said to the team, you have 307 yards, you break a school-record for single-game rushing at this place with the tradition around here, it's pretty big," Pelini said. "[Helu] obviously played a heck of a football game."

Highlighting the performance for Helu were touchdown runs of 53, 66, and 73 yards. Helu was always a back who could pop off long runs, and on that day he made Missouri's gambling defense pay big time. The win helped the Huskers clinch the North Division title for the second year in a row under Pelini. Helu finished the 2010 season as a second-team All-Big 12 running back with 1,245 yards and 11 touchdowns to go along with his impressive 6.6 yards-per-carry average.

Helu probably won't go down as one of the top five running backs in school history, but his record-breaking performance against Missouri certainly will be remembered as one of the greatest single-game efforts by a Husker, especially considering the Tigers were ranked inside the top 10.

"He was a warrior for us and he did a great job," Watson said. "He never complained. He played hurt, and for him to have a day like today, nobody deserves it more."

99 Black Friday Football

In 1965 Nebraska played Oklahoma in Lincoln on Thanksgiving Day. It was the first time the Huskers played a regular season game on a non-Saturday in program history. NU won that game 21–9 against the Sooners, and it marked the start of a tradition where Nebraska began playing games on either Thanksgiving or Black Friday.

NU and OU played on Thanksgiving from 1965 to 1967, and then from 1968 to 1970, the game was moved back to a Saturday. In both 1971 and 1972, the Huskers and Sooners played again on Thanksgiving. The first Black Friday game in school history wasn't played until 1973, but then in 1974 and 1975, the game was moved back to Saturday before being played again on Friday in 1976 and 1977. There was no rhyme or reason for the date shifts other than the whims of television programmers.

In 1978 Nebraska ended the season with Missouri because originally it was supposed to play Alabama on the final weekend, but the game was moved so it could be aired on ABC. From 1979 to 1989, NU would only play one game on Black Friday while the rest were against Oklahoma (and Colorado in 1987) on traditional November Saturdays.

It wasn't until 1990 that the Huskers began playing on Black Friday every year, starting with OU from 1990 to 1995—the final years of the Big 8 conference. Because the Sooners and Huskers were not in the same Big 12 division, they no longer played on an annual basis, and the Colorado game took over the Black Friday tradition for the Huskers in 1996. Basically the Big 12 told Nebraska that Colorado had to become their new designated rivalry game, and because Oklahoma was struggling at that time, the Sooners didn't really have much of a leg to stand on. "Colorado decided to declare us a rival, and I never did quite understand it," former head coach and athletic director Tom Osborne said. "We didn't feel it was a rivalry. They did."

The two teams would go on to meet on Black Friday 15 times from 1996 to 2010 with the Huskers holding a decisive 11–4 advantage. Some, however, might say the 62–36 thumping the Buffaloes handed the Huskers in 2001 is something Nebraska has never fully recovered from.

When NU moved over to the Big Ten in 2011, Osborne made a request to league commissioner Jim Delany that the Huskers continue their Black Friday tradition with Iowa being the most logical opponent. The league took Osborne's advice, and the Hawkeyes jumped on board. The league even designated the rivalry as "The Heroes Game," and the two teams play for the Heroes Trophy. This kept Nebraska's Black Friday tradition alive but gave it some Big Ten flavor by designating it a trophy game.

The two teams met during the 2011 and 2012 seasons with Nebraska winning both contests. After a poor student turnout in Iowa City for the 2012 matchup—along with some logistical issues Iowa had never faced before—there was some concern that the series could be moved to a Saturday, ending NU's 23-year run of playing on Black Friday.

The opportunity, however, to have a nationally televised game on Black Friday was something Iowa athletic director Gary Barta and head coach Kirk Ferentz could not pass up. "Our experience with it has been positive," Barta told *The Cedar Rapids Gazette*. "When we went into it, the reason we limited it to two years is because Nebraska has had Friday-after-Thanksgiving games for a long time in their history and we had never done anything like that on our campus. We wanted to make sure that it worked. There's some disadvantages, but overall it's been great. Nebraska and I have talked. [Ferentz is] on board. So it's something that both schools have recommended to the conference that we continue, and we have recommended that we continue it indefinitely."

100 Your Guide of Where to Stay and Eat for Husker Games

As I close *100 Things Nebraska Fans Should Know & Do Before They Die*, no trip to a Husker game would be complete without knowing where to stay and eat in Lincoln. When looking for a place to stay, there are different routes you can go when attending a game. If money is less of a factor, staying at one of the four major downtown hotel properties makes the most sense.

The Embassy Suites is considered the flagship hotel for Husker game weekends as it's a stone's throw away from Memorial Stadium on 1040 P Street. The Embassy Suites offers spacious rooms and an excellent pregame party with live music for every Saturday home game. An average room, however, runs anywhere from $279 to $399 per night on a gameday weekend.

The Cornhusker Marriott is about a 15 to 20-minute walk to Memorial Stadium on 333 South 13th Street. The one cool thing about staying there is that it is also Nebraska's official team hotel, so you will get a glimpse of the players and coaches as they make their final game preparations on Friday and Saturday. The Cornhusker is a very nice property that is walking distance to nearly everything but does not feature the same festive atmosphere as you might find at the Embassy Suites. The chance, however, to get a glimpse of the players and coaches makes it a pretty good trade-off.

The other two downtown properties are the Courtyard Marriott and the Holiday Inn. Both are located in the Haymarket District. The Courtyard is a brand new hotel that was put in with the Pinnacle Bank Arena project in the Haymarket and is located on 808 R Street. The Holiday Inn sits on 141 North 9th Street, and it also sits in a prime location within walking distance to several bars and restaurants.

If you are trying to keep your budget in check, staying near the Lincoln Airport or off the 27th Street interstate exit is a viable option as several hotel properties sit in those two areas. You can also stay in South Lincoln but be prepared for about a 20-minute drive to downtown Lincoln and a fairly expensive cab ride if you choose to go that route.

Another possibility is to stay in Omaha for game weekends. The La Vista exit off Interstate 80 features an Embassy Suites, Courtyard Marriott, and a Hampton Inn, and it is just a short 40-minute drive from Lincoln. There is also a brand new Cabela's right off the exit. The popular outdoors store has its worldwide headquarters in Sidney, Nebraska.

If you are looking for a distinct local restaurant on a game weekend, you can't go wrong with Lazlo's Brewery & Grill in the historic Haymarket District, Misty's for world famous prime rib, The Oven for nationally renowned Indian food, and Dish for classic American cuisine. All four of these options are located near Memorial Stadium and are known as some of the more popular places to eat in Lincoln.

For a great slice of pizza, Isles in Havelock is a spot as is Yia Yia's on O Street. Isles has a throwback feel to it, and many consider it the best pizza in Lincoln. Yia Yia's serves more of a thin-crust, gourmet-style pizza along with 375 different kinds of bottled beer.

Misty's is the most well-known steakhouse in Lincoln, but Venue and The Lodge at Wilderness Ridge are also two of the better places to grab a good cut of meat. If you are looking for great bar food, it's hard to beat the Watering Hole and its famous char-grilled wings. The Watering Hole is located downtown and has recently undergone renovations. It doesn't have quite the same hole-in-the-wall feel as it once did, but you still won't find a better wing joint in Lincoln. The N-Zone, Brewsky's, and Barry's in the Haymarket also offer excellent bar food near Memorial Stadium.

One of the best-kept secrets in town is Phat Jacks BBQ on 244 North 11th Street. Phat Jacks is owned by world championship pit master Matt Burt, who has won multiple awards for his ribs, brisket, and pulled pork. You'll thank me once you try it.

Acknowledgments

This book could not have been completed without the outstanding work and contributions of other writers much before my time covering Nebraska football. A special thanks goes to Husker historian Mike Babcock for the countless feedback he gave me throughout this project.

I also want to thank Randy York of Huskers.com and Steven M. Sipple of the *Lincoln Journal Star* for their advice and feedback as I put together this book.

Thank you to Nebraska media relations director Keith Mann, Boyd Epley, Charlie McBride, Dave Rimington, Milt Tenopir, Matt Hoskinson, Paul Meyers, Supreme Court Justice Clarence Thomas, Don "Fox" Bryant, Joe McMenamin, Ralph Brown, Gary Sadlemyer, Dean Kratz, Tom Ruud, and Scott Downing for each taking some time to talk with me as I completed this project.

I also want to thank my entire staff at Rivals.com and HuskerOnline.com of Robin Washut, Mike Matya, Dan Hoppen, Gregg Peterson, Nate Clouse, and Eric Winter for giving me the flexibility to step away and finish this project.

A thank you is also extended to Jeff Fedotin and Don Gulbrandsen of Triumph Books in Chicago for approaching me about this project and working with me to get it completed.

Thanks to both my parents, Pat Callahan and Micaela Moriarty, along with my sister, Maureen Gregor, for always pushing me in life and making sure I had every opportunity I needed to succeed.

Lastly, I want to thank my loving wife, Lisa, for showing me support and always being there for me. Without her love and support, I could not have finished this project.

I've dedicated this book to all the great teachers and coaches I've had in life at Saints Peter & Paul Grade School and Daniel J. Gross High School in South Omaha who always pushed me to get the most. Often teachers don't get the recognition they deserve, and it was important for me to let them know their value in my life.

Sources

Here is the sourcing for all 100 chapters:

1. Cordes, Henry & Rubek, Nick. "Take a Bow. Husker Backers Switzer Says NU Has the Best Fans." *Omaha World-Herald* 27 September 2009. PopCulture.us "Remembering 1962."

2. "Osborne, Tom." Tom Osborne retirement party. 9 March 2013.
    "Alvarez, Barry." Tom Osborne retirement party. 9 March 2013.
    "Snyder, Bill." Tom Osborne retirement party. 9 March 2013.
    "Switzer, Barry." Tom Osborne retirement party. 9 March 2013.
    "McBride, Charlie." Tom Osborne retirement party. 9 March 2013.

3. Hammel, Paul. "Farewell, Coach Bob Devaney Dies in Lincoln At Age 82 The Life and Times of Bob Devaney." *Omaha World-Herald* 10 May 1997.
    "Ruud, Tom." Personal interview. 22 March 2013.

4. Hoskinson, Matt. "Personal interview." 8 April 2013.

5. Pivovar, Steven. "Glover still remembers fierceness of competition." *Omaha World-Herald* 1 January 2000.
    Tramel, Berry. "Remembering the Game of the Century." *The Oklahoman* 1 November 2008.

6. Barfknecht, Lee. "NU walk-on program succeeds as quantity brings quality, unity." *Omaha World-Herald* 30 August 2009.
    Sherman, Mitch. "Past has Jamrog primed for duty. The former walk-on aims to revitalize the program for NU." *Omaha World-Herald* 17 January 2008.
    Hoskinson, Matt. "Personal interview." 8 April 2013.

7. The best ever? 1971 vs. 1995 Huskers "Best college football teams of all-time." Page 2. ESPN.com 2002.
    "Top 10 College Football teams of All-Time." *Parade* magazine 2002.
    Shatel, Tom. "Knock on '71 doesn't offend." *Omaha World-Herald* 19 December 2006.
    Shatel, Tom. "'95 NU vs. USC? Don't forget '71." *Omaha World-Herald* 1 January 2006.
    Olson, Eric. "Many Say '95 Huskers Greatest Team Ever Who's NU's Best?" *Omaha World-Herald* 4 February 1996.

8. Sipple, Steven. "Making the grade Pelini's top priority." *Lincoln Journal Star* 14 April 2008.

9. "Charlie McBride, Charlie." Personal interview. 15 January 2013.
    Babcock, Mike. "History of the Blackshirts." Huskers.com.

10. "1970 National Champions." Huskers.com 26 June 2009.
    Bryant, Don. *Tales from the Nebraska Sidelines.* 2001.
    Porter, Larry. "1971 ORANGE BOWL Nebraska 17, Louisiana State 12 Recruiting class of '69 makes early mark." *Omaha World-Herald* 25 December 2004
    Hambleton, Ken. "Championship Timeline." *Lincoln Journal Star* 31 December 2010.

11. Barfknecht, Lee. "NU Works Overtime, Finishes Business." *Omaha World-Herald* 4 January 1995.
    Barfknecht, Lee. "An Unbeatable Finish Schlesinger Caps Rally With 2 TDs." *Omaha World-Herald* 2 January 1995.

12. "The Last Hurrah." *Sports Illustrated* 12 January 1998.
    "Huskers give Osborne one last hurrah." *Sporting News* 2 January 1998.
    Hambleton, Ken. "Huskers rumble over Vols." *Lincoln Journal Star* 2 January 1998.

13. "Schmahl, Jeff." Personal interview. 11 January 2013.

14. Barfknecht, Lee. "Presence of Johnny R Gave NU Confidence." *Omaha World-Herald* 19 August 2001.
    Kenney, Colleen. "Rodgers 'Humbled' by Honor Player of the Century." *Omaha World-Herald* 1 January 2000.
    Ash, Tom. "Devaney's Farewell Is Romp Over Irish Johnny R Turns Smiling Irish Eyes to Tears." *Omaha World-Herald* 1 November 1999.

15. Hambleton, Ken. "Nebraska football legend 'Trainwreck' dies." *Lincoln Journal Star* 2 November 1998.
    Rimington, Dave. "Personal interview." 21 January 2013.

16. "Meet Mike Rozier the Heisman Trophy winner." Independent Press Services 6 December 1983.
    Kaipust, Rich. "Door opens for Rozier After being bypassed a year ago, the ex-Husker is voted into the College Football Hall of Fame." *Omaha World-Herald* 17 May 2006.

17. Barfknecht, Lee. "Lasting Imprint Nebraska Fans Won't Forget Tommie Frazier's Final Game The Great Escape: Tommie Frazier's 75-Yard Touchdown Run." *Omaha World-Herald* 4 January 1996.

18. Pivovar, Steven. "Solich Says Husker Unity Intact Coach says rumors swirling after selection of Newcombe to start ahead of Crouch are not ripping apart the team Nebraska Football Opener." *Omaha World-Herald* 31 August 1999.
    Sherman, Mitch. "Crouch Gets Top QB Job Bobby Newcombe, the starter for the first two games, moves to wingback." *Omaha World-Herald* 15 September 1999.

19. Callahan, Sean. "Where are they know: Craig Sundberg." HuskerOnline.com 23 June 2010.
    Shatel, Tom. "'84 Orange Bowl call shoed T.O.'s mettle." *Omaha World-Herald* 28 December 2006.

20. "Epley, Boyd." Personal interview. 26 January 2013.
    "Strength and Conditioning timeline." Huskers.com 28 April 2003.

21. "Epley, Boyd." Personal interview. 26 January 2013.
    "Tenopir, Milt." Personal interview. 22 March 2013.

22. Nebraska media guide

23. "Switzer, Barry." Tom Osborne retirement party. 9 March 2013.

24. Gierhahn, Trenton. "The story of the first black athlete in Nebraska history: George Flippin." Examiner.com 2 February 2009. "'Flippin Project' to honor UNL's first African-American Student Athlete." UNL News Release 9 September 2001.

25. Rimington, Dave. "Personal interview." 21 January 2013.
"Tenopir, Milt." Personal interview. 22 March 2013.
"Boyd Epley." Personal interview. 26 January 2013.

26. "McBride, Charlie." Personal interview. 15 January 2013.
"Brown, Ralph." Personal interview. 19 February 2013.

27. Christopherson, Brian. "How to humble a Bear." Lincoln Journal Star 30 May 2012.
Bryant, Don. Tales from the Nebraska Sidelines. 2001.
Washut, Robin. "NU great Glover says Huskers can rebound with pride." HuskerOnline.com 27 December 2012.

28. Bryant, Don. Tales from the Nebraska Sidelines." 2001
"Nebraska Athletics to honor Bob Brown." Huskers. com 9 November 2004.

29. "Tom Osborne." 2013 Nebraska Football Coach's Clinic. 30 March 2013.
Big Ten Elite "1994 Nebraska." Big Ten Network 30 October 2012.

30. Maisel, Ivan. "Hallowed be his name." SportsIllustrated. cnn.com 12 Nov. 1997.
"Miracle catch helps Nebraska clip Missouri in overtime." CBSSportsline 8 November 1997.

31. Callahan, Sean. "Nebraska falls short against Texas." HuskerOnline.com 6 December 2009.
Callahan, Sean. "The Suh tour moves on." HuskerOnline.com 8 December 2009.
"Ndamukong Suh to donate $2.6 million to the University." Huskers.com 18 April 2010.

32. Rosenthal, Brian. "Corso says NU fans the best then, now." Lincoln Journal Star 14 September 2007.
York, Randy. "Sportsmanship alive and well at Nebraska." Huskers.com 14 September 2007.
Schapiro, Morty. "Morty Shapiro interview." 15 October 2012.

33. "Huskers historic 1959 upset over Oklahoma was the greatest one ever." Huskers.com 9 November 2009.

34. Sipple, Steven M. "Personal interview." 3 April 2013.
Kaiput, Rich. "Rimington says firing of Solich upsetting." Omaha World-Herald 14 December 2003.
Sipple, Steven M. "Solich Fired." Lincoln Journal Star 30 November 2003.
Sipple, Steven M. "Solich's last pep talk has players set on winning bowl for him." Lincoln Journal Star 2 December 2003.

35. "Nebraska football team's visit to Michigan Stadium in 1962 was the start of something special." Associated Press 17 November 2011.

36. "Tenopir, Milt." Personal interview. 22 March 2013.
"McBride, Charlie." Personal interview. 15 January 2013.

37. "Tom Osborne on Leadership." 2012

38. Nebraska media guide

39. Big Ten Elite "1994 Nebraska." Big Ten Network 30 October 2012.

40. "Origin of the Cornhusker nickname." Huskers.com 26 July 2009.
Rowell, Rainbow. "Herbie's retro look wins new fans." Omaha World-Herald 4 September 2010.

41. Callahan, Sean. "Gill leaves NU as final chapter of a Husker era." HuskerOnline.com 3 December 2004
Sipple, Steven M. "NU assistant coach Gill resigns." Lincoln Journal Star 4 December 2004.

42. "Brown, Ralph." Personal interview. 19 February 2013.

43. "Fryar, Gill and Rozier to return for 'Scoring Explosion' reunion." Huskers.com 8 April 2005.

44. "McBride, Charlie." Personal interview. 15 January 2013.
"Brown, Ralph." Personal interview. 19 February 2013.

45. "McMenamin, Joe." Personal interview. 22 March 2013.
"Downing, Scott." Personal interview. 20 March 2013.

46. Tenopir, Milt. "Personal interview." 22 March 2013.
Hoskinson, Matt. "Personal interview." 8 April 2013.
Banderas, Tom. "Personal interview." 4 April 2013.

47. Nebraska media guide

48. "Perrett, Becky." Email statement from Runza corporate offices. 20 February 2013.

49. Pivovar, Steven. "Colorado hands Huskers worst defeat." Omaha World-Herald 23 November 2001.

50. "McBride, Charlie." Personal interview. 15 January 2013.
York, Randy. "Texas native Walker gets his dream job." Huskers.com 15 October 2010.
Schmitz, Brian. "Nebraska fans give deaf lineman a silent salute." Orlando Sentinel 26 December 1990.

51. "Ruud, Tom." Personal interview. 22 March 2013.

52. Callahan, Sean. "Kiffin, Carroll paved the way for Pelini." Rivals.com 24 January 2008.

53. Big Ten Elite "1994 Nebraska." Big Ten Network 30 October 2012.
"Brown, Ralph." Personal interview. 19 February 2013.
Callahan, Sean. "Where are they now: Matt Turman." HuskerOnline.com 26 May 2010.

54. Bryant, Don. Tales from the Nebraska Sidelines. 2001.

55. Big Ten Elite "1994 Nebraska." Big Ten Network 30 October 2012.
"McBride, Charlie." Personal interview. 15 January 2013.

56. Big Ten Elite "1994 Nebraska." Big Ten Network 30 October 2012.

57. "McBride, Charlie." Personal interview. 15 January 2013.

58. Shatel, Tom. "Bremser's calls shaped the game for many." Omaha World-Herald 18 April 2010.
"Mackiewicz, Alan." Personal interview. 19 March 2013.

59. "McBride, Charlie." Personal interview. 15 January 2013.
"Brown, Ralph." Personal interview. 19 February 2013.

60. NU Media Relations. "Osborne makes his decision on Callahan." HuskerOnline.com 24 November 2007.
"Husker coach's deal extended through 2011 season." ESPN.com 4 September 2007.

61. "Schmahl, Jeff." Personal interview. 11 January 2013.
"HuskerVision." Huskers.com 15 September 2009.

62. "Brown, Ralph." Personal interview. 19 February 2013.
Crabtree, Jeremy. "Clutch return gives Blinn title."
Rivals.com 6 December 2010.

63. Callahan, Sean. "Stuntz stays positive despite lack of
opportunity." HuskerOnline.com 11 November 2004.

64. "McBride, Charlie." Personal interview. 4 June 2013.

65. "Jumbo Stiehm." Huskers.com official bio.

67. Talman, John. "Former Husker, Wisconsin AD talks
game." HuskerOnline.com 28 September 2011.

68. Sehert, Walt. "The amazing Ed Weir." *McCook Daily
Gazette* 7 July 2008.
Babcock, Mike. "The Nebraska Football Legacy"
Huskers.com.

69. "History of the Rose Bowl." TournamentofRoses.com

70. Babcock, Mike. "Fact and fiction with Mr.
Touchdown." Huskers Illustrated 28 January 2012.

71. Personal visits

72. "Downing, Scott." Personal interview. 20 March 2013.
Babcock, Mike. "How it was: Remembering's
Nebraska's JV." Huskers Illustrated 18 January 2012.

73. York, Randy. "'82 Penn State one of Osborne's greatest
regrets." Huskers.com 11 November 2011.
Shanker, Jared. "College football's three worst calls of
all-time." *The Patriot-News* 3 June 2010.

74. Piersol, Richard. "Bob Logsdon was Lincoln's host with
the most." *Lincoln Journal Star* 5 June 2012.
"Babcock, Mike." Personal interview. 19 March 2013.

75. "Orange Bowl History & Honors." OrangeBowl.org.

76. Callahan, Sean. "Kris Brown praises Alex Henery."
HuskerOnline.com 11 November 2009.
York, Randy. "25 years later Klein's seven field goals
at Mizzou still an NCAA record." Huskers.com 30
October 2010.

77. "Brown, Ralph." Personal interview. 19 February 2013.

78. Hillgrove, Bill. "Personal interview." 17 September
2004.

79. "Babcock, Mike." Personal interview. 11 March 2013
"1955: 6-0 win at Nebraska Rainbows biggest upset."
Honolulu Advertiser 26 August 2009.

80. HuskerOnline.com "Nebraska, Adidas agree to an
8-year contract." 24 January 2005.
HuskerGameUsed.com, "Jersey History."
Christopherson, Brian. "Huskers eyeing five year
extension with Adidas." *Lincoln Journal Star* 8 March
2013.

81. Merrill, Elizabeth, "What rumors? NU's focus pays
off." *Omaha World-Herald* 30 December 2003.
Callahan, Sean. "Pelini answers final questions in San
Antonio." HuskerOnline.com 30 December 2003.
Callahan, Sean. "Gill says practice got off to a sluggish
start." HuskerOnline.com 24 December 2003.

82. "Thomas, Clarence." Personal interview. 5 February
2013.

83. "Sports Illustrated Magazines." huskerj.com

84. Bryant, Don. *Tales from the Nebraska Sidelines*. 2001.
"Pavelka, Kent." Personal interview. 22 February 2013.
Rosenthal, Brian. "18 yards: Touchdown, Tokyo style."
Lincoln Journal Star 28 July 2012.

85. "Meyers, Paul." Personal interview. 8 February 2013.

86. KOLN TV. "Team Jack presents $275,000 check for
pediatric brain cancer research." 16 January 2013.
Hoppen, Dan. "Burkhead ends NU career with a
bang." 3 January 2013.

87. "Kratz, Dean." Personal interview. 29 January 2013.
"Sadlemyer, Gary." Personal interview. 4 February
2013.
"McBride, Charlie." Personal interview. 15 January
2013.

88. Callahan, Sean. "The final breakdown of the Colorado
game." HuskerOnline.com 28 November 2008.

89. "History of Misty's." MistysLincoln.com.
Pascale, Jordan. "Pregame favorite Sidetrack Band to
move down the street." *Lincoln Journal Star* 17 August
2011.
"About us." Barry's Bar & Grill website.

90. "Kratz, Dean." Personal interview. 29 January 2013.

91. Dodd, Dennis. "Cornhusker motto against the Irish: 'In
Crouch we believe.'" CBS Sportsline.com 10 September
2000.
Christopherson, Brian. "7 yards: South Bend turns red
all over." *Lincoln Journal Star* 8 August 2012.
Weiss, Dick. "Crouch's dash beat the Irish in OT."
New York Daily News 10 September 2000.

92. Olson, Max. "Unanimous vote sets move toward the
Big Ten." HuskerOnline.com.
Cordes, Henry. "The Big Ten Decision." *Omaha
World-Herald* 30 August 2010.

93. "Pelini gives his final thoughts on the Sooners."
HuskerOnline.com 3 December 2010.
"Stoops gives final thoughts on the Huskers."
HuskerOnline.com 3 December 2010.
Callahan, Sean. "The final breakdown from the Big 12
title game." HuskerOnline.com 4 December 2010.

94. Callahan, Sean. "Championship runs can be defined by
breaks." HuskerOnline.com 3 November 2012.
Callahan, Sean. "Just stop trying to figure it out."
HuskerOnline.com 10 November 2012.

95. "Mann, Keith." Personal interview. 13 February 2013.

96. Bock, Hal. "Holy BCS, Batman! The Gotham Bowl
was a real joker." The Associated Press 2 January 2003.
Bryant, Don. *Tales from the Nebraska Sidelines*. 2001.

97. "Nebraska has longest Super Bowl streak." The
PostGame Blog 23 January 2012.

98. Callahan, Sean. "Helu runs wild in 31–17 win over
rival Missouri." HuskerOnline.com 30 October 2010.

99. Morehouse, Mark. "Osborne: Iowa and Nebraska will
eventually be a rivalry." *Cedar Rapids Gazette* 2 May
2011.
Dochterman, Scott. "Iowa, Huskers seek to make Black
Friday permanent." *Cedar Rapid Gazette* 13 February
2013.

100. Personal visits